Pluriverse an Essay in the Philosophy of Pluralism

Benjamin Paul Blood

Copyright © BiblioLife, LLC

This book represents a historical reproduction of a work originally published before 1923 that is part of a unique project which provides opportunities for readers, educators and researchers by bringing hard-to-find original publications back into print at reasonable prices. Because this and other works are culturally important, we have made them available as part of our commitment to protecting, preserving and promoting the world's literature. These books are in the "public domain" and were digitized and made available in cooperation with libraries, archives, and open source initiatives around the world dedicated to this important mission.

We believe that when we undertake the difficult task of re-creating these works as attractive, readable and affordable books, we further the goal of sharing these works with a global audience, and preserving a vanishing wealth of human knowledge.

Many historical books were originally published in small fonts, which can make them very difficult to read. Accordingly, in order to improve the reading experience of these books, we have created "enlarged print" versions of our books. Because of font size variation in the original books, some of these may not technically qualify as "large print" books, as that term is generally defined; however, we believe these versions provide an overall improved reading experience for many.

PLURIVERSE

An Essay in the Philosophy of Pluralism

BY
BENJAMIN PAUL BLOOD

WITH AN INTRODUCTION BY
HORACE MEYER KALLEN, Ph.D.

BOSTON
MARSHALL JONES COMPANY
1920

TO MY FRIEND
SPENCER KELLOGG

AUTHOR'S FOREWORD

IT was in the year 1860 that there came to me, through the necessary use of anæsthetics, a Revelation or insight of the immemorial Mystery which among enlightened peoples still persists as the philosophical secret or problem of the world. It is an illumination of the cosmic centre, in which that field of thought where haunt the topics of fate, origin, reason and divinity glows for the moment in an inevitable but hardly communicable appreciation of the genius of being; it is an *initiation*, historically realized as such, into the oldest and most intimate and ultimate truth. Whoever attains and remembers it, or remembers of it, is graduated beyond instruction in "spiritual things"; but to those who are philosophically given it will recur as a condition which, if we are to retain a faith in reason, should seem amenable to articulate expression, for it is obviously what philosophers fail of.

After fourteen years of this experience at varying intervals, I published in 1874 "The Anæsthetic Revelation and The Gist of Philosophy," not assuming to define therein the purport of the illumination, but rather to signalize the experience, and in a résumé of philosophy to show wherein that had come short of it. My brochure was indifferently reviewed, except that William James treated it seriously in the *Atlantic Monthly*. But afterward submitting it to the poet Tennyson, I immediately received from the laureate a cordial and explicit confirmation out of his own occasional abstractions, while not in a fully normal state, yet impressing me as likely to be of identical illumination. Many other responses came to me in the course of time, announcing similar strangely inexpressible memories, until I learned that nearly every hospital and dental office has its reminiscences of patients who, after a brief anæsthesia, uttered confused fragments of some inarticulate import which always had to do with the mystery of life, of fate, continuance, necessity and cognate abstractions, and all demanding "What is it?" "What does it all mean, or amount to?" Such is what is known esoterically, or among its comparatively few illuminati, as the anæsthetic revelation.

I let it drift along for years, for there seemed nothing to be made of it, or out of it, except that it drove me more and more to the realization of philosophy as "of all our vanities the motliest," while yet the confirmations of the homogeneity of the experience came faster and more various.

For there comes a wondrous and congratulatory sense of *reminiscence* with the experience itself, which exalts this immediate mental phenomenon to the solemnity of fate and prehistoric necessity; a sense of life and the world falling of its own weight into the vacuity of the future, rather than as an ejected superfluity or surfeit of the past; a sense that it was always so, and has to be so. It is this reminiscence of the *immemorial*, the "time out of mind," which only later could have become the Adamic and aboriginal, that makes it supernally the

AUTHOR'S FOREWORD

Revelation. It is this, too, that *secularizes* the ancient mystery, and leaves it congenital and familiar with the humor and pathos of life; that gives the weirdness and thrill to occasions of birth and death and marriage; that makes the rustic halt and keep his countenance at the most absurd occurrence; that puts a sting of danger into the homeliest of proverbs; that makes us cheer when the awkward horse wins the race, and when Portia's picture is found in the leaden casket; when fair Titania yields the flower of her cheek to the hairy and grotesque Bottom; when we call the heaven-inspired weak-minded person a "natural."

This singular insight obviously belongs to, or implicates or calls for, what is known as philosophy. But turning thereto, one finds philosophy itself in such a vagarious and unsettled condition, as having no tribunal nor generally acknowledged authority, that its promiscuous precepts have no judicial standing. In fact, philosophy, at least of the unprofessional sort, has largely deserted the field whereon alone this topic can be exploited. What it most needs is language; but almost disqualifying logic, philosophy seems to have turned for light and guidance to biology and the inarticulate instincts of mere life.

The plain truth is that the modern student of philosophy has been baffled, daunted and discomfited by a fake esotericism, arbitrarily technical in terms and presumptions, wholly problematical in its own coteries — delighting, as Kant protested, in the confusion of the plain man. The thoughtful spirit finds the interest of the problem unabated, although so

AUTHOR'S FOREWORD

many novelties invite the popular attention that there is left even for him but little of that fine old leisure in which philosophy was once the pride and the prestige of the race.

It is this problem, and the Revelation of it, which is the import and background of my book.

In the popular sense the book begins with a proposition of positive science, one that the astronomers rarely consider, although it involves the determining element in all their wonderful calculations, the proposition that a numerical or limited set of movable stars, pervaded by a uniform attraction, would all come together in one conglomerate mass; and that those which we do observe must be either held apart by others still beyond them, and these others still by others indefinitely without end, or else by some arbitrary and superstitious and unscientific agency.

And the fact is clearly apparent, to common sense, that if the stars in their multitude do thus go on and on interminably, there can be no comprehension nor comprehender of them as a whole, or as a one, or as all; and that no pressure or formation or management can come to them from without. But this inference, seemingly so sure, is conditioned upon the natural understanding that the space which contains the stars would go on, whether with or without them; and this understanding has been rudely shaken by "idealism," a doctrine that outer things are at least partly determined by the knowing of them, and that space is not physical extensity, but mental or spiritual freedom to extend.

This doctrine (which Mr. Herbert Spencer rankly characterized as insanity) badly shatters the integrity of all objective things; and it is abetted scientifically by the microscope — for instance in the important matter of size — showing that all sizes are determined by the lenses of vision, which they surely are. Color and form and tangibility also are found to be referable to organic structure; the difference of things is not a property of things themselves, etc., so that for an *explanation* of vision and distinction and space we have to go behind both the eye and the mind, to "metaphysics."

And although reality as a whole (a one, an all, or totality) may not be known by a comprehension from without — since full comprehension must include the spirit which comprehends — yet the psychologists insist that it can be comprehended from within by self-relation; that it is at once in-itself and for-itself, a subject-object, and they appeal to the common "self-consciousness" as its empirical proof.

All these topics have long since been treated with a desperate persistence and an astonishing ingenuity, which have necessitated and must condone the possibly tiresome chapters which follow. But however these chapters may disqualify the philosophy of the past, they do not assume to replace it by a better on the same lines. The leading expectation of this book is to signalize the anæsthetic revelation.

The most overt and beaten path into philosophical curiosity is at its division of reality into static and dynamic, as these notions are exemplified in eternity and time, and in the duplexity of the one and the many. To this duplexity we now devote our first working chapter.

BENJAMIN PAUL BLOOD.

CONTENTS

CHAPTER	PAGE
INTRODUCTION	xv
I. DUPLEXITY	1
II. IDEALISM	38
III. MONISM	65
IV. CAUSE	88
V. SELF-RELATION	110
VI. THE NEGATIVE	156
VII. ANCILLARY UNITY AND THE PRESENT TENSE	172
VIII. JESUS AND FREE WILL	182
IX. THE ANÆSTHETIC REVELATION	204
SUPPLEMENTARY ESSAY: THE POETICAL ALPHABET	246

INTRODUCTION

I

WHEN, in *As You Like it*, Shakespeare makes Touchstone ask William, "Hast any philosophy in thee, Shepherd?" the thing that Touchstone means is a certain wisdom and vision of life, serenity and resignation mingled, such as Jacques possessed and Hamlet yearned for, and whose perfect example in the works of Shakespeare is Prospero. Its varieties in the tradition of European thinking are not numerous, systems of philosophy exhibiting always the temper of serenity or of resignation, with the missing member of the twain replaced by acquiescence or ecstasy or sorrow or security or bitterness. The overruling quality in each system, the essential of its tone, no matter what its type, is tranquillity. The mind may be that of Seneca or of Schopenhauer; in and through its philosophy it has found repose, its problems solved, its seekings successfully at end.

This aspect of the temper of philosophy has, however, another side, a complement psychologically and historically antecedent, logically later, a sort of father-brother who divides the mastery of the house of thought. Philosophy is a quest no less than it is an attainment, a battle no less than it is a peace. Its wont is that of an appetency and a yearning, as its use is that of a fulfilment which is the consummation and dissolution of appetency and yearning. Its history is of system replacing system, argument argument, in the ambition to affirm that state of enlightenment and security which outlaws both system and argument, and constitutes what Benjamin Paul Blood, the subject of this essay, calls "the satisfaction of philosophy." There is, as he truly perceives, a satisfaction beyond philosophy which philosophy seeks, which only philosophy can seek, and which, it may be ventured, only philosophy can attain. To the relation between that satisfaction and the hungry reasoning that pursues it there pertains a high comedy, perhaps the most piteous and ironic of all the comedies into which the human spirit propels itself. It is the comedy of a deliverance, whereof, always, "the rest is silence." There is hardly a supremely great thinker who does not exemplify it. Plato, aiming by dialectic at possession of the absolute good which is the ineffable repudiation of all dialectic; Plotinus, at endless trouble to demonstrate the indemonstrability of the ineffable One; St. Thomas, Spinoza, Hegel, Bergson, any philosopher you will; each is in one way or another at great pains to reason out the ultimate nescience of reason, the swallowing up and termination of reason: to reason out a state where the act of reasoning no longer signifies and its end and beginning are joined in one. The attainment of this state is somehow an initiation. Its being is a mystery. Its attributes are totality and eternity and goodness. Its apprehension is a revelation of the instancy of time, of the interpenetrative simultaneity

INTRODUCTION xvii

of the primary and the ultimate inwardness of being, of nature at once immemorial and inveterate, the first thing and the last thing, and the real essence of man.

Much of the ratiocination of the philosophic tradition consists of recounting the aliency of mankind from this, its proper essence, and of providing the instruments and the technique of its self-recovery. Sometimes these instruments are forged and authorized by the discrediting of reason and the justification of faith or instinct or intuition. Sometimes they are provided by the transmutation of reason itself. But however they are fabricated, their use is to establish and sustain a security already assumed, regarding the goodness, the unity and the eternity of being, and requiring rather the rejection of its contraveners than its own demonstration. Ultimately, this security is the ultimately desirable revealing its self, and in the act convicting those whom it illuminates of its veridiction. It is ever an object of faith rather than of proof, and faith, as Mr. Blood says in the "Anæsthetic Revelation," "comes not by doubtful tests, but is ever a foregone conclusion."

It is such a foregone conclusion that Mr. Blood pursues. His pursuit differs in many important respects from the traditional one. But most of all in this — that he makes it *knowingly*. "The Hound of Heaven," he declares in his device for *Pluriverse,* "is on his own trail, and the vestige still lures the scent of a foregone conclusion." What he means — and takes the whole of this one book to say — is that the mystery of existence is not a hidden thing like a face behind a mask, but is existence itself, its actual process, both as search and as satisfaction. That, therefore, men seek what they already possess, like a dog hunting its own tail. There is nothing behind, Mr. Blood would reiterate. The face and the heart of being are in identical place and of identical substance; men are self-deluded when they attempt, as philosophers or otherwise, to uncover an essence or a principle different in nature from that which science apprehends or the daily life encounters. And he would say it as one speaking with authority, authority ineluctable as the "anæsthetic revelation," its source and sanction, wherein, at the moment of awakening from anæsthetic sleep, there gets accomplished that "stare of being at itself," of which all revelation must consist. The reliance on experience of this kind, which can be suggested, pointed to, designated, perhaps even shared — "signalized" is Mr. Blood's word — but cannot as yet be analyzed or described, makes of him a mystic; and indeed his doctrine abounds in the qualities wherewith mysticism is distinguished — notably the rejection of ratiocination as the ground for security, the warranting of security upon ineffable experience, the subsequent use of ratiocination to persuade of the inescapable authority of this experience. But also, Mr. Blood's teaching in certain respects differs from the mystic type to the point of uniqueness. He holds the revelation, overwhelmingly convincing as it is, a thing *commonplace* and *secular,* confirming instead of outlawing, the daily life of men. The world it yields him seems somewhat ambiguous, but it is a "pluriverse" far more definitely than a "universe." In a word, Mr. Blood is a mystic of the commonplace, his certainties are certainties of the ineffable truth and reality of the changeful flux and disparity and multiplicity of the daily life.

The latter variation from the tradition particularly impressed William James. Discussing Mr. Blood's philosophy in the *Hibbert Journal* (July, 1910) he celebrated him as a "pluralistic mystic." "The practically unanimous tradition of 'regular' mysticism," he wrote, "has been unquestionably *monistic;* and inasmuch as it is the characteristic of mystics to speak, not as the scribes, but as men who have 'been there' and seen with their own eyes, I think that this sovereign manner must have made some other pluralistic-minded students hesitate, as I confess that it has often given pause to me. One cannot criticise the vision of a mystic — one can but pass it by, or else accept it as having some amount of evidential weight. I felt unable to do either with a good conscience until I met with Mr. Blood. His mysticism, which may, if one likes, be understood as monistic in this earlier utterance (the Anæsthetic Revelation) develops in the later ones a sort of 'left-wing' voice of defiance, and breaks into what to my ear has a radically pluralistic sound." This sound is somewhat tempered in "Pluriverse," but it is resonant and definitive enough to justify the book's title, even though the existence it designates is not shown with certainty to be either monistic or pluralistic.

II

The causes of Mr. Blood's divergence and novelty are more easily guessed at than accounted for. They were not in variety of scene and society. He hardly ever ventured far from home. Born in the second decade of the last century, most of his long life of eighty-six years was spent in and about the dingy town of Amsterdam, New York. He held almost as close to his native scene as Kant and there was as little therein to motivate and to explain his thinking as there was in Königsberg to explain the latter's. His life is marked by a normality unusual in a mystic. Neither do his ancestry nor his education enlighten us. His breed was Scotch-Irish, that pre-Revolutionary type of tough mind, obstinate will and rigid faith which had early in the eighteenth century been driven by famine from Ulster to these shores. It carried with it a resentment against Britain which animated the Revolution and saved it from disintegration during more than one crisis. It imported a pattern of congregational organization that influenced the form of polity which, after the Revolution, the country adopted. These things aside, it was not further distinguished. It had the normal endowment of practical competency in affairs, and speculative regularity in theology. The bulk of it pioneered, constituting the westernmost wave of the European strain that has now won and possessed the North American continent. A percentage settled, took root, found an equilibrium of life capable of transmission and continuity, and used up its surplusages of energy in feud, evangel or philosophy.

INTRODUCTION   xxi

The descendants of this percentage are to be found, from its migratory beginnings to the present day, all along the Appalachian range, from the Adirondacks and Catskills to the Ozarks. Thus, the ancestral farm, situated in the town of Florida, had been in the possession of the Blood family some one hundred and thirty years when it came at last in the hands of Benjamin Paul, to work as his fathers had worked it before him, for the family's provision and continuance. His education appears to have been as normally American as his breed — the public schools of Amsterdam, Amsterdam Academy, a period at Union College. No precocity is recorded beyond a far from unusual speculative propensity in adolescence, a sensibility to language, and the itch of authorship. The last seems to have found relief in letters to such locally-known newspapers as the Amsterdam *Gazette* or *Recorder*, the Utica *Herald*, the Albany *Times*. The letters dealt with an astonishing diversity of subjects, from local petty politics or the tricks of spiritualistic mediums to principles of industry and finance and profundities of metaphysics. Almost the whole of Blood's mental life, from his eighteenth year to his eighty-sixth, has found record and expression in these letters. The qualities of thought and style which had attracted William James to him, appear, prior to 1874, to have been but foreshadowed in them. Their fulness seems to have come into being only with the composition of "The Anæsthetic Revelation."

Nor does the range of Mr. Blood's independent reading appear to have been wide. His references and allusions show an intimate knowledge of Shakespeare and of Plato, and a customary familiarity with the Bible. He has read the German philosophies current during his young manhood — notably Hegel. He is conversant with Hegelians at home and abroad. He knows the American transcendentalists, particularly Emerson, to whom he defers. He has sharp things to say about W. T. Harris, *quondam* Commissioner of Education, for whose *Journal of Speculative Philosophy* he rewrote a number of philosophical letters, and he pounds the "Universology" of Stephen Pearl Andrews as if it were important. On the other hand, he is, after 1874, in epistolary contact with a great many men of personal eminence and literary distinction — with Stirling, the English interpreter of Hegel, with Edmund Gurney, with Sir William Ramsay, with James, with Emerson, with Tennyson. Most of the correspondence touches the inwardness of the anæsthetic revelation. Mr. Blood had sent about copies of this tract — printed, like all his things except his letters, at his own expense — and for a time conducted an extensive correspondence anent its subject-matter. The exchange of letters led in cases eventually to a circulation — in the instance of William James to an exchange — of photographs, and to subsequent amenities of which two are evidential: Tennyson's "the face is that of one born to grapple with difficulties metaphysical and other," and James's, "I am so delighted to find that a metaphysician *can* be anything else than a spavined, dyspeptic individual fit for no other use."

It may be that the constitutional vigor recorded by the photographs is the beginning and end of the idiosyncracy of Blood's genius. He is declared never

INTRODUCTION xxiii

in the course of his long life to have known illness of any kind or to have been confined to his bed as an invalid. He is that unusual event in the tradition of mysticism and metaphysics, a healthy mystic. The point of departure for his mysticism seems to have been an anæsthesia induced by nitrous oxide or ether. Its effect on him was not unlike that of a religious conversion. The experience which came in waking from this artificial slumber reset his consciousness and made of him a poet and philosopher and mystic. His first and most beautiful attempt to signalize it he composed at the age of forty-two as "The Anæsthetic Revelation," after, he declares, "experiments ranging over nearly fourteen years." His second and final attempt is "Pluriverse," a modification, expansion and elaboration of the essentials of the first. The interval between them is filled with letters to the press, letters and still more letters (signed mostly "Paul"), a poem or two, the more or less voluminous correspondence already mentioned, and the quiet almost anonymous life in Amsterdam, New York. He was waiting, he wrote his friends, waiting for the necessary terms and expressions, fearful always of being "too soon at last." He had high hopes of what might come of an adequate expression of his insight: "Thus you may see," he declared in a letter to the Springfield *Republican* shortly after William James had died, "that this mumbling and mouthing mystery of the cosmos still hovers over hospital and laboratory, awaiting articulation; like the wild hawk of Walt Whitman, untamed and as yet untranslatable, it sounds its barbaric yawp over the books of the world. If I can

INTRODUCTION

express it, as I may in a year or two, or in a decade or two, as it shall happen, my book will be more than one of the 'Books of the Week,' for therein the fact may appear that Sinai and Calvary were but sacred stepping-stones to this secular elevation where free thought may range hereafter, when the old scares of superstition shall have vanished to the limbo whence they came."

As a matter of fact the composition of "Pluriverse" took nearly a decade. What fell between it and "The Anæsthetic Revelation" appears to have mattered little. Both essays signalize the same essential experience. Each sucks up from the philosophic atmosphere of its generation the prevailing metaphysical tone. In each this tone is tempered by a certain resilient straitness which is of the unrelenting taste and predisposition of "Paul" alone. By these the monism of the "Anæsthetic Revelation" is keyed down with the observation that "each and every one of us is the One that remains." By these the high flights of Hegelian rationalism of the same document are made to culminate in the pronouncement that "the naked life is realized outside of sanity altogether; and it is the instant contrast of this 'tasteless water of souls' with formal thought as we 'come to' that leaves in the patient an astonishment that the awful mystery of Life is at last but a homely and a common thing." By these, again, the pluralism of "Pluriverse" is mitigated with the hope "that the fond monism that we have dialectically disparaged may be at least transcendentally rehabilitated." As the monism is a reverberation of the transcendentalism current in the latter half of the nineteenth, so the pluralism is an absorption of the Jamesian metaphysic of the twentieth century. Analogously, as the gist of philosophy was declared to have been confirmed or paralleled in revelation during the seventies and eighties of the last century, so it is, in its intellectualistic aspects, both required and rejected in the generation of James and Bergson. Whatever the age, the conclusion — foregone — is the Revelation, "given you as the old Adamic secret, which you then feel that all intelligence must sometime know or have known; yet ludicrous in its familiar simplicity, as somewhat that any man should always perceive at his best, if his head were only level, but which in our ordinary thinking has grown into a thousand creeds and theories dignified as religion and philosophy."

III

If, in his serene obscurity, Mr. Blood can be said to have had a vocation, it was to celebrate this revelation "ludicrous in its familiar simplicity." His style as celebrant has the hymnic quality, and the meaning of his diction — particularly when most metaphysical or when closest to the revelation — that tang of suggestion and overtone which ally it to the utterance of feeling by music rather than to the denotation of ideas by words. This quality he shares with all mystics, as is natural he should. The range and the depth of the mystical experience, its completeness of emotional transformation and intellectual readjustment, the total loosening and overturning of the psyche which the experient undergoes, cannot fail to initiate in any man or woman a mode of rhythmic vocalization and imaginative statement at once exalted and colorful. But here again Blood varies from the type in that the power of such utterance is in his work something more than occasional. His style is conscious, not reflex, an effect of will rather than of passion. He is not, as his reader must see, a constructive writer, even in a work so sustained as "Pluriverse"; James describes him as "aphoristic and oracular rather . . . sometimes dialetic, sometimes poetic and sometimes mystic in his manner, sometimes monistic and sometimes pluralistic in his matter." Nevertheless there is that even in his dryest passages which never fails to capture heart and ear with a felicity of cadence and of precision that points to the disciplined mastery of medium attainable only through the training and perfecting of a gift inborn. Blood, like Poe, has a philosophy of style, a far profounder and more subtle philosophy, with declared affinities to the observations of Burns and of Swedenborg and the suggestive analysis that Plato made in the "Cratylus." The ideas constituting this analysis appear to have occurred to Mr. Blood altogether spontaneously, when he was a young man just out of his teens. They are incorporated in the Supplementary Essay to "Pluriverse" under the title "The Poetical Alphabet."

That the subject-matter of the essay is not remote from the preoccupations of the book is conclusively established with the declaration that "logical truth is held to the arbitrament of language, the production and determination of which are therefore of prime importance in philosophical explanation." And forthwith the problem is attacked in the form of the question "why the word *icicle* is not a fit name for a *tub*." Its answer is an exhibition, not an analysis or an explanation, of felt and observable harmonies between things and the names of things. These names, in their sound and in their form, are somehow the reverberations and the shadows of the things they stand for. How, Mr. Blood has not been at pains to work out, and perhaps never was equipped to do so. The matter is one for the precise technique of the psychological laboratory. But its principle — the rule underlying observations of writers so diverse as Plato and Swedenborg and Burns and Blood, and tongues so different as Greek and Swedish and English — however difficult to demonstrate, should not be difficult to state. It might be formulated as follows: The human organism, as a unit and in its separate organs, is something like a sounding-board. Knowingly or unknowingly it as a rule responds to, refracts and gives back whatever stimulus impinges upon it. The specific responses and reproductions which it is conscious of are only a tiny fraction of the generalized reverberations which it is not conscious of. There are "emotion," constantly modifying the breathing and the state of the vocal chords and of the other organs involved in the production of sound and speech. Now between all bodily activities and their causes and occasions both physiologists and psychologists have observed a certain vibrational similarity, or even identity. This is most noticeable in both conscious and unconscious imitations of rhythms and movements, but

INTRODUCTION

it is to be observed as well in such unnormal experiences as color-audition. In those experiences sound seems to be translated into and accompanied by color; it is this order of succession which renders the experience unnormal. But the reverse succession, in which color is translated into and accompanied by sound, incipient or actual, is far more frequent. Indeed, it is an unobserved commonplace of the daily life. It takes place, moreover, not merely with respect to color, and movement, but with respect to line and shape as well. What is seen is also sounded; it is the unheard melody sweeter still. And therefore icicle is *not* a fit name for a tub and "each of the sounds represented by several letters of the alphabet is specially effective in conveying a certain significance; and wherever language is popular and happy it is so in accord with these early intuitions."

"These early intuitions" are synonymous with the transmutive sensibility of any word-master to the fugitive phases of the changing world about him; they are the initial endowment of the poet. And Mr. Blood was a poet, whether he wrote verse or wrote prose.[1]

---

[1] James, in "A Pluralistic Mystic," quotes from Blood's "Apostrophe to Freedom," his "Nemesis," and from "The Lion of the Nile." The latter two were printed, through James's interest, in Scribner's Magazine, 1888 and 1889. "The Lion of the Nile" is a very remarkable piece of writing both for thought and diction. Concerning the former it is worth while quoting a letter from Blood to James, dated March 31, 1887: "I have a letter from Dr. Stirling — full of kindness, and a shake of the head about the Lion; he sees much beauty, etc., in it, but says: 'I am hopeless of the one thought which connects it altogether.' Damme but I will prove the connection, the potential connection, right here:—We all believe,

INTRODUCTION xxix

With Blood's sensibility to word-music there goes also another quality not usually associated therewith but having in fact, as Blood himself adumbrated, connections as intimate as they are obscure. This is logical skill, dialectic power. It came forcefully under the attention of William James, reviewing Blood in 1910, and what it has lost in vigor since that date, readers of "Pluriverse" will concede, it has gained in grace. Although "Pluriverse" gives, within its wider structure, the total effect of a mosaic rather than of an architectonic, there weaves through the notable apothegms, reflections and imaginative flights into which it lifts again and again

poetically, in metempsychosis, and the Socratic reminiscence, and the unity (Emersonian) of intelligence, whose idol is the Sphinx. The poem says, for the spirit of championship, or the champion spirit of the world: I drew my life from the dugs of one that lived on blood alone, and my consciousness is the accumulation [translation] of many. I trace back through the streams of this blood to episodes of individual life (which ran together in the milk of my all-rapacious dam, and be damned to her). I feel as Cæsar felt — as Antony and Cleopatra had gall enough to feel that Cæsar felt. I was Coriolanus, I was a gladiator. I was a condor — and for the matter of that I was the whale that swallowed Jonah. Will any call this pretence a dream? . . ." If so, dignity and freedom are, no less. As the poem concludes:

Nay, now is but the dream,
When things of greater heart and wider mould
And deeper life and patience here conspire
To claim this reminiscent verse a phase
Of the world's championship. — Let be what may.
The gods are dreary as the worshippers:
As the wide cycles tire they too have changed.
Faint 'neath its newest garb of charity
Flutters the heart divine in these last years,
And low the purple trails, and justice stoops
To mercy weaker than the sin forgiven:

INTRODUCTION

from levels of the commonplace, a swift and competent dialectic whose force and influence are of the nature of overtone and suggestiveness rather than of explicit conviction. They do not coerce by proof, they persuade by implication. As in Blood's diction Shakespeare, the Bible and the slang and vernacular current mingle their lights and invest with the glow of strange familiarity new perspectives of thought and feeling, so in his argument commonplaces of illustration and habit are suffused with indications of the ineffable, and grip and redirect, without forcing, the mind: as when he says, speaking

> *Yet the patrician pride, the red disdain*
> *Self-sustenant — more gracious in its scorning*
> *Than e'er, alas, Christ-love in pitying tears,*
> *Remembers me on the Judean banners,*
> *O'er lands Levantine rampant without peer:*
> *The shuddering wilds grew firm; the haggard cliffs*
> *Where conscience flings her troubled victims down,*
> *Caught peace from my sane eyes; e'en vulgar life,*
> *That knows no other charm, was great through me.*

> *And still my worship lives in longing hearts,*
> *Human or brute or bird, — for these are one*
> *In love and longing, as my sphinxes know*
> *That lie along the sands and watch the River.*
> *Many are the altars but the flame is one;*
> *Of every hell the misery is fear,*
> *And every heaven is mockery but mine.*
> . . . .
> *Doth thy pulse, quivering thro the pose of Ajax,*
> *Defy the lurid blood of the strong gods*
> *As one with them at last, and one with Him —*
> *The longest wing in heaven, the deepest crown.*
> *Who, ever vanquished, fighting as he falls,*
> *Still proves himself immortal? —*
> *Lo, it is I, the Lion of the Nile,*
> *The mystery of the wingéd human brute*
> *Couchant — the CHAMPION spirit of the world.*

of the astonishment that the homeliness of his revelation produces — "the astonishment is aggravated as at a thing of course, missed by sanity in overstepping, as in too foreign a search, or with too eager an attention: as in finding one's spectacles on one's nose or in making in the dark a higher step than the stair." Deliverances of this kind, again, are naturally accompanied, according to the wont and use of the mystic, with a certain lordly impatience, a highhandedness in the discussion of the opinions and teachings of other men, such, for example, as Kant. But this is an incident.

Less incidental, because truly implicated in the idiosyncrasy and personal flavor of the man is a certain specific contemporary irrelevance. Mr. Blood's contemporaneity is of atmosphere warmed by personal glimpses, it is not of contact and comprehension of the living movements of the day. Readers will miss reflection of the vivid and poignant social concerns of the times; of the reticulated conceptions of the new realistic philosophies and of the momentous development and implications of the biologic and physical sciences. What to other readers is most coercive in Bergson's doctrine — the ordered biological material — is negligible to Blood, and his observations in physiology, and his one use of physics in the argument for the endless manyness of the world he set great store by, are naïve. And who shall say that there is any harm done? Firm on the rock of his revelation, Blood, in but not of an age that has prevailingly spoken from without inward, speaks from within outward. His vocation has been truly metaphysics; he is a dialectician vindi-

xxxii   INTRODUCTION

cating in ordered words a faith in which serene certainty and disillusion mingle and are one. Hear his last word: "And now inexorable time admonishes me to have done with this world. I am thankful at having seen the show; and although after eighty-five years, the stars are still flickering slightly, and the winds are something worn, I am still clear and confident in that religion of courage and content which cherishes neither regrets nor anticipations."

IV

The overture to this finale is the exposure of philosophy's incompetency and the enthronement of the brute datum, the fact and givenness of being, through the anæsthetic revelation, exfoliating in a more pertinent philosophy. Mr. Blood begins his exposure with the consideration of the well-known antinomianisms, made familiar by Kant, of the traditional descriptions of the world. From the beginning thinkers have built inwardly coherent and mutually contradictory metaphysical systems. These have been criticized by Kant and others, but their critical review is itself only a dialetical negation of their dogmatic grounds, and cannot, therefore, establish itself as having transcendental and hence superior authority. Experience is self-contradictory, and any proposition may be affirmed or denied of it. Not, however, absolutely. This could be absolutely so only if the world were truly static and inalterable. But it is not that. Its staticism must be proved; its dynamicism can be observed. The oppugnance between the two works itself out em-

INTRODUCTION xxxiii

pirically, somehow, in favor of a cosmic doing. This doing is a thing of chance and freedom, whose essence may be apprehended in the unaccountable gains of force or motion in the phenomenon of momentum, in the ineluctable infinitude of stars and suns whose reciprocal outward pull alone could keep them from falling together as the inward pull of "gravitation" would compel any finite number of them to fall toward a common centre. The gravitational pull, the force or motion of momentum is each an action which takes place. That it does take place is a free gift or eventuation of being, a chance, which as chance is the only sure thing: "The reliability and permanence of chance are the most consolatory elements of philosophy. The notion that, left to chance, all would go wild and undependable, miscalculates experience and . . . calls for a positive malignity to overweigh the just indifference or stolidity or essential inertia of things in themselves. There needs a positive and peremptory *why* the ace should come up an inconvenient number of times. Justice is balance. The Good is not best, upon the whole; it does not appear to have been deserved, and it is unjust, by comparison, to the indifferent and the commonplace; it shows heat in the bosom of fate."

Nor do the static, the necessary, or the eternal come off better through the demonstration of idealism. One aspect of the contentions of that way of thinking, Mr. Blood maintains, is correct and commonplace. The mind's activity, or the body's, does make a difference in the thing it acts on, and the show and pageant of our living world cannot help being a show and pageant determined by our point of view and the organs of our seeing. But once this relativity is conceded, what then? The enterprises of doing and thinking go on as spontaneously, as inexorably, and as provokingly as before, demanding explanation. Idealism has but given a back to the pigment or added a frame to the picture. The form, matter and articulation of the stuff upon the canvas, the sequence of line, shape and color, the whole processes, of the picture within the frame — and these are the problem — have still to be accounted for. Atlas may uphold the world, but the order and connection of what takes place upon the face thereof, or in its caverns underneath — what have they to do with Atlas, or Atlas with them? Idealism is no more competent to resolve duplexity than any other idea of the tradition. Something always escapes and stands out, a distinct and ineluctable Other to any system of inclusion that may be formulated or felt. Each is an eventuation of chance whose opposite might be equally good, and, as it appears in the history of philosophy, seems so. Thus with all monisms. Their psychological original is the constitutional egoism of the spirit of man; their production is a process of limitation; their ultimate nature must be that of "self-relation" (an idea known to Mr. Bertrand Russell as "the class of all classes" and rejected also by him as impossible) in which the container is no addition to the contained but identical with it, as men are supposed to be self-identical when they know that they know. Monism, it would appear, is but a recessional of the philosophic problem which calls recession, solution.

In the end, it also begs its datum and leaves it unexplained. Its effect, hence, has been that of "a needless barrier to explanation," since where it does not intervene that impulsion of being which we call *causation* may be discovered and acknowledged immediately at hand, as "in the self-respect of some great emotion or agonism that should *feel* itself worth while." But too much reliance must not be placed in *causation* either. Also that is implicated in self-relation, with its asserton that *this* is *the other*, or that *the different* is *the same*, as when we say water is hydrogen and oxygen. For *this* and *the other* and *different* and *same* are all data, things given, *facts,* to which "cause" is added, for the assuagement of our unrest in their presence, as inference or explanation; and added, not as increase but as reduplication without increase, such reduplication as is supposed to take place when you know that you know. Such reduplication is no more than "self-relation."

"Self-relation," in Mr. Blood's view, is the heart and goal of all philosophy, its dialectic motive and contemplative illusion. It is the "foregone conclusion," the begged question whereof the actuality and potency are already assumed in its own proof. Systems of philosophy are no more than such proof. However else they may differ, they are alike involved in the circular argument that, since cause and effect must be somehow identical, being has to be its own ground; that difference, therefore, is the same as identity, negation as affirmation: reality is its own other and all relation is self-relation. Whether you think of this relation as the identity of knowing with

INTRODUCTION

what is known; or, after the fashion of the theologians, as the identity of the mover with the moved, the causer with the caused; or, after the fashion of the metaphysicians, as the identity of past, present and future and the instantaneity of time, you do not, by the use of it, solve the problem of being and becoming: you only delay and postpone it, you pass the buck to God. "The grudge of science as against the pretense of self-relation is that our highest claim and achievement, namely, knowledge, is therein made to countenance with its full authority and significance a claim to have attained the comprehension and mastery of that which halts our curiosity, controls our interest, and occasions our discontent, while in fact it does not fundamentally understand the least and simplest thing in the world. Our consciousness, even as it glows, is a helpless projection from an alien energy, bottomless in its regard, utterly unqualified to declare or to determine anything as necessary, and therefore wholly incompetent to radical explanation."

What, when "self-relation" is discredited, is there that remains competent to "radical explanation?" Nothing. At various instants in the European tradition philosophers have seized upon this nothing, have made a principle of it, and used it as an instrument of explanation. The foremost among them was Hegel, who, resting his dialectic upon the dogma that being and not being are the same, agreed that "the vitality of the negative is essentially the life of being and that negation is positive in its results." Hegel and his kind have, however, been merely deluded by the feeling that nothing, *as a word*, is something, and have attributed to the discursive substantiality of the term a metaphysical potency that is merely fanciful, like the potency of any shibboleth. Sesame, which opens doors in the fairy story, opens no doors in fact. There is nothing in negativity: non-entity is a thing purely verbal and logical, a topic in dialectic. What force it has accrues to it only by reason of "its positive given force," as the force of the wind on the sail of a tacking ship, whereby it goes in the wind's own face. The diversification and richness of existence does not need for its explanation the equilibrium of contradictories, of "entity" and "non-entity." "Contrast may come as well from new excess in nature as from the negation and non-being of the passing and the past." There is, and there comes to be, difference and distinction without antagonism: "being gets vital distinction in the oncoming future and becomes itself the negative or background in a world new-born. . . . There is no struggle for mere being. . . . but rather the bounty of a miraculous becoming, ever new, and ever more."

Does then, with monism discredited, idealism doubtful, the negative incompetent, the world stretching indefinitely anywhere, ever exceeding, exceeding, exceeding, its Midst everywhere, does then duplexity dichotomize existence into confusion, and is the last word of thought, *agnosco?* Not for Mr. Blood. If analysis and dialectic do not reveal an organic and absolute cohesion of the world's multifariousness, observation compels the recognition — nevertheless — of a certain "ancillary unity" of being, a certain contact and mutual interplay or interpretation of

xxxviii   INTRODUCTION

the diversity of existences. If the universe is not a block, neither is it a chaos. There are no absolutes in it: "contradiction cannot utterly contradict nor can being exclusively be." The very essence of "the bounty of miraculous becoming" is that everything shades off into something else with whose nature its own mingles, as the present mingles inextricably with the past and future and the *then* creeps up and overtakes the *now*. "There is a penumbra which defeats the exactitude of every assumed connection," and it is only in the ignoring of this penumbra that the gratuitous paradoxes of philosophy arise. Mr. Blood expands this proposition by means of an analysis of the moot-point of current philosophy — the nature and reality of motion and time. His treatment of the famous Zenonian paradox of Achilles and the Tortoise is typical. "Let," he says, "Achilles himself propose the paradox that he cannot overtake the tortoise, and we see at once that to be a philosopher he has to be a knave; the mathematical requirement of the feat is wholly impertinent to its empirical accomplishment."

"The theoretical puzzle of Achilles is that in the punctual unity of each repeated effort he must achieve the distance between himself and the reptile at the outset — during which accomplishment the latter will of course have advanced *somewhat:* and this recurring somewhat, however short its space, renews the whole problem — for Achilles' next effort is assumed to be spent in the covering of *that* space, while the tortoise gains a new one, offering the same difficulty in the mathematical impossibility of exhausting a whole by taking away successive fractions of it, since the remainder will ever be a whole. The absurdity of the story appears in the assumption that the athlete is intellectually hobbled, in his repeated efforts, punctually one by one, so that he may not continue to do his best as in the first endeavor, but must waste a whole unit on the little space which his rival has added to the course; and it is this restraint, which in practice he would never dream of (and which might be in another country), that encumbers an empirical proposition with a conceptual impossibility, uncalled for and impertinent."

With the exposition of "ancillary unity" Mr. Blood's dialectic concludes: We are now on the verge of the anæsthetic revelation. Yet to make the transition not too abrupt, he turns for authority and justification to the central figure of the Christian tradition. He claims the sacredness of Jesus for the side of his secularity. As each one of us carries an ancillary penumbra which sucks up and deindividualizes our entity, a penumbra shading into the aliency of the endless pluriverse, and funneling its concentration through us, as light through a lens, so Jesus also carried the cosmic penumbra. He also repudiated man's responsibility, self-sufficiency, self-relation. Thus in the narrative regarding the woman taken in adultery — "the pertinence and motive of the legend can obtain only in the divine purpose of the gospel to relieve the human conscience of any responsibility to the inspiring power whose behest it powerlessly fulfils." Thus, again, in Jesus' remark concerning himself that of himself he could do nothing. No sum, no category of human conception is adequate to the solution of the riddle of existence, to the abolition of "duplexity": "freedom, originality and reason, as in equation with the Mystery, shall be the last hopes of mortal explanation." And so "the Mystery" is upon us. It is heralded with the significant remark: "our hope is not so much to philosophize the mystery as to signalize in it an unequivocal *impasse* whose obstruction can be neither obviated nor defined. . . ." It is the rock-bottom of reality whose uniqueness is irreducible and whose very recollection yields only a sense of initiation, of "now you know." The realization that comes to an animal passing over blood freshly spilled on the ground is of its sort; the animal is "arrested and entranced, seemingly by some exhalation from the vital fluid." Of its sort may be the spell that holds a calf to its place in the absence of its mother, or that constrains a brooding hen, or that, at the point of death, is indicated in the "stare of seeming recognition, as of some wonderful import, just before but distinctly not inclusive with the 'setting' of the eyes." What is found in the revelation is "no static unaccountable equation, but rather a constant excess, a going on simply *because* it is going on, in which the natural endeavor to account for itself proves to be of a piece with and containing the same stuff that it is meant to account for. . . . There never was a time that did not recognize the presumption of time and the push of its own necessity, and also that any question of its motive was itself a sufficient reason at once for its continuance and its precedence, but with no relation to a beginning." What validates this philosophic commonplace as Mystery and as Revelation is "the immemorial ata-

INTRODUCTION xli

vism, the sense of initiation, the voice of the blood, the unique assurance that it *is* a revelation of the historical and the inevitable and the time out of mind." It may befall each man differently, according to his nature, and no one man's befalling is ever reducible to another's. If it be unique for each, it is so because it shows him the commonplace secular stretch of time where his own being is but the instant firing-point of an advancing line. All this through anæsthesia, the right psychology of whose remission is stated, in Mr. Blood's judgment, by Xenos Clark:

"It is the one sole and sufficient insight why (or not why, but how) the present is pushed on by the past, and sucked forward by the vacuity of the future. Its inevitableness defeats all attempts at stopping or accounting for it. It is all precedence and presupposition, and questioning is in regard to it forever too late. It is an *initiation of the past*. The real secret would be the formula by which the 'now' keeps exfoliating out of itself, yet never escapes. What is it, indeed, that keeps existence exfoliating? The formal being of anything, the logical definition of it, is static. For mere logic every question contains its own answer — we simply fill the hole with the dirt we dug out. Why are twice two four? Because, in fact, four is twice two. Thus logic finds in life no propulsion, only a momentum. It goes because it is a-going. But the revelation adds: it goes because it is and *was* a-going. You walk, as it were, round yourself in the revelation. Ordinary philosophy is like a hound hunting his own trail. The more he hunts the farther he has to go, and his nose never catches up with his heels, be-

INTRODUCTION

cause it is forever ahead of them. So the present is already a foregone conclusion, and I am ever too late to understand it. But at the moment of recovery from anæsthesis, just then, *before starting on life,* I catch, so to speak, a glimpse of my heels, a glimpse of the eternal process just in the act of starting. The truth is that we travel on a journey that was accomplished before we set out; and the real end of philosophy is accomplished, not when we arrive at, but when we remain in, our destination (being already there) — which may occur vicariously in this life when we cease our intellectual questioning. That is why there is a smile upon the face of the revelation, as we view it. It tells us that we are forever half a second too late — that's all. 'You could kiss your own lips, and have all the fun to yourself,' it says, 'if you only knew the trick. It would be perfectly easy if they would just stay there till you got round to them.'

"The Anæsthetic Revelation is the Initiation of Man into the Immemorial Mystery of the Open Secret of Being, revealed as the Inevitable Vortex of Continuity. Inevitable is the word. Its motive is inherent — it is what has to be. It is not for any love or hate, nor for joy nor sorrow, nor good nor ill. End, beginning, or purpose, it knows not of.

"It affords no particular of the multiplicity and variety of things; but it fills appreciation of the historical and the sacred with a secular and intimately personal illumination of the nature and motive of existence, which then seems reminiscent — as if it should have appeared, or shall yet appear, to every participant thereof.

"Although it is at first startling in its solemnity, it becomes directly such a matter of course — so old-fashioned, and so akin to proverbs, that it inspires exultation rather than fear, and a sense of safety, as identified with the aboriginal and the universal. But no words may express the imposing certainty of the patient that he is realizing the primordial, Adamic surprise of Life.

"Repetition of the experience finds it ever the same, and as if it could not possibly be otherwise. The subject resumes his normal consciousness only to partially and fitfully remember its occurrence, and to try to formulate its baffling import, with only this consolatory afterthought: that he has known the oldest truth, and that he has done with human theories as to the origin, meaning, or destiny of the race. He is beyond instruction in 'spiritual things.'"

And so end philosophy and its perplexities and its contradictory solutions that do not solve. The Revelation itself is, according to Mr. Blood, not a solution either. It is a satisfaction. It is a satisfaction because it shows that what seems to be really is, that the question is the answering, that the answer is the questioning itself.

To many, what is attained here must seem no more than the blind autonomy and naïve acquiescence in which consists the consciousness of the beasts of the field. This needs no denial. It is the manner of the attainment that counts, that must be added to the goal, and that being added alters its nature and significance. The beasts of the field are not mystics and men who become mystics do so only by the force of the philosophy with which they justify their becoming. It is in this addition, in this power of dialectic circling that our manhood resides. The vindication through philosophic questioning of undoubting consciousness of the beast is the victorious self-preservation of the doubting consciousness of man.

H. M. KALLEN.

PLURIVERSE

CHAPTER I

DUPLEXITY

SECTION FIRST

The Critical and the Dogmatic

PHILOSOPHY, as the science of explanation, naturally assumes the coincidence of the possible and the rational, and as well of the rational and the logical. But experience rudely jostles this amicable adjustment. The human finite, as a local and ephemeral parasite, finds his prime concernment in causes and beginnings and ends, while the stable cosmos can afford only vibrations and compensations. To Sufficient Intelligence all things always are; only in a nightmare could it dream of a radical beginning or an utterly ceasing. And as for logic and expression, these can claim only as imitation or re-presentation, which at best may attain similitude, while "truth" is what likeness explicitly lacks, and what identity only could supply.

Reality itself, in and as knowledge, would have no essential being. Knowing is not being — not "thing in itself" — unless, always, knowledge is self-known. It is a fair conjecture that finite rationality is not consistent with cosmic conditions, and may factually be called upon to tolerate the rationally impossible.

Philosophy proposes a weird partnership or equation between man and the world, as subject and object, and these two prove strangely convertible and interwoven. That the transient subject, for all his legends of rainbow "covenants" and conversations face to face, "as of a man with his friend," should fail as a divine correspondent, is not surprising.

Yet duplexity is the main parenthesis of philosophy, signalizing a more or less explicit duality, a kind of sex, suggestive of attrition and process and result, with their thousand proverbs of reaction and compensation, even of strife as the father of things. Duality is especially the fated nature of consciousness, but whether instantly such in itself, or by a process of shifting viewpoints, making the wonder of a self to itself, is one of the most annoying and persistent problems of philosophy. A rational unity would require an intelligence that is such as an object or topic to itself; it should comprehend and include itself, even in the contradiction that the other is the same. But then, what is the use of contradiction?

We must call upon Emerson here:

"It is all idle, talking. Life is made up of the intermixture and reaction of two amicable powers whose marriage appears beforehand monstrous, as each denies and tends to abolish the other. We must reconcile the contradictions as we can, but their discord and concord introduce wild absurdities into our thinking and speech. No sentence will hold the whole truth, and the only way we can be just is by giving ourselves the lie: Speech is better than silence — silence is better than speech — things are and are

DUPLEXITY

not at the same time — and the like. All the universe over there is but one thing, this old Two-Face, creator-creature, right-wrong, of which any proposition may be affirmed or denied."

To a man on the street (if one could be supposed to stop and listen to it) this diatribe, seeming to discountenance all literary expression, even as confession, were but rigmarole or absurdity, possible under poetic license; but so far from all this, it has to be recognized as the basis of all responsible criticism.

From this classic substratum rose the reluctant confession of Kant: "It is sad and doubtless provoking, that reason, the only tribune for all conflicts, should be in conflict with herself."

We read in Schwegler also: "Only in the last of days can history account itself a work of reason."

Herr Eucken exclaims: "Scarcely anything repels so much as the impertinence of representing the world as it is as a realm of reason." And for this he is awarded the Nobel prize.

It makes good reading too in the *Hibbert Journal* (July 1910): "There is no complete generalization, no total point of view, no all-pervasive unity. . . . There is no conclusion — what has concluded, that we might conclude in regard to it? . . . The mystery remains as somewhat to be dealt with by faculties more akin to our activities and heroisms than to our logical powers."

In his exhaustive study of "Parmenides" Plato seems to have driven human rationality entirely from the field of explanation: "Whether one is or is not, one and the others in relation to themselves and one another, all of them, in every way, are and are not, and appear and appear not."

Popular civilization gets a call-down here. How has it responded to this esoteric arraignment of its power of expression and conception, in presence of the old Two-Face "of which any proposition may be affirmed or denied?" And either way under the handicap that no one sentence will hold the whole truth! Think of the numberless writers and teachers and preachers, with very liberal salaries and considerable reputations, taking themselves quite seriously: how has been condoned or compromised the inconsistency of their pretensions with possibility and rationality radically dissociated? Under what apologies or exceptions do the universities assume to have accomplished their thousands of graduates?

We should have expected in such an imbroglio that some determined spirit would long ago have come to the front with either a clarion denunciation of philosophy as the headline of the intellectual program, or with some *tour de force* in "method" wherein an expert might succeed in expression, even under the handicap that his opponent *on his own ground* might be as knowing as himself, with an equal standing in court. Why not a "commission" on the subject?

So far from any such ingenious *éclaircissement* appearing in the record, the position is stalled and camouflaged in a myopic pretence that there is nothing to be concealed — or if there is any inexplicable complication in the premises, it shall redound the more to the glory of God, with whom all things are possible. "Metaphysics" gets but a sinister shrug. "Religion out of church is sacrilege":

DUPLEXITY

it is bad form, such as would be discussion of the sacred privacies of the family physician. But *in* the church, safe from the free lances of the club and the clinic, rank exhorters who know little of the idealism that alone might tolerate their pretensions, speak as familiarly of God as Master Shallow spoke of John of Gaunt: "he might have been born brother to him."

It is fairly up to criticism and book-reviewing and reputation-making to adjudicate this challenge of reason by reason. Is the problem of true thought and expression — the classic "truth" — so obdurate as the professional thinkers have left it? Literature as well as metaphysics shall find its prestige at stake upon the question, whether this of Eucken is really the last word of truth — "the difficulty, indeed, *the impossibility of its appropriate representation in thought and conception!*"

Experts find it easy enough, however idle or inconsequent, flirting between equivalent viewpoints — ideal and real, static and dynamic, and dogmatically setting up half-truths which, when depended upon, directly topple over in their own partiality. Society has helplessly consented that certain oppositions shall be ignored. We cloak over our inconvenient discoveries and suspicions. The astronomer speaks of the "sunrise" quite childlike and bland; and the profoundest idealist constantly confesses to the integrity of matter. A rap on the head gives a conviction of reality that no idea can come forth of it and refute. Criticism of the common sense comes back in its own face; like the wasp and the hornet, it leaves its sting in the wound, and is fatal to itself.

For there does seem to be in the world, and more or less *as* the world, an *essential opposition*, which throws truth into contradiction. And the opposition is elemental, integral, punitive, entitling vitally opposing viewpoints, and encouraging antagonistic creeds. Down upon the practical field it entails the survival of the fittest. In metaphysics we see being and not-being insisting upon and pervading each other. We read of "negation positive in its result."

Such is really the genius of being, such the burden of philosophy. If possibility will stand for essential opposition it must stand for logical contradiction; there must be contrary knowledges at the same integral point. But opposing knowledges (not mere opinions) at the same point are null except upon one condition: *the reality shall not be objectively determined,* not a thing in itself, but rather what it is known as, the subjects themselves furnishing any apparent difference. But these knowledges may be good and sufficient for their subjects — half-truths perhaps, but wholes to half-natures. A man may stake life and soul that the sun goes around the earth; "to whom a thing appears that thing is," said the ancient; but for this to be true and not an illusion of sense reality must be subjectively determined, and not an alien thing in itself.

Reality by right should *be essentially,* or in and of itself; but for philosophy, which is a kind of impertinence, it can be only what it is known as. In truth being and essence should be identical, but in philosophy they are merely the same, and dialectically the same is another (there needs two for sameness). Though it were a re-presentation it were not truly the same though similar, or at best a likeness, and "truth" is explicitly what likeness lacks: pure being, rightly same in its identity, without limit or distinction, for philosophy becomes "one" — a being of limit and comprehension; and when philosophy would comprehend its all as one it has to negotiate the anomaly of somewhat limiting and comprehending itself. For, as said Philolaus, "one is made by limiting," and if all is one or a whole it is such by the limiting and comprehension of itself. The whole has no environment or room containing it: these if necessary shall be in the whole's own essence; and hence its comprehension is from within, spiritual, as of an ego or personal intelligence.

In taking the world as a problem philosophy necessarily raises the question, whether reality is objectively essential — a thing in itself — or merely what it is known as; and this again becomes under criticism a double question. Knowledge itself will in turn be called upon as to whether it is authentically such, or only what it can be critically proved — possibly only secondary and given.

For idealism reality has no objective integrity; or if at best it has position the same is questionable and indifferent. For pure philosophy the world *must be* what it is known as; and if knowledge itself is in question it must be self-determined.

That reality is identical for only what it is known as, consider the matter of its different sizes.

All sane human beings are agreed as to the apparent sizes of different things as something genuine and reliable; the world (we assume) is real as in and of these sizes. But when we subject an object to the microscope and enlarge its size many times, and find potentially in it beautiful features, and perchance living creatures for which the unaided eye is inadequate, we learn that in true æsthetic value our sizes are but arbitrary and accidental determinations of our own lenses, and that the world may have as many sizes as it has observers, and that it is identical only as position in some occult order of being, with no size at all of its own, in fact that *all things in themselves (if there are such) are the same.*

For instance we may say categorically that light and darkness are the same. Every one knows the sense in which they are different, but he may need to be advised of a vital sense in which they are alike, to wit, that neither is essential, or anything at all in itself — and further that there may be *no* reality in itself, but specifically only what it is known as.

As for light and darkness, we know that if all the light should go out there would be left no distinction — no form nor line nor shade of difference. But consider: *if all the darkness should go out*, the pure light would be equally void of any line or form or difference. It should appear then that neither light nor darkness essentially affords distinction, nor one more than the other, but that distinction in itself is a property of intelligence. The difference of two things is not a property of either.

In practical life we easily condone our opposing viewpoints. We assume a duplex consciousness of the sun going around the earth and the earth going around the sun; we allow them to mingle their motions,

Forever singing as they shine:
"The hand that made us is divine."

But we are not quite so ready in accepting as half-truths universe and pluriverse, or theism and atheism, as they arise in the consideration of space as either going on-and-on beyond comprehension, unity or personality, or as being in itself nothing, save by the voluntary occupying of subjective spirit. Concurring freely with Herr Eucken as to the impertinent presumption of the finite in assuming that the cosmos, to be at all, must be rational, or consistent with its parasitical nature, and agreeing generally that the rational and the possible are not necessarily coincident, we regard it as no heroic undertaking, holding theism and atheism as half-truths equally defensible.

Said Novalis: "Philosophy can bake no bread, but she can give us God, freedom and immortality."

By baking no bread he doubtless alluded to our utter ignorance of any natural law, the fact being that we know nothing of natural causes or elements; but for idealism (which was his only intention as philosophy) the world is not an alien imposition upon consciousness, but rather is determined by (or through) consciousness; and the seeming extensity of space is a mirage of spiritual liberty — the room and possibility of the spirit's action, and nothing at all in itself, nothing "out there."

The advantage of this absorption of space is to the spirit's unity and comprehension. Philosophy as explanation requiring a being that is sufficient in itself, and unity or one being due to limitation and comprehension, the vagary of a mere space-comprehension, a one in an unlimited other, would not be the *one of all* that supremacy and safety require. The one must furnish or contain its own limit, and philosophy as idealism proposes this in the self-knowing, self-limiting and every way self-determining (they would say self-creating if they dared) of the one.

(For scientific purposes it is better to understand here by the popular words, God, freedom and immortality, the plainer meanings of unity, spontaneity and safety.)

All turns here upon the notion of space — whether it is concrete objective extensity, or else the spirit's reflection of its own capacity and freedom of achievement, in a world where things are not alien and integral in themselves, but are what they are known as, determined by or through the lenses and forms of personal organization.

If space is physical extensity — *out there*, a concrete terrain whether it be occupied or empty, going on and on with nothing to stop it — then there is no more to be said of unity or comprehension, no more of "all" or "the whole." *Pluriverse* is the word, the everywhere as here, the democracy of the many, the impossibility of autocracy or supremacy or general personality.

(There needs care here to avoid the whim of "the infinite." We vacantly see space going on, and let it go at that: "infinite," because we neglect the finishing and carrying out of the thought of it. But it makes a radical difference in theology whether our outlook is mere indifference and negligence or a concrete continuum beyond comprehension. If

DUPLEXITY

the spirit determines its own space and unity and comprehension [as self-consciousness is supposed to demonstrate] then there *is* a possibility of God, freedom and immortality, self-centred and safe from any dangerous environment.)

Obviously there are here two ostensible viewpoints from which to rationalize a no less formidable opposition than that of theism and atheism. To the average culture pluriverse is inevitable; space goes on and on, and there is no comprehension nor limit nor unity, and no whole save the solipsist's whim of another than himself. But against this rises the world of idealism, which from its viewpoint cannot be disqualified.

The seemingly necessary and logical going on of space can be countered by an equally fated necessity of intelligence itself, whereby thought has a centripetal and self-relating tendency, a transcending excess of its own essence as knowledge in and of itself (possible if not rational) whereby it may constantly revert from the true tangent of extensity to the down-curving water-level of the planet-born, and prove the space which is conceived of as outward extension to be the freedom of its own will to extend, and that its limit and its wholeness are its own property — not framed or stayed by otherness, but essential as self-related.

Of course we of the scientific world know how this trick of orbicular intelligence is played upon us in the water-level, and we know that while in our logic nothing can be related to itself, yet we do constantly entertain the conceit of knowing ourselves without definite objectification, and of having an independent autonomous spontaneity of power — such as someone or something somewhere or somehow should afford for explanation. And as for our so confident assurance that space goes on and on whether occupied or not, let us see by an easy psychological experiment how Novalis would prove that philosophy can "give us God, freedom and immortality."

He has but to show that space-extensity is mental, and then all the objective world will respond to the subjective spirit, and dwell in the sphericity of a freedom in which it may advance equally and infinitely in any direction — a universe founded from within, not prescribed or framed by otherness, but having in itself essentially the otherness wherein reason or fancy would produce or sustain existence.

Let the experimenter then resolutely set forth to walk off the planet into space and prove its endless outward extensity an objective reality.

We should foresee that in achieving this field or route our protagonist as an ingenious spirit will, as we might say, have one eye upon himself; and while, on his passage, he will at first measure this achievement by the bounds and barriers which he passes, he will also credit himself with the exertion that he puts forth; and in this regard he might well perceive that a blind man on a treadmill would be covering space at the same rate, and to the same extent. In the outer field of the empyrean our experimenter's eyes will be useless as to his advance; there will be no guideboards to pass, and he will be ready to confess that space so demonstrated or accomplished is literally nothing, and that the only considerable thing or fact to be objectified in the premises is his own liberty of action, which he has been erroneously construing as an atmosphere in which he lived.

As an intellectual problem, this proving space by units of outer exertion is the same as would be the proving of possibility by inward steps of the infinite divisibility of number. Our traveller (for the higher thought) is only marking time, and proving that space is his own freedom, while for the lower or pragmatic thought he is pursuing the water-level of the planet-born, and like the compass-foot that is ever returning while advancing, he will but identify his position by process, and prove that "unit and universe are round."

Nevertheless, over against this demonstration of orbicular intelligence, the pluriversal continuum stands immovably transcendent of all unity, comprehension or personality, and in the name of science protests that only the boor and the bigot bow to the rising sun.

Science can have no quarrel with Novalis for recalling space into himself, for we shall find under "Idealism" that all our world is a deposition of consciousness; but what we claim for duplexity is that the reverse of his doctrine is an equally plausible argument from grounds whose reality is as invincibly real as his own. We are not taking a side, but rather claiming that philosophy has been an inconsequent excursion. Our exclamation, Pluriverse, is here preferred to Universe only as emphasizing the clumsiness of those who live constantly in the dream of Novalis with no scintil of the idealism without which it is crudely irrational.

It is peremptorily obvious to the modern man, whom the astronomers have driven to the Copernican viewpoint, that facts as sure as the rising of the sun have to pass as illusions in order to give sanity and "sense" to doctrines that have grown out of unquestionable accuracy of thinking, which none the less stands loyally by the old ideas from the old viewpoints, which can be neither ignored nor superseded. The best form will not necessarily take a side in the theistic controversy. When the insistent dogmatist puts his question, "Is not one or the other of these propositions absolutely and exclusively true?" the best culture can but smiling put the question by, or like Socrates refer it to the professional experts.

Surely whatever is to be admitted in our world of thought should be expressible in words; we do no consecutive thinking otherwise than in conventional terms; but we are to consider that language is an invention slowly produced, and our philosophy infers the morning of the times. So far it is an inconsequent excursion in the hope of comprehension.

It is confessedly a strenuous and thankless *rôle* of thinking assuming the equivalence of opposing hypotheses in the same premises, and allowing a fighting chance to half-truths while denying any unity of generalization. Consistently we could never speak at all in the presence of the old "Two-Face," under whose countenance "any proposition may be affirmed or denied"; but convention has politely shelved these ultimate questions in the presumptive interest of religion, and before advancing

DUPLEXITY

to scientific idealism we shall speak more popularly of duplexity, less as of the critical and the dogmatic, and more as of the static and the dynamic.

SECTION SECOND
Static and Dynamic Relations

Only confusion can result from the exploitation of any philosophical topic without a previous appreciation of the ineluctable duplexity which involves all thought and things, and which primarily and most portentously divides the field of speculation into time and eternity; demanding two opposing viewpoints, to be severally characterized as the static and the dynamic, equally defensible.[1]

From the static viewpoint all things always are. For sufficient reason nothing could newly become; for becoming is in a time process, and in it the identical might only partly be, except under the startling concession of a reality both being and not being in the same instant, congenitally splitting the tongue of truth.

We may notice here, and perhaps as fitly as if anywhere else, that in the matter of a complete being between the past and the future (neither of which presently is), or of complete being as embracing being and not-being in contradiction, the understanding of Hegelism is that the truth of the absolute fact is process, or transcendental nature, in which being and not-being (logically apprehended) are moments, or mental elements. These, in the Hegelian exposition of the topic, appear and disappear in a tergiversation *between* the static and

[1] See Chapter IX.

dynamic viewpoints, either of which may be dogmatically defended — although they can be reconciled only in a confessed contradiction — by unifying identity and difference, and by claiming as (logically) instant a self-relation confessedly achieved by a lapsing process of the "in-itself" to the "for-itself." His dexterity in this tergiversation is "the secret of Hegel."

We may as well here notice especially the duplex nature of man.

Note firstly in his make-up the primeval equation of substance and form, or extension and thought, as he stands visible and invisible, apprehensible only by the joint faculties of sensation and reflection, of sense and spirit. Next see him double and opposed as male and female; and curious science has gone so far as to detect in either of these orders a rudimentary incipience of the other — as if, were one sex destroyed, the other might project the lost one from itself. Note further the duplexity of his two sides, right and left. From head to foot he seems put together as two variously independent parts, each with its leg and arm, and eye and ear, and its side of the organs of taste and smell — each with its half of the brain, the lungs, kidneys and heart; each with its system of nerves and vessels; and one of these sides may be at least partially paralyzed while the other is working comparatively well.

More intimately observe how each of the sides in turn is double in the method of its construction, in that it is throughout tubular — hollow and filled, container and content; the binding web, of which we might say, it is the man proper, is filled with blood and juices and food increment, formally *accessory;* the food and the juices inhabit their proper channels, and with regard to the integral man may be said to enter the form but not the substance: like a knife stabbed into a billet of wood, it may dynamically knock but it does not chemically enter.

The same persistent duplexity characterises the tubular web; for this in turn is made up of tubes. As in the ancient homoiomeria hair was made of lesser hairs, and feathers of lesser feathers, and stones of lesser stones, and the world at large of lesser worlds, so every tube seems made of lesser tubes that are made of tubes themselves, until, beyond the limits of microscopic observation, the sensible identity fades in the infinite divisibility of matter, lost in the bottomless well where, according to Democritus, Truth disappears from mortal view.

From the dynamic viewpoint, whence we naïvely recognize Nature and becoming, and seem to visualize change and increase and diminution, the static schema excludes any such idea of intelligence as we can admit or understand; and it vacates the reality of all human experience. It denies the possibility of novelty in nature and consciousness, and imposes an All-knower, with a "general" personality, yet competent to identify individual idiosyncrasies of thought and feeling within a compass as small as their own. If a man were down, in life's battle, and had "taken the count" up to nine, this All-knower should himself be within one tick of the knock-out. How else could he realize the finite measure of such a consciousness?

Wavering between these adverse viewpoints, philosophy develops various "activity situations," in which being and change are so confused that a logical statement of the case involves an *identity of difference*. Our conscious experience of life and time is of a continuüm of process and change, growth and decay, becoming and deceasing, in which philosophy raises a question as to what really is. She must insist that only what fully is is real, and she challenges a condition of becoming for somewhat that has fully become. We are loth to admit that any reality can only partly be — as if it were half in and half out of the real world, or as if the world were but half real, or as if what we mean by identity *is* difference and process. All these questions arise from any careful consideration of what we thoughtlessly call the present tense.

A contract for a working model, or even a "side elevation" of the present tense, done under all its scientific exactitudes, would drive the best inspired architect to either a madhouse or the ultimate surd. He would have to first effect a compromise with the static viewpoint, which can only under protest countenance any present tense at all. For to Sufficient Intelligence (and no other can obtain) all things always are, and the form of eternity excludes any form of time. An "eternal present" is a whim which the sure method quickly evaporates. But adopting the dynamic viewpoint, as the only feasible one for us, his first outlook would encounter *two cross-universals*. The spacial universe cuts like a disk at right angles across the universe of duration, and the crux of reality is at the instant junction of the two.

DUPLEXITY

Around this point swarm like bees and hornets the positive and negative queries of speculation. Here the time current offers to criticism its three moments of present, past and future, to be construed under the requirements of community, contrast, opposition and compensation; and at the same intersection the spacial universe presents to the wavering time element the sympathy of a problematic unity of matter and form, of real and ideal.

We shall not dwell upon this crucial collocation just here, but will offer a suggestion as to "the nature of things," always intending by the word *nature*, the gerund or noun-participle, as the act, fact and substance of *being born*.

An object of sensation is presumptively such in the present tense only; but as subject to the passage of time it is also presumptively in continual change, and therefore never wholly identical, never quite the same; but since it may not at once be wholly other in its change, the object as such is a *quasi* identity of changing aspects, and the endurance of similarity in any one of its aspects constitutes it as a "thing." A cross-section, or a breaking-off of the stream of time at any given instant, would show an aspect on its hither end.

As a merely provisional simile I will instance the body of time as a confectioner's batch of candy, made to be drawn out into the usual "sticks." In making up the batch (ordinarily of 25 pounds), the expert makes a fasces or rope of rolls of differently colored stock, so ingeniously disposed that when drawn out, and broken at any point, the ends of any stick will present a picture, possibly of a star, or a rose, or a bird. If these various strands of the fasces may represent the elements or laws in the body of the stream of time, we may envisage a thing in the present tense as an aspect or a picture *done on the hither ends of the laws.*

Certain thoughts in passing are inevitable in view of the present tense, or of its genius as we apprehend it. Our first necessity is, in attempting to assume a definite present as distinct from the future and the past, we materialize or embody it, and subject it to the infinite divisibility — the real centre of the ideal centre, etc. (*i. e.* reconciling matter and form). But when we pause in satisfaction at the present tense in its three stadia of present, past, and future, the same acumen which proposes these divisions finds itself called upon to grade the three into one another: there are as many degrees between the present and the future as there are between the future and the past. Infinity, the bottomless well, intercepts every possible distinction.

It was our thought to apply these necessities to practical music. The maestro may pride himself on his distinction of tones and semitones, and so determine the *matter* of music, but the genius of music holds its carousal between his lines, in infinite division. Here it is that we learn how the violin is queen of all instruments. The piano, the organ, the harp, are fixed at given intervals; only the violin finds the infinite difference, where even the pulse of the artist varies the pressure on the string, and denotes the soul.

The recognition of these opposing viewpoints is

DUPLEXITY

the most venerable characteristic of the sagacity of our earliest historical past. Long before the Greeks had contemplated the problematical aspects of the One and the Many, or of being and not-being, the Semitic genius had detected the subtlety and the fatality of truth's double tongue. Even to the Talmudic sages the legend of Job was antique, yet therein the duplexity of the ultimate was as distinctly pronounced as it was by Parmenides or Zeno.

In the Vulgate translation of this ancient scripture we read that Zophar the Naamathite, said unto Job: "And that He would show thee the secrets of wisdom, that they are double to that which is." (Job xi, 6.)

The last clause here rather exaggerates the duplexity intended. In the correct translation of the original Hebrew (as I am instructed) it is wisdom, not the secrets, that is double; and further, the clause here is incomplete, and this as to its most relevant and ingenious import. I may be permitted to offer a more accurate translation:

"*And that He would reveal unto thee the secrets of wisdom — for it is double to that which is really in our comprehension.*"

The last word is convertible as either physical possession or mental comprehension. The sages of the Talmud have used "toosi io" as synonymous with wisdom itself:

"Thine eyes did see my substance, yet being unperfect; and in thy book all my members were written, which in continuance were fashioned, when as yet there was none of them." (Psalms, cxxxix, 16.)

Another translation:

"My undeveloped substance did thy eyes see, and in thy book were all of them written down — the days which have been formed while yet none of them was here."

Again the Preacher said:

"That which hath been is now; and that which is to be hath been already: and God requireth that which is past."

These ancient sentences overhang our lucubrations, warning us how old is philosophy — how early man tried to turn upon himself — to put being into thought, and thought into language, to objectify an ultimate generalization, a one of it all — only to find, at second-thought, that at best he was other to his one, and that his ultimate unity was duplexity at last — that the *truth* of his knowledge was a vanishing phantom of endeavor to know — to effect a self-relation, to *realize* being in thought, matter in form, the divine spirit in the Word, and the Word in the flesh. All this comes down to us in the confessed failure and discontent of philosophers: for modern instance, in the dream of Fichte, of "being out of its being," as *into* "existence," or the claim of Schelling that "something deeper than science he certainly did *know*," or the despair of Jacobi that there was a light in his heart which failed when he would bring it into his understanding, even as Saint Paul's law in his members antagonized the law in his mind.

These troubles will in course recur to us as we advance toward the revelation of the Mystery, wherein the unique must fail to be articulate and

DUPLEXITY

factual, because there can be nothing comparable as either like to it or different from it — it being feasible in personal experience alone.

Right here, for a *modus vivendi*, we must apologize and if possible conciliate. We began by disqualifying philosophy at its ostensible best — not promising on our own part to philosophize any better, but rather intimating another kind of satisfaction — and still we are in a way philosophising. We acknowledge the discrepancy; we have to dogmatize even in declaring our ignorance, using an intelligence whose finality we question: a kind of knowing that we do not know.

A claim of Sufficient Intelligence would assume the radical solution of the philosophical problem, while all the intelligence that we know of is secondary and unaccountably *given* to us — so that our course is ever wavering between an ideal of certainty and a practical plausibility. We shall hold that there is no "sufficient reason" short of a self-relation which we cannot admit; and while we deplore our uncertainty we cannot greatly admire a consistency due to an arbitrary and meretricious partiality for either horn of an incorrigible dilemma. We have simply found the problem of its practical unity insoluble in the philosophic methods of the past; and our treatise is not necessarily impeached by the adoption, more or less satisfactorily, of a different standard of satisfaction and a different method of attaining it. We admit equally the horns of the dilemma, and by the adoption of a name for it hold it in a merely nominal though philosophically useful existence.

When we say that to a Sufficient Intelligence all things always are (since for it all causes or rational principles shall have emptied their effects, and forestalled from it all novelty and surprise), we are entertaining *an ideal of intelligence higher than our own practice exemplifies;* and only by a degradation of this reason (as knowing all causes or fertilities exhausted) can we admit the reality of our ever-becoming world, which nevertheless our pains and pleasures so positively and even punitively authenticate.

Nevertheless such an all-knowing intelligence is a transcendental presumption. Critically considered, *no* intelligence as merely such is sufficient for fundamental explanation. Intelligence, as we exemplify or acknowledge it, is *after the fact known* — except upon a condition which we shall find inadmissible: to wit, that *there is no lapse or passage of time between the intention of the subject and the existence of the fact known.* Any such lapse, for the thinkers whom we shall prefer and defend (as opposed to "self-consciousness," so called), is a merely nominal "identity of difference," a clever logical puzzle which would meretriciously annul all distinction, since, forsooth, difference must be (to be at all) *identically* such, while identity itself has "all the difference in the world" from difference — making strife the ill-begotten father of things: a fact, if fact it is, of little credit to philosophy as satisfactory explanation.

The dialectic position best appealing to us would assume a chasm between the static and dynamic viewpoints, the breadth and potentiality of which

DUPLEXITY 25

vary with the cultural and temperamental differences of philosophers themselves, some of whom have fancied "truth" as in absolute contradiction — resolutely holding being and not-being as the same — while others have shaded or mellowed direct opposition by a bias diversion of it into process (through time's becoming), or else making conceptual abstractions serve for perceptual or empirical uses — which Kant forbade.

It may amuse, however little it may edify us, to observe how *quasi* or half truths and flimsy abstractions have in their ingenuity, and their novelty in the growth of thought, lulled temporarily the yearning for absolute explanation. In this humor we shall propose a substitute for creation out of nothing, which shall give full credit to Sufficient Intelligence while yet saving the vital experience of the Many.

We saw in Section First, under the hypothesis that reality is what it is known as, that the sizes of things are determined by organic lenses, and that knowledge through the lenses is to that extent ostensibly creative.

The popular supposition is of the One's divinely creating Many in a time process, and credit herein is given to some occult activity or fertility from which things come as out of nothing. Mere knowledge seems incompetent to produce, and rather fitted to witness or attend. In the case of the sizes, as determined through the organs, the effective power is left a mystery within or behind the subjective spirit; but as for the One creating the Many, or being creditably responsible for the Many, we shall see that in the nature of things, without any dynamic action or fertility, the Many *belong*, and are potential in the One, as a necessity seen in its nature from the static viewpoint of Sufficient Intelligence, whence all things always are.

We are now to suppose a human eye placed just without the perimeter of the revolving earth, which would pass it at a speed of 1,000 miles per hour. In the unity of the intelligence behind the eye there is the many-ness of 1,000 miles. If now, in the freedom of our hypothesis, we increase the intelligent unity by enlarging the eye to the size of the earth, the 1,000 miles, as a reality of organic consciousness (a Many), would fade into a mere potentiality in the unity of the larger consciousness. For the earth would be, to the larger consciousness, not larger comparatively than a lady's watch, so slow that the hour-hand, though taking all day for one revolution and hardly seen to move, would beat her two to one. *To the Sufficient Intelligence the Many belong in and are as real as the One.*

The One of identity, or pure being, shall hold involved and nullified all difference and form. To illustrate this position:

Taking a bushel of crude stones, we may beat them down to say three pecks of dust, a smaller bulk; but while the crude stones, piled as a cairn upon a windy knoll, might so endure for many years, the dust in the same exposure would soon be blown away.

This familiar fact becomes curious when we consider that the particles of dust are likely, each by itself, to be of the same specific gravity essentially as the bulk it helped to constitute, if not heavier, for presumably the bulk would have taken fracture where it was least substantial. But a moment's reflection warns us that the particle of dust has a larger surface-exposure in proportion to its weight. When you cut a body in two you expose two new surfaces, while the weight remains unchanged; and the wind, having the advantage of pressure upon a greater superficial area, more easily carries the particle away.

We are concerned here with two units of identity in the same environment. A stone is a stone, surely, but in this experiment it appears that the larger stone is not only more but *more in proportion* than the smaller; and if we ask, in proportion to what? the answer is, to the show it makes in the sensible world. From the viewpoint of mere appearance, increase is creative of identity by the degradation or absorption of form; the accretion of the one bulk vacates the discretion of the many of the dust; it takes in all of their form, which as an abstraction enhances the identical and concrete. And if identity appreciates by the accretion and destruction of form, the supreme One, the identity of totality is, within, dark and formless; for all externality or marginality or aught of discretion must disappear—unless, always, the One is not only one, but other to itself, and in so far not itself; *i e.*, its "truth" is contradiction.

We may well rest a moment amid these baffling subtleties to better account for them. They do not explain; we can at best discover the grounds of their plausibility. There is no standpoint from which philosophy can be despised. The cosmos is a momentous affair, and we are ourselves so clever, we cannot repress the presumption that it can be understood. We have but to watch the stars to believe in "perpetual motion," at least with their assistance. But our immediate interest is in the *quasi* principles or half-truths, abstractions partway across the dialectic chasm, which have been meretriciously posed in their day as explanatory. There is no great risk of credit in quoting from Pythagoras that number is the substance of things, or from Aristotle that matter is by the degradation of form, when we see Kant with no other first principle than "spontaneity" — just an empty word, presuming fertility; or see Hegel and Fichte impregnating negation and self-relation; or see the modern Germans, discomfited by a stale personality, depersonalizing the popular attributes of God, and using them *sans* credit; or see M. Bergson investing life and time and evolution with all the efficiency of creative intention. We do not disparage the ingenuity of these professors, at least not so much as we distrust their veracity, or regret their shortsightedness in deeming their results "philosophy."

Resuming consideration of the *quasi* power of abstractions: When we reflect upon our utter ignorance of the origin of the world's dynamic forces, and recall that the most ambitious account of the metaphysical forces halts at an inane "spontaneity" — a pseudo-fertility of emptiness — or at best at a "free will" whose freedom is essentially its exemption from any native influence or tendency — we are startled and interested by any hint from the dy-

DUPLEXITY

namic world that *force* may be due to *liberty*. It seems at first a rather hopeless resource, but some admissions are necessary to unaccountable fact.

The amateur in dialectic may well need some coaching here, lest he too hastily retort that getting force out of liberty is nonsense; the sophist may catch him if he does not watch out. All talk is dangerous. The amateur might not hesitate in saying that nothing can create — he meaning that creation is impossible; but the sophist will stare in mock admiration at the oracle: he is interested in production, and wonders at this account of it, and he proceeds to magnify it with his largest lens: "Nothing can create! nothing, nothing, NOTHING!" By capitalizing nonentity, and "taking you at your word," and pretending that the oracle is worth while, he finds a *position* in your amateur *negation*: NOTHING, logically, is "something" (*i. e.* something for discussion); and indeed a professor of capital reputation has held half the civilized world for a hundred years staring at the paradox (transcendentally true) that "negation is positive in its result." The cue of the dignified skeptic is possibly rather silence than dogmatism. And as a sop to Hegelians we may mention an instance where the negative seems to have positive effect, not merely as logical but as empirical. We allude to the tacking of a ship against the wind, an everyday affair.

With the wind blowing, say directly from the west, the expert skipper faces his sails diagonally to its pressure, and so, by tacking alternately to the right and left, glides forward by degrees in the direction of its very source. When we consider how the water is entirely negative or inert, while the wind is the only motive force, the fact that the west wind blows the vessel to the west calls for an explanation of the "dialectic" of the skipper, which out of the negative water achieves his positive advance. Now all this involves a curious question of our practical experience of physical motion and momentum. When I was young, in almost any attic in our Eastern States there was liable to be found the débris of some device for "perpetual motion." The latter is not a necessarily extravagant dream. The stars seem to exemplify it; and even if one could not independently produce momentum for mechanical uses, still with the help of the motion everywhere apparent he might hope to "hitch his wagon to a star," and get the benefit of its impulse. And a certain striking fact in physics encouraged the hope of an absolute production of momentum from freedom, as if thereby one might share the fortune of the stars themselves, however they come by it.

This fact is certainly occult at least, however it may be ultimately demonstrated as superficial. In any event it seems to have been the spur to many fruitless Yankee inventions. The fact was this:

A pound-weight falling to the platform of a spring balance-scale will, in a fall of twenty inches, gain about nine pounds; it will deliver the impact of a ten pound weight; or practically it will weigh ten pounds. Whence are the extra nine pounds? The earth itself weighs but one pound less while the pound weight is free and falling; and of course, to that extent, "the belt is off," the moon gets away, etc., but the impact, the blow, the momentum, seems wholly

DUPLEXITY

due to time and freedom, which have no material cost. The hope of inventors has been to so use the momentum gained as to replace the fallen pound for another fall, with some advantage won for mechanical uses. But unfortunately the time required to replace the pound weight is as exacting as the time of the falling was liberal, and the experiment fails.

The lesson is not unimportant for us. If the stars are a limited set, the outermost orbs in their circular courses may advance toward the unlimited and unoccupied space, against the general gravitation of the system as a whole, in this false hope that the momentum gained will restore them to perihelium, so that their motion, however originally given, will be retained forever. But this hypothesis has no standing in any rational court. Gravitation admitted as a general principle of matter will "hold the universe together" with a vengeance! No gain of momentum from "freedom," no series of motions within a limited set of stars, can withhold the whole system from falling to a single center. There must be as much gravitation outward as inward, to keep the stars apart; and the conception of space as wholly subjective does not reach the problem at all, for transcendental and empirical realities alike are necessarily subject to the same *a priori* rules. Sidereal orbits are possible only in a limitless field.

Still this growth and momentum, born of freedom (which metaphysically costs just nothing), awaken curious reflection. You may see a woodsman with his axe by a mere twist of his wrist sever a three-inch limb by use of momentum, though the steady pressure of all his strength might not sever it in an hour. So a man with one blow of a sledge will crush a stone that may have upheld a temple for a thousand years. *Why did not the still pressure of the temple accumulate momentum from time, as does the free swing of the sledge or the axe, or the falling pound?*

And there is a psychological momentum of the same kind. A man may wind up his resolution for an emergency, as the boy cries "One, two, three," and "Go!"

There is such an instance in the play of "Othello," which Shaksperian critics seem to have disregarded. Just before stabbing himself, and after having protested his hard fate, the Moor says:

Set you down this;
And say besides — that in Aleppo once,
Where a malignant and a turbaned Turk
Beat a Venetian and traduced the state,
I took by the throat the circumcised dog,
And smote him — thus.

I find no historical warrant for the precedent here cited. I rather suspect that the great dramatist depended upon his audience to realize that in this rigmarole, possibly preconcerted for such an occasion, the desperate hero was screwing his courage to the sticking point.

Our Americans may well regard it as an endorsement of our ostensible freedom that a little more than a century of it has evoked more patented inventions than are recorded in the whole history of England, saying nothing of our more liberal religious thought.

We may infer that idle freedom is a more prolific mother of invention than is the proverbial necessity.

An Italian peasant enters the lofty vestibule of St. Peter's with bowed and uncovered head; before him, in the dim religious light, the pillared silence stoops from arches vast to uplift the melody of the finest voices to be gathered in Europe, while haply the great organ, yearning in the pathos of its theme, shudders at the memory of Calvary and the Via Dolorosa. On every side around him appear the loving contributions of a thousand years of art and culture. Who or what is he among these æsthetic treasures, which for his unsophisticated reverence have an equal date with Andes and Ararat, to question or to criticise the doctrine that he hears? An original thought if he could have one would be anomalous, even profane; he is both mentally and materially overborne and outclassed. Meantime, in a land far from this sacred establishment,

A land where the mountains are nameless,
And the rivers all run God knows where,
Like the lives that are erring and aimless
And the deaths that just hang by a hair,

the plainsman, with his rope and his gun, takes the withers of the bay mare lovingly between his calloused knees for the long lope that covers her thirty leagues between sun and sun. Your thousand years are but as yesterday to him, and if he wants a church he must build it, under no other authority or inspiration than his own.

These philosophical controversies, so confident and at times so bitter, what are they more or other than cultured and temperamental preferences vibrating between the static and dynamic viewpoints, as in turn matter and form, identity and difference, and all the other nominal abstractions are allowed to exchange places in an incorrigible duplexity which in turn stultifies its claimant as of an ultimate generalization? How shall one claim the "world" as *thus* or *this* and no other, with the deeps of being as other behind his eye? What hope of explanation remains when the last word of dialectics shows an equal alternity of being and not-being, identity and difference, reality and appearance, and finally of reason and unreason?

The coil is about us, and at once we are and are not the coil. Can this be "true"? or if true is it worth while? Since it seems that whatever we may say will from some point of view pass as true, we shall venture the paradox that chance is the only sure thing.

The vulgar reverence which accounts him an imbecile who accepts anything as referable to other than personality, or in fact to fate, is subject to criticism as a psychological and possibly erroneous conceit; and we take occasion to say a word for chance, as quite as explanatory as any other hypothesis — as essentially just, and certainly exempt from the whims and vagaries whose possibility is the chief prerogative of spontaneous and independent personality.

It can be only through positive injustice and partiality if all being and becoming have not an equal chance; for chance is a daughter of justice, if justice should be, and her deformity would be a scandal to the cosmic empyrean.

Chance could be only half-bad at the worst — surely as apt to be good as bad — and experience, in all our human policy, finds it dependable and sufficiently fair. Be it as blind as you please, all business defers to it. And why not? Is it not obvious that only some monstrous malignity could permanently overbalance the normal equality and indifference of things in themselves? *Why* should they go crazy, and destroy value (so opposing the Good, which was Plato's first principle of possibility and continuance)?

(We are not assuming to explain, but proposing to the reader the contingency under which the question, why things are, is no more important than the question, why should they not be.)

With three true dice, marked respectively *G, o,* and *d,* you will, *as a rule,* in six throws get the name, God, with no intention of so doing. With the appropriate nine dice and letters you will in 362,880 throws get the sentence, *God is good;* that is to say, the fact will be extraordinary and remarkable if you do not; failure of such a result would prompt the player to seek, and usually to find a malformation of the dice. The sentiment suggested to him by the disposition of the letters infers no bearing of its intention on the result. It would be irrational, saying you should not expect such a result. Similarly reasoning, the elements being given, in x throws one should get the universe (if it were a whole); and any sentiment of wonder arising at its contemplation would be overborne by the afterthought that, given any conservative principle of value, there is an equal wonder why it should not be.

The popular doctrine of evolution is a coarse-hand script of the persistence of value, or the Good, whereby the fittest survives in heredity. Given such a conservative principle, in the profusion of nature which affords a host of germs as against one that survives, the aggressive force of the fittest must hereditarily improve the species by selecting the most vivacious; and not so in general, but in every detail of animal organization the conservative principle must adopt the betterments which happen; and in the limitless time, which costs nothing, chance and heredity will have rationally contributed all that, afterwards, appeals to æsthetic appreciation.

We are not to wonder then, when the æsthetic parasite, ingenious and capable on his own account, flatters his vanity as a representative or model of the genius of the cosmos, and attributes all things to personality — forgetting, or rather not thinking, that under criticism personality is the greatest wonder of all.

Thus we may readily suppose him misconstruing, under a claim of "final cause," an appreciation at the end of things into an intention at their beginning.

The reliability and permanence of chance are the most consolatory elements of philosophy. The notion that, left to chance, all would go wild and undependable, miscalculates experience, and (as before noticed) calls for a positive malignity to overweigh the just indifference and stolidity or essential inertia of things in themselves. There needs a positive and peremptory *why* the ace should come up an inconvenient number of times. Justice is balance. The Good is not best, upon the whole; it does not appear to have been deserved, and it is unjust, by comparison, to the indifferent and commonplace; it shows a heat in the bosom of fate.

CHAPTER II

IDEALISM

THE word *idealism* has been so drawled through perfunctory and irresponsible discourse that one must speak by the card if he would not be undone by the reckless equivocation. Fortunately the most fashionable authority in the premises has left a categorical definition of the term that will bear criticism as well as will any statement of an insoluble problem.

In the year 1840 the editor of Hegel's works issued a small volume specially composed or selected by Karl Rosencranz, presenting Hegel's original outline of his course of lectures in the gymnasium at Nürnberg in 1808-11. We quote from his exposition of the "Phenomenology of Spirit," as delivered in the second year of the course:

"Our ordinary knowing has before itself only the object which it knows; it does not at first make an object of the knowing itself. But the whole which is extant in the act of knowing includes the object and the ego that knows, and the relation between them, namely consciousness.

"In philosophy, the determinations of the knowing include not only the determinations of objective things (as such) but also a determination of the knowing to which they belong — this likewise in common with things. In other words (always there are other words), they include both objective and subjective determinations; or rather (sic) definite species of relation of the object and the subject to each other.

"Since things and their determinations are both in the same knowing, it is quite possible, on the one hand, to view the same (the original) things as in and for themselves outside of consciousness, given to the latter as foreign and already existing material for it; on the other hand, however, the view is possible that consciousness itself posits this world, and produces or modifies the determinations of the same, through its mediating relations and self-activity, either wholly or in part. The first mode of view is called Realism, the second Idealism.

"The subject, more definitely apprehended, is Spirit (the mind). It is phenomenal when essentially relating to an existing object; it is so far consciousness. The science of consciousness is therefore called the phenomenology of Spirit.

"But the mind, according to its self-activity within itself and in relation to itself independent of all relation to others, is considered in the science of mind proper, or psychology."

This private outline for a course of public lectures is a kind of soliloquy, in which the lecturer forecasts clearly for his own guidance the substance to be amplified in his future discourse. Its rugged and categorical sentences call down literature from its vague and æsthetic atmosphere to scientific analysis of experience, and the precise meaning we intend in the language that we use. We find that we have been making objective topics of particulars which are internal and spiritual, or else are so blended of matter and mixed as to fail of right identification.

Experience more and more aggravated the antagonism between sense and reliable understanding, as to whether reality was external or internal, or partly each. Things of many kinds, which should be real and identical of themselves, not only change constantly in time but become different through their environment and the subjective conditions of their observers. The summer haze doubles the size of the sun, and a moral haze magnifies the two mites of the widow. "Things are not what they seem"; we are at a loss in locating reality, whether mental, material or moral.

A tree falls in the woods, and there is a roar — *i.e.* if any creature hears it, but not otherwise. The discrepancy here, between the popular and the ideal notions, comes from neglect of the distinction between sound, as in our experience, and vibration of the air, which becomes sound only as affecting auditory nerves; and this prompts the awkward assertion of the idealist, that there is no sound unheard. But when he says there can be no pain unfelt, the former assertion seems less anomalous. So when we say a lemon is sour, we are only locating externally our own sensation; the *lemon* will not be sour if left alone. We find that we have given to experience an externality which must be identically lived, to be at all — not but that there may be external ingredients involved with the experience.

So in the case of certain relatives. We say of a certain body, it is hot, or it is cold; but it is neither hot nor cold by itself, but only by a standard. The same body may seem hot or cold according to the patient's temperature. A cold-blooded fish may be warm in water that would chill an animal to death. There is no absolute thermometer on which cold is a degree.

Now while this proposition of Hegel, that "Consciousness may posit this world," is altogether too rank when taken for the world's rational explanation — for consciousness, to be explanatory, should be wise and designing and efficient, and every sane man knows that he does not designingly and voluntarily posit his world — and further, there is no popular or even esoteric understanding of a *universal* consciousness to which the positing could be rationally attributed (and the rationale of all consciousness is still left as an unknown root), still, I say, the categorical sentence, "Consciousness posits this world," is capable of a striking defence, and one quite satisfactory to a faith that will admit primarily the miracle of it all, or hold with the good Bishop Berkeley, that all consciousness and all ideas are due to the instant inspiration of God. For I must hold that so far as "this world" can be resolved to color, form, size and tangibility — and I will include all difference whatsoever — it is determined through (if not by) consciousness. But this declaration shall evade, so far as radical explanation is concerned, any power or fertility or cause behind consciousness, and (for the moment) any account of the objective and historical order of experience in whose presence alone consciousness is found to determine for spirits the things of this world.

Beginning with color, I say categorically that color is determined by the eye; I do not mean caused or produced in an explanatory sense, but only that it is phenomenally according to the eye, and awaits its presence.

In voicing my experience I have to assume a rôle of authority here, because my personal vision, although not singular, is rather extraordinary, exemplifying a binocular paralogism, in which quite frequently each of my eyes sees for itself, making for me two objects out of one; and either of these objects is the reality, as confirmed by its tangibility, although they differ in color. When I look at a lighted lamp, say seven or eight feet away, I see two lamps, a foot apart, one giving a white or clear light, the other appearing yellow. An ordinary iron stove has for my left eye, singly, the color common for both eyes when in normal focus, but to the right eye singly it appears bronze. Nickel ornaments are to my right eye of a beautiful brass. Surely my eyes determine these colors, even as stained glass colors the landscape; but the wonder is that the lens of the eye, unlike the glass with its one color, discriminates a myriad of tints and shades.

But it is not the mere color of an object that concerns me most. When I see two frames of one picture on my wall, and can hold my focus on either of them, I advance and place my hand upon it as the real frame, and am ready to stake and soul that I *touch the real*.

This conception of the phenomenality or ideality of objects becomes yet more impressive when we consider their size. Here we have the whole city claimed

IDEALISM

and owned and mapped to the fraction of an inch, and recorded in the courts, according to standard measures that are guarded with locks and seals. An inch is an inch and a pound is a pound *by law*. If the earth should lose part of its gravity unaware, all justice would be frustrated. The merchant who had contracted to deliver a pound would instantly become an idealist; your pound is not such in itself, but is related to and determined by an external intention; it is to be adjusted to the scheme of things, like Shylock's bond.

The literal truth of a size in and of itself would set the whole world crazy. Here is a pea — the whole race of men are of one opinion as to its size, as established in a universal environment; its alteration would derange the procession of events. But the truth is that this magnitude of the pea is but an arbitrary selection from its myriads of sizes, in this case determined by the common visual lens. This the true size! or the *real* size! Place it in the microscope and instantly it shows the size of a cannon ball. Is this a trick, an illusion? So far from it, we have lived the illusion hitherto. The glass has not merely exaggerated or distorted the features visible to the naked eye; the ball has grown, not like a bladder at the expense of its walls, but as the womb grows, essentially; new features and perhaps living creatures appear upon it. If any credit is to be allowed for beauty and ingenuity and use, the experience demonstrates the mechanical lens as an improvement on the natural eye, yielding, if not an ultimate size, at least a higher grade of appreciation or the assumed reality of size, as somewhat in and of itself. At any rate the fact is manifest that size is phenomenal, and determined by physical organism. Consciousness does "posit" it.

This is a simple truth, comparatively stale, to be sure, amid the growing wonders of science, but if the reflective mind will philosophize and make the most of it the inferences are overwhelming. The moment we admit that size is according to the lens of vision, "things in themselves" become conjectural.

The ideation of form is rather handicapped than staminated by the intrusion of tangibility, until both are subjectivized. Plato, being pressed for a definition of color, ventured the opinion that color is "an effluence of form commensurate with sight, and sensible"; we should say, rather, an effluence of surface; and that we rather think than see form, which is a kind of eclectic construction. Of course sense and understanding are inseparable, but when we propose analysis we are well advised to keep them separate. Even a worm or a clam is not so exclusively sensuous as not to show some understanding when its ground is jarred; but it seems a fair distinction to say that while a realist knows what he sees, the idealist sees what he knows — or that sense is amenable to identity, while difference is due to thought. Perhaps one cannot see what he does not know, but he surely may know what he does not see — for instance, familiar things when his eyes are closed, or in the darkness of the night. He knows (or at least assumes that he knows) by memory and conception, while he has no corroborating perception, and may be deceived.

We shall find, upon due reflection, that we have

IDEALISM

been very inconsiderate in our notions of form. For instance, we have a general notion of a table, obviously due to the average height of our viewpoint, and the ordinary position and use of the article. But we may assume that there are creatures on the floor, and on the ceiling of the room, to which the table presents a very different formation; those overhead may have never seen the legs, and those below may have never seen the various objects which the table is made to support. Theoretically the table has numberless viewpoints, from either of which it has a different form — constantly different, as well as also successively different by natural change.

Now as no one of these viewpoints can claim an authenticity superior to that of any other, the table has no integrity of form, taken as an observed thing in, or of, or by itself; all of its forms are solipsisms, each peculiar to a different intelligence. The thing in itself therefore fades into a mere position in the objective order of nature, identical only as a reliable potentiality in whose presence one of the table-forms becomes actual in the presence of a homogeneous spirit.

For the idealist, identity is blind; the "truth" of reality is distinction, which can be only in intelligence. It is very old philosophy, that "one" is made by limiting — *made*; the distinction is vital. There is no dead limit-ed; there is only the unlimited and the limiting. Draw with chalk a circle on a piece of cloth; the circle is limiting, or limit; but if you ask for the limited, the only answer is that it is essentially the unlimited, the cloth, which is the same without as within the circle. For idealism, distinction is alive, vital. The difference of two things is not a property of either, but is rather the property of that which relates them, or holds them in distinction. Here are two stones, distinguished as the big one and the little one; are they such in and of themselves? Surely, no; for I can change either as such by increasing or diminishing the other. Or in the case of number: here are six counters — are they six in themselves? Each is now a sixth of the number; if I surreptitiously remove one, I do not intrinsically affect the others, yet each of them will become a fifth; and if a thing is indifferently a sixth or a fifth, or is the same whether it is number six or number five, it can hardly claim number in itself. Number is a property of some one who can count.

So form is not a dead objective thing in itself, that may persist without thinking; it is not of stuff, but of mental relation. Here is a "puzzle picture, showing an Arab and a camel; find another Arab." Around the two obvious figures the artist seems to have indulged in scribbling, mere trash to transient observation, but which, nevertheless, is all that is to be merely *seen*. If you find the Arab in question you will have constructed his form by selection and unification, *after* which the form has become visible. We draw a triangle on a blackboard, and habitually assume that we see it by the eye, regardless of its idea, or the genius of its construction. But can a horse see a triangle? Take its base line: why shall he connect that with the two converging sides above? Why not rather affect the parallel with the edge of the board below? How shall he care where those lines go or end, while there is no form in his mind? He can

IDEALISM

no more see a triangle than he could see a picture of the Crucifixion. He has not the thought-forms through which the rhapsodies of sense become things.

The idealist will contend that only the idea, or the class, can be real and consistent, while the particular or participant is contradictory and confused; that the general cannot be asserted of the particular thing, but at best of thought or spirit only.

Idealism seems to have originated with the Greeks over the question whether the class or universal was merely an aggregation of particulars, each a separate value individually, or a unit from which their value came by participation. There are various beautiful things, but whence the common adjective that determines the class, beautiful? Is it an entity that can be thought as by itself? Taking the largest generality, we assume an entity of the many; but when we ask for the reality, instead of the name — when we ask "Many what?" we discover that the many are a mere rhapsody and confusion, of which the whole stock and substance is unity — it is nothing but ones, and is itself nothing, if not resolved to one. It was a question between Socrates and Parmenides, whether everything had or helped to constitute a class, or took stock in an idea. Socrates favored a certain objectivity in beauty and truth and justice, as general ideas that could have participating specimens, but at such examples as filth or nastiness he demurred; they seemed wholly subjective postulates or opinions. There is nothing against the real contents of filth, or even nastiness; it is only matter out of place; a basket of garbage may be of royal cuisine, only broken and disordered — every bit of it a dainty morsel by itself. The nastiness is in our appreciation of its incongruity with conventional fitness. But, then, could there be ideas wholly subjective? — and so forth.

We yield too readily to the claim and appearance of motion — perhaps too readily to the "science" that denies it. A wheel rolling on the rails at sixty miles an hour certainly presents as sure a demonstration of motion as the nature of things may afford — the wheel going bodily on the line of its route, and at the same time revolving on its axis. But questions arise: If the wheel moves, it must *all* move, or else go to pieces? It must. And the track is still? It is. But if the wheel moves, while in contact with the motionless track, the wheel would *grind* the track; but now a changing particle of the wheel at the bottom serves as a pivot for the motion of the other particles. Strip off the rim of a wheel and roll it on its spoke: we see at once that each spoke holds its position on the track until the next spoke comes down. If the wheel were lifted from the track and then revolved, this motionless part would fly to the centre and the other parts would go up and down and right and left around it; set the wheel upon the track again, and then the forward moving centre assumes also the backward motion of the bottom, the top doubles its speed, and the bottom is as still as the track.

But stillness, and centre, and bottom are all general ideas, which refuse sensible expression. Is there a bottom or a centre of a wheel, as a material thing? Or are these conceptions in the mind only? Surely the latter. The perimeter of the wheel is a curve,

IDEALISM

and no section of it can be so short but it will curve up from the track and present the anomaly of being both top and bottom; and no portion of the wheel can be so small as to be wholly a centre, but if sensible it will be so large as to have an ideal centre of its own.

Now in declaring the subjectivity or ideality of form we found the integrity of the idea threatened with frustration by the tangibility of its ground; we can sensuously *touch* the material that owns and presents the form, and so prove its objectivity as awaiting consciousness, rather than determined by it; let vision be never so illusive, touch seems a sure test of substance; let the night be ever so dark, touch proves the objective reality of things whose inherent form awaits only the kindly light to reveal them.

Well, sensation, that involves pain and pleasure, should seem the surest criterion of reality. But somehow, as at the discharge of a gun the report comes later than the fact, the scientists will insist that the nerves carry sensation only 180 feet per second, so that a material man might be dead before he knew it, as they tell of a star still visible that perished thousands of years ago.

But that touch is less phenomenal than vision, that its objects show a substantiality not relative to or determined by subjective organization, is an untenable hypothesis. The attestations of substance by tangibility and impenetrability are variously contradictory. We have but to notice the different penetrative forces of electricity and light. Light goes through glass, and stops at iron, while electricity goes through iron and stops at glass. If our visual faculties were electrical, glass would be phenomenal, and iron would be no object; while if our vision had the penetrative quality of light, iron would be an object, while pure glass would be invisible. We see only what we cannot see through.

We gather from these reflection the potential significance of Hegel's definition of idealism, as the doctrine that "consciousness posits this world," with the careful reservation, "wholly or in part." Only the "absolute" idealists, of the Fichtean order, go so far as to say that there is nothing in the visible and tangible world but what is placed there either by or through consciousness. According to Kant there is something at least mentionable as a thing by itself, but how qualified he neither knew nor ostensibly cared to know. His vocation was science, not explanation, and science as a fact for criticism, regardless of its unknown root. But the more moderate idealists — such as appreciate the reflections above noticed — are for their own part very willing to avoid the responsibility of consciously *making* this wondrous world, or even their own share of it, and insist that there must be somewhat independent of our parasite consciousness — some objective and historical order, in the presence of which, and according to which, consciousness has or makes or determines these phenomenal revelations. Either this or else the whole fact is a divine miracle.

The static and dynamic viewpoints are likely to remain in contrast, if not in opposition, as long as men shall countenance the possibility of a particular and of a universal intelligence, or the masque of humanity shall continue. That we live in the new-

IDEALISM

ness of time, that creation is continuous, that things are born and grow old, and that life in its process is vitalized and realized by sensations of immediate and temporal and even sacred experience — all new, and with the prestige of a divine accomplishment of historical purpose and intrinsic worth — it were stultification to deny; the denial would be a flippant assertion that we are but such stuff as dreams are made on and that we do not really know, or feel, or exist. (Yet to deny the supremacy of reason and Sufficient Intelligence, in which all things must always be and be known and felt, is to declare a condition in which existence itself would be so precarious and confused as to be hardly worth while, and one requiring a suspense of judgment at its very best.)

The dilemma is the same, or analogous, between idealism and realism. If we agree with Parmenides, that "one thing are being and thinking"; or with Protagoras, that "man" (as intelligence) "is the measure of all things"; or with Hegel and the earlier Fichte that the absolute totality is the self-relation of "thought"; or with Kant, that our external world is projected from (or at least determined through) our personal organization, and that our objects are not things in themselves; or finally, with more modern critics, that there are no things in themselves — common sense and sane metaphysics alike require some account of the region where things at least seem to be, and some sort of objective and historical order of reality in the positions before which, and some way determined by which, the individual spirits are so uniformly given the same phenomena in the same place and time. It is certainly remarkable, if spirits project their own phenomena, that in any given presence or position they all project the same apparitions, in the same stages of growth and decay. There should be either a unity of inspiration from behind the different spirits or else there is presumably an objective integrity before them.

For example, take the discovery of our planet Neptune. At least two astronomers had realized that in the objective consistency of the solar system there was required in a certain position the gravitation proper to a certain bulk of matter. The practical fact of the "thing" (Neptune) had never appeared in human knowledge, and was realized only after science and mechanism had caught up with a reality which historically preceded them.

These contrasting viewpoints of idealism and realism are as such quite as defensive severally as are those of the static and dynamic, and it is but fair to materialism, in the face of the idealist contention that consciousness posits the apparent world, to consider occasionally what a wonderful world it is, and what a staggering proposition to the average consciousness its production or even its comprehension must be. We have no use for the truism that each man's world is "all the world to him." We are not solipsists; we have to believe in other people, and in history, in "alien energy," and a venerable establishment at which, as ephemeral visitors, we may take our glimpse, question its conditions, its origin, purpose and permanence, and inconsequently pass on.

It is under the spur of these or like considerations

IDEALISM

that solid people like Mr. Spencer revolt at "the insanities of idealism." Yet Spencer himself, when philosophising, will not forego these anomalies. In his "Psychology" he says: "What we are conscious of as properties of matter, even down to its weight and resistance, are but subjective affections produced by objective agencies which are unknown and unknowable." No idealist can say more; and if any property of matter is not such a subjective affection, but a reality apart from subjective spirit, the sensible world may exist as truly without experience as within it.

But the sense anomaly will persist. Here is a great painting which has for the moment but an uncultured observer. Now I am free and prompt to say that color, form, size, tangibility (and even all difference whatsoever if you please) are determinations of conscious spirit, and that apart from such determinations there are no "things," any more than there are color and beauty and perspective in the night on the hind side of the earth; something must come there — light as well as vision — to afford intelligent experience; still the ground of possible experience may be objectively determined. The culture of the boor is the measure of the picture only for him. The picture has objective potentiality for a larger culture; and so the idealist, with his one dogmatic and unquestionable claim, may well inquire, if reality evolves "things" only according to his subjective categories, the material limiting, if not the formal constructing element of experience may be on the objective side so far as he is concerned. A critic might say to the average perfunctory idealist, even as he might to the boor before the picture, "you see all there is in it for you, and ignore what a fundamental explanation requires of its position — in which event you are a solipsist and a bigot, up in the tree of life indeed, but sawing off the limb that supports you."

Idealism and realism, in their literature, have shown a very unnecessary and even contemptuous antagonism. The idealist, obsessed with his right claim that objects are not yet "things" in themselves, seems to the realist to be clearing his perspective of everything save, perhaps, of subjective dream — at any rate that he makes the visible world "in itself" unreal; whereas the true idealist should mean no such fact; he opposes not realism but materialism. Fully admitting the external reality, he philosophises the *making* of the reality, claiming that experience is not wholly due to mere crude stuff, but partly as involving soul in the world, and possibly God; that experience of phenomena is a composition of matter and form, and that the matter becomes "things" (out of the formless dark) only in the presence of divine light and organic vision. But idealism has been mainly (and perhaps helplessly) at fault, in not scientifically explaining what the noumenal ground, the matter-side of the exhibition, is, before the show, and in itself — what it is that impregnates the position in the objective historical order, and makes it potential of the same "things" to all organized spirits alike in the presence of the same position. Kant's idealism is not opposed to the reality of things but only to their utter materiality:

"The ideality of space and time (and of their contents) leaves the truthfulness of our experience (as well as the ground or cause of it) quite untouched, because we are equally sure of it, whether these forms are inherent in things by themselves, or by necessity in our institutions of them only."

It is just here that "absolute" idealism puts in its claim, that the noumenal side of reality is totally implicated in the divine subjectivity, and that matter or the negative shall have no essential credit in itself, but only as critically posed in the shape of a non-ego in the ego regarded as self-related spirit. The exploitation of this idea into a system, involving the working world, became the life vocation of Fichte, and continued until its possibilities and as well his own powers were hopelessly exhausted, and ended in his renunciation of the whole problem, in his "Vocation of Man."

"I know that if I am not merely to play another perplexing game with this system, but intend really and practically to adopt it, I must refuse obedience to the voice within me. . . . I will not do so. I will freely accept the vocation which this impulse assigns to me. I will restrict myself to the position of natural thought, in which this impulse (faith) places me, and cast from me all those over-refined and subtle inquiries which alone could make me doubtful of its truth."

(This determination changed his claim of knowledge as self-relation, or knowledge of knowledge, to simple faith in Kant's canon of pure reason, "I think.")

Yet *malgré* this renunciation by Fichte, absolute idealism is the only goal and full accomplishment of dialectic philosophy. The soul cannot pose as a mere spectator of any object, however real. It must draw the object up into itself, where no mere copy or representation of it before the Highest shall, under the name of "truth," pretend to absolute science; only identity with the object can be trusted. Truth, to the absolute, is a false pretence. Its very name stamps it as paper, not gold which cannot be substituted, however conventionally represented. The question is about knowledge, not about correct or passable likenesses; and truth is only asserted of likeness, not of identity with the object. Truth can pertain only to representation, which can never be equivalent to the genuine original. It is a word too much, unless the object as subject is self-related.

I do not observe that our materialists, who are halted by the spiritualists' claim that no matter can be refined to mind (since substance cannot serve as relation), have made full use of these phenomena of light and color, which were to Plato the prime wonders of the world. For how indeed can we think of light, at whose presence all the form and beauty of the world appear, as less than half of what we call intelligence? Without it "subjective" vision were impossible; we cannot imagine color. Nor are compound colors chemical. A blue ferruginous sand and a yellow silicous sand combined will make a green, although all the particles retain their integrity, and can be separated by a magnet. And the common light, which plays such an intellectual part in the phenomena of beauty, is a chemical element; it is as rankly material as any acid, as well appears in its action upon collodion in the making of a photo-

IDEALISM

graph, and in its mechanical effects upon vegetation. The distinction shall be very fine between such substance and relation, in a mechanical green.

All our conceptions of light are crude and immature. How inconsiderate and puerile is our notion of a star: a bright point, sending a ray to us. But is it not at the same time sending a ray to every point of the universe? Not a singular gleam, but a limitless globe of light — an atmosphere, yet to be distinguished among a myriad of such, and occupying the same space. Our star is but one of its infinite manyness. And we read that it may be only the ghost of a star at last.

If the apparition of the star be really a ghost, there is a globe of light (assuming it to have had a beginning) in which a dark sphere is swiftly expanding a ring of light which still contains it.

Frankly speaking, it is not in our present vocation to explain, even if we easily could, the confusion in which our concession to the plausibility of Idealism may seem to have involved our discussion. The purpose has been rather to philosophically show wherein philosophy has failed. And just here particularly should appear its shortcoming, as having not clearly distinguished between realism and "materialism" — a notion beyond the possibility of thought.

Kant took pains to acknowledge and give warning that an idealist proper does not deny the reality of what he depreciates as mere phenomena (to whose basic stuff he was presently indifferent), but insists upon the intellectual and relational element in its composition. Said Kant: "It must not be supposed that an idealist is one who denies the existence of external objects of the senses; all he does is to deny that the existence is known by immediate perception, and to infer that we can never become perfectly certain of their reality by any experience whatever."

Kant himself was stoically indifferent to the unsettling consequences of his doctrine. If it made knowledge solipsism — if the things of this world are only as they are in spiritual appreciation that may be commingled of conception, memory, dream and illusion — he would but fall back upon his sure method, and warn the acolyte of the ineluctable necessity of empirical experience, and of the fact that only the accompanying assurance of perceptive sense could make a whole of knowledge.

When the materialist says then, "these things are real, whether observed or not, and are no less real in the dark on the hind side of the earth," the idealist may well inquire for his meaning, not only as to the "things" but as to reality itself. For consider the things as to their sizes: the materialist will not long persist in the integrity of these sizes, but if he does not hold the things to their apparent sizes they will vanish; they have none of his "matter" if they have no determined size; all that he can claim of matter without color, form, tangibility, and above all, difference — all of which we have found determined by organs — falls into the curiosity of what *causes* the mental experience, and matter, as dead, negative stuff, gives little promise of explanation.

It will be but courtesy on our part to kneel in

IDEALISM

spirit and confess the fatuity of any presumption of having made explanation easier. Newton may find a pretty pebble on the shore, still lost in wonder as to what the great ocean covers. We rather like the notion, shallow though it be, of primordial forms in the elements of things, which crystallize readily of themselves: it spares a little of anxious intention. And we are comforted by the rupture of aristocratic heredity, when we see that a divine descent through the line of the acorn is not absolutely necessary in the lineage of the oak: since, as we have noticed, both root and branch of the same plant may have grown out of its environment, and represented an illegitimate succession. But after evolution has congratulated itself on its main stay of the survival of fitness, through the push of self-love — seen the mere paws get fingers and indurated nails, finally reinforced by the afterthought of a thumb, to enclose (in order to climb a vine, for instance); after it has seen the blind anxiety of the pushing worm wear through the skin to a focus so sensitive and responsive to the interest within that it has developed a lens and can really see, realized the cordage and leverage of the bones and joints as time and the vital push have accomplished the creature for his position — all this and so much more — then to see the wonder of all wonders, the recreation of the species — to see the mere orgasm of the cock and the hen, drawing from all the streams which out of the wild time delivered this creature, deposit in an egg a white speck in which the whole history is recorded in a potentiality so vital that mere impersonal heat may in twenty-one days render it actual as a bird of paradise — there philosophy, as we regard it, should consent to one very important fact: it is most unlikely that any man (at best any man that we have known or heard of) has in his intelligence any cosmic relation to this world, or as an inheriting son has any unique claim to the estate. Yet that he may have a glimpse of the record we surely know.

Another thought which may be a part of philosophy hereafter is that time must be regarded as a dynamic principle. These wonders of history and development argue so long a process, give a sense of so much being due to process, that when we reflect that time as such can have no beginning, we seem driven to regard it as in itself fertile, objective and concrete, and to conceive Idealism as a private affair. A cultured appreciation finds the world so utterly beyond finite comprehension that, taken as a subjective effect, it would incur a contempt that is due only to the subject himself. While Idealism, for its ingenuity, will be ever safe from the charge of "insanity," it is most likely that the faith in objective reality will prevail,[1] and that the ultimate

[1] There was a piquant and memorable controversy, lasting more than twenty years, between Thomas Hobbes (author of "The Leviathan," etc.) and certain of the professors of Oxford University, over the possibility of the quadrature of the circle, which has a metaphysical interest as involving the relative authority of sense and understanding, and so liable to personal predilection and preference. The discussion was at first conducted in Latin, with classic dignity and decorum, but waxing hot in consequence of opposing viewpoints — so hot that Mr. Hobbes, arguing from the sensuous and popular side, did not hesitate at calling his opponents not only fools but liars — he decided that he could more roundly abuse them in their native tongue, and continued the contest in English, whereat the Dons

duplexity will be of time and space as respectively male and female principles.

Having granted all that may be rightly claimed in Hegel's definition of idealism, we have to notice what it lacks of explanation, in the large discourse of reason.

---

rather wittily, if not very elegantly, protested that he had resorted to Billingsgate because "he had not the right Latin for stinking fish."

(This, by the way, was a rather disingenuous claim of such thorough scholars, for Hobbes' translations of both Latin and Greek have been generally approved. Pope declared that his versions of Homer and Thucydides were the best ever written. Hobbes' idiosyncracy, if such it was, is best expressed by Sir James Mackintosh as his inability to discriminate between the intellectual and the emotive faculties of man, as determining metaphysical certainty.)

It was this peculiarity, perhaps, that led to Mr. Hobbes' final comment upon the refinements of his adversaries, that "if he had been as learned as they were he would probably have known no more than they did."

This jibe appears superficially no more than a retort of common sense and experience upon highbrow technicality and finesse; but it is this and much more.

It was a characteristic saying of Kant that we may think certain facts while yet we do not know them. This he would call transcendental thinking, wherein words and symbols are assumed as concrete realities. Language is an invention and a growth, which has not yet attained the limits of insight and intuition; but at the same time the mind can disport with mere conceptions which have no corroborating perceptions of sensuous experience — although according to Kant (and Aristotle as well) a whole of thought must have both matter and form — the sensuous experience being taken up into intellectual forms, and so made a whole of knowledge.

But while Kant plainly instanced the transcendental extravagance wherein we may verbally think what we do not concretely know (making play upon words as real things), he did not remark upon the converse fact that we may really know what, for lack of the appropriate language, we cannot

When the idealist, as a philosopher or observer, finds Consciousness (a name in capitals) "positing this world," wherein is *he* the wiser? Intelligence as such can but accept what is given to it, and there

---

articulately think. I suspect it was as exploiting one of these unspeakable surds, or as giving it rational interpretation, that Hobbes claimed, if not the technical quadrature of the circle, a pragmatical value "just as good."

Hobbes' proposition assumes to show the tangent that is equivalent to any given arc, and so to determine the area of a curvilineal figure in quadrilateral form; and in doing this he would encounter an incapacity of mathematics to express an obvious geometrical space. His demonstration is of exceeding length, and of troublesome intricacy to the layman, and although we have its language, the appropriate drawing or diagram seems to be lacking from American libraries. One can only conjecture, therefore, whether or not he made good, or in what sense; but such a claim is obviously an intrenchment upon the "fourth dimension."

Let us first approve, by collating geometry and mathematics, the converse of Kant's very pregnant assertion that we may think what we do not know, to wit, that we may know what we cannot articulately think, our conceptual and formal mathematics failing of terms that should respond to, or accord with our geometrical perception, in this instance to the side of a double square.

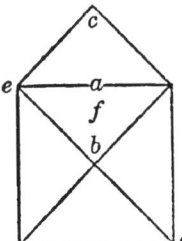

The diagonal of any given square is equivalent to the side of a square of twice its area.

In the figure the diagonal *a*, of the square *bc*, is a side of the double square *de*, for the triangle *f* is half of the square *bc*, and a quarter of the square *de*, which obviously has twice the area of the square *bc*.

Now, mathematically, the square *bc* is to the square *de* (its double) as one is to two; and a side of *bc* is to the diagonal *a* (a side of *de*) as one is to that which, squared, would equal two — that is, to the square-root of two, expressed thus: $\sqrt{2}$.

Or similarly, if the side of the smaller square be taken as 2 (which squared is 4) the side of the double square would be

IDEALISM 63

remains inscrutable the ingenious and productive power which consciousness can only be said to represent. The worth of things being transferred to consciousness affords no explanation or account of

---

a number which, squared, would equal 8 — it would be the square-root of 8; *i.e.*, that which squared would equal 8.

But our mathematics afford no such number as, squared, would equal either 2 or 8. We can with decimals approximate ever nearer and nearer to the square roots of these numbers, but the process is in vain, because no digit, squared, produces a cipher. Whether some other than our decimal system might thwart the infinite regressus of these mathematical surds is a question for professors; it is enough for our purpose here to *see* in the diagram the result of a proportion which we cannot mathematically *express*. We may, as a *modus vivendi*, for practical purposes, wrap the problem of the infinite regressus in a symbol (as $\sqrt{2}$), but the fact remains that the "truth" of the matter is at the bottom of the "bottomless well" of Democritus. Still it is readily obvious that a controversy might arise over the relative sufficiency of percepts and concepts of the same object, since the diagonal of a square, taken as representative of the double square, is as such demonstrable geometrically, but inexpressible or surd mathematically.

This fact affords the hint that in other and more important instances sensuous intuition may transcend intelligible expression. Reverting to Mr. Hobbes and his proposition, in the absence of his diagram, I can but conjecture that he used some such geometrical value in defiance of the professors' mathematics. For he says in his final comment: "I have used a more natural, a more geometrical, and a more perspicuous method in the search of this so difficult a problem than you have done in your Arithmetica Infinitorum." But I have to think that any angular equivalent of the circle is debarred by an inexorable proportion, which I will formulate in the following theorem: *The area of any figure is to its perimeter as the uniformity of its extension.* It is the uniformity of dimension diametrically that appreciates either surface or solid. It is uniformity that constitutes what is called, more or less in a hopeless jest, the "fourth dimension." Perhaps we may sufficiently illustrate this fact without diagrams.

them, either as to their coming or to their order or connection. Even if consciousness were original instead of merely a gift, its criticism but opens the way to fundamental explanation.

However, the discomfiture of its devotees will not make idealism less than the most startling discovery of the human race.

Conceive a square, six by six inches, and beside it a parallelogram, seven inches by five. The two figures have an equal perimetrical straight lineage of 24 inches, and four equivalent right angles; yet the area of the square is 36 square inches, while that of the parallelogram is but 35. Some other quality than mere extension must determine the containing capacity of this 24 inches of lineage. Again, measure with a tapeline any circular disc; a dinner plate will serve; then cut from cardboard a square of the same perimeter, and impose it upon the disc. While the corners of the square will extend beyond the circle, the area of its extrusion will obviously fail to compensate the lunes apparent between the circle and the sides of the square; the discrepancy is even greater than that between the square and the parallelogram. In the same way, a sphere of plastic matter, pressed into the form of a cube, would require a more extensive receptacle to contain it.

We should learn from these experiments that *form* is an element of extensity; that excentricity of outline involves a diminution of areal content; and that the circle, in the perfection of its uniformity, has a dimension which any possible angularity must degrade and diminish.

Whether the first circle was a concept or a percept — whether some genius thought of a point central in a horizon of points, or a caveman twirled it with a forked stick in the sand — is likely to remain a question.

CHAPTER III

MONISM

MONISM, popularly intending the unity of totality, might be defined as obsession of finite limitation — a fate of the planet-born or orbicular intelligence. In philosophy it implies egotism and self-relation.

As a culture it is incapable of any direct or tangent thought or outlook, its expectation reverting ever to the subjective interest and viewpoint. Compassing no object in its mere freedom to advance, it orients its vision as if to freedom itself as a property of its own nature, rather than the objective extensity of the vulgar space.

Instead of recognizing everywhere as a here, it locates space behind the mental eye instead of before it — finds the only answer to its outward quest — a *quasi* other to itself, and says with Brahma, "When me they fly I am the wings."

Its burthen is ever the "universe," exploited by some theological cosmography which leaves it but a limited object in an unlimited field. It will of course ignore the anomaly herein cited — that of the stars as a limited set in a limitless space that hungers for exploration and occupancy.

A mere makeshift in metaphysics, its psychological

plausibility renders it the most alluring recourse of speculative thought.

For a treatise on monism one may start bravely from the saying of Philolaus, "One is made by limit" (plausibly a circle then, or a sphere), and forthwith conclude that all cannot be one; for any such one, however great, leaves a margin unoccupied; it does not fill the canvas. Or if regarded theoretically and rationally, rather than pictorially, or imaginatively, such a one cannot be all, because comprehension, as of all, must include that which comprehends, and the observer of the fact is not yet included in its observation.

But this conclusion will be confronted by the idealist with the undermining charge that it is a judgment based not upon reason but upon impertinent imagination. He will say that the margin by which the one is pictorially exceeded is due to a false pretense of space being objective, instead of being subjective — which it certainly (or also) is; space (in his sense) is not extension, but merely room or mental freedom to extend; so that the one (he assumes) can be founded centrally, or wholly within and related to itself alone; and what imagination regards as space and margin shall be but the freedom of the supreme or absolute subject; the required limit of its oneness shall be self-determination, and its unity and universality shall be the perfection of a harmonious whole. Infinity is but a false greatness: "that that which is should be infinite is not permitted."

Then as to one failing of all because its observer

is not included in its comprehension — assuming that comprehension as universal must include the being that comprehends — the charge confronts the main ground of transcendental idealism, namely, that all knowledge contains or includes self-knowledge, and that any totality is necessarily self-related, subject and object at once. The limit of the One of Philolaus is thus assumed as the self-determined, and the imagined margin is resolved into the infinite liberty of the free subject.

(It will, of course, be seen that a universe thus established from within, with no regard to outer space, would not hinder the existence of other universes; and the claim of its being *the* universe would be solipsism. The One of Fichte and Hegel and Harris, the absolute ego, is such a centre, whose outlook or infinite is potential in freedom.)

These are the two chief problems of philosophy: to get the world into an absolute whole, self-comprehended, and to prove that knowledge is what it pretends to be; *i. e.* that as knowledge it knows itself as it knows other facts — comprehends its own being as essentially its own ground. Our safety, in dread of fate, requires the assurance proper to this information; and the cogitation of its possibility has been the main industry of modern philosophy — occasionally satisfied with results which have invariably been outgrown and discarded.

The average citizen is content to believe that he is at least so far whole and original as to be socially responsible; but those whom we prefer as the great thinkers of the race have decided otherwise — not but that man shall render unto Cæsar the things which are Cæsar's, but that for or against the government of God, "of himself he can do nothing."

The capital advantage hypothecated in monism is that it makes a "universe," symmetrical, dependable and manageable, all within reasonable bounds; but unfortunately it implies a "universal intelligence," which, if unlimited, or unfinite, could hold no relation to personality as we conceive and represent it. The "universal ego" of Fichte and Hegel is not like the human ego, nor fitly suggested thereby. It is posed as a formal, transcendental, *quasi* vision or fetich, an institution, an enfolding atmosphere, countenanced as a logical necessity — a concept which, as Kant would say, has no staminal substantiation in a possible perception. And being sole, it must have all its sufficiency in self-relation; there is none to know or sustain or reflect it but itself, subject and object at once (if ever), but for Hegel by degrees and process which Fichte's instant insight forestalled.

Against this scheme has been opposed the opinion that a universal reason is not a reason at all, and that universal personality is more than contradictory, in fact absurd, although announced by Hegel as "the highest, steepest thought."

In lieu of a managing personality modern thought has conceived of necessary laws, under which what we call "design" should appear as due to an appreciation at the end or accomplishment of things, rather than to an intention at their beginning. In other words, that the requisite necessities of mechanism are less mysterious or astounding than the contradictions involved in a primary and self-related intelligence. We know secondary intelligence as an empirical fact, but its primacy or originality would merely double the wonder, as calling for similar necessities to avert its logical contradictions. A necessary machine is as plausible as a self-related mind; for a principle of reason can have no contradiction. Materialism holds that if knowledge is not essentially grounded, is not self-related, mind-stuff is no more explanatory than matter; that God becomes but a convenient limb or fetich whereon to unburden the Mystery. The wilds of nature are as fertile and luminous as are the Elysian fields. [We recall the scientist who grieved that he could not find within him the God whom he recognized everywhere without.]

I can but think that monism will come to be regarded as a needless barrier to explanation — a mere mirage of limitation, a projection of our egotism, through a false psychology of personality as an original principle. There is no louder voice from antiquity than that which declares that One is made by limit; and there can be nothing more convincing to the average thinker than that any One is transcended as but a spot on the true universal. Let there be gods and gods in the "lower cases," the universe will not stand for the capital G. The true universe is too great for a "personal" God. The margin beyond the One (even as liberty) is an abyss wherein the bats of chance wing blindly in dreams of potential cataclysm and disaster.

The management and comprehension of wholeness seem to be the main difficulties of explanation. When we are once rid of these, which to any second thought are clearly impossible — when we frankly admit that there must be an *everywhere* as plausible as any *here* — we are freed from the exaction of management by impossible comprehension, and are at liberty to look for principle, fertility, explanation in the monads and centres of the Midst, where everything for itself must be. One may then "look into his heart and write." We may possibly find the monads giving explanation without comprehension — find a vast democracy working by immediate contracts and local managements of individual energy, regardless of any autocratic heredity, or any cosmic process or purpose. Get rid of this impossible wholeness and the impossible "purpose of eternity," and we may find in heart and life something so noble, so willful, so self-sacrificing and magnanimous in suffering, that our most critical curiosity shall call it in itself worth while, sufficient for being — in fine, pure Cause.

It may well be that this bewildering immensity, which yet is not a whole nor demanding treatment as a whole, has exaggerated the dignity or profundity of sufficient explanation. The Mystery may be more homely and secular than our fear and ignorance have come to regard it. Perhaps "He is not far."

What we would infer is that the notion of wholeness, as of a One, throws all the hope of explanation into the possibility of a universal personality, which could be one only from the inside, by solipsis. Experience teaches us the possibility of monads, Ones of *quasi* original power, which, while not fully explanatory, still carry the Mystery as feasibly

MONISM

as a God may carry it; but a universal One is objectively impossible, save in a transcendental concept of pure solipsism.

The conception of a continuous democratic many, everywhere as here, vacates the contradiction of a universal objective One, and is embarrassed only by the familiar Mystery which all intelligent monads are to themselves. And this Mystery I have tentatively presumed to alleviate (adopting as the canon of pure reason the empirical "I think"), in the self-respect of some great emotion or agonism that should *feel* itself worth while — as when Ajax would defy the lightning, or when Job should curse God and die. The conjecture seems to open a vista which, pursued with resolution, might lead toward finite satisfaction, if not to explanation.

The miracle of originality or principle is no more astonishing, theoretically, in a monad than in a god. We are personally conscious and accustomed to a certain amount of "creation"; and we should be well contented in finding the world at large so accounted for; but when the difficulties of universality cut us off from that satisfaction, the immense aggregations and consistent systems of things still get no explanation from the energy and intelligence of mere monads. The stars for instance, and their revolutions: men do their work, making cities, as the coral insects build great reefs, and the instant efficiency is in some degree satisfactory; but even ignoring the One whole, or assuming it as impossible, there are lesser wholes too great to be accounted for by individual and unconcerted agency. There seems to be required some fitness in the *elements* of things, by which mere aggregation should result in admirable forms and harmonious masses and movements — possibly to be countenanced by the concession of all-enduring time.

To faintly illustrate the intention here: Most people have seen what are called "alum baskets" (rock candy is of the same nature). They are forms automatically constructed or determined upon cottoned wire immersed in a solution of alum or sugar. Regular cubes, usually about a quarter of an inch in diameter, accumulate around the frame of the structure, until each wire is loaded with crystals, and averages about an inch and a half in thickness — the whole capable of any fanciful design. The philosophical spirit, curious as to what or who produces these beautiful and wonderful things, is loth to sing "the hand that made us is divine"; for they are not divinely worth while, at least, a more mechanical reference would be acceptable. What hinders the thought then, that the planes and angles of the elemental atoms of the solution are such that the aggregation gets its form from the adjustment, through a uniform attraction, of all the planes and angles? The wholes, then, would thus be simplified, so far as their greatness is concerned, by reference to the mechanism of the elements. A multiverse might thus be construed, though a universe were impossible.

So in the growth of a plant. If we consider the sap within it as rising, by the general expansion of heat, in tubes of a valvular formation, which hold all they get, against the cooling process of the

MONISM

night, and then, in the returning light and heat, exude the sap into the similarly crystal atmosphere at the ends of the fibres and tendrils, we may indeed admire the grown result, but we look at it as rather scientifically than spiritually mysterious. We see beautiful ferns produced in this manner; and then, on a frosty morning, we may see the nightly dew on the pavement for miles and miles thrown into precisely such fronds and ferns. Our science in the premises, while it does not fully explain as yet, abates the necessity of the superstitious personal intention; it reduces the individual peculiarity to a generalization; it gives the wonder of the many a trend toward a single however mysterious principle.

Why are we so egotistic and suburban as to require for our mental environment a "universe" as limited to unity, rather than a multiverse of cosmopolitan, democratic and uncentred continuity? The rims of the philosopher's spectacles seem to determine a monism in his outlook. It would seem a not difficult viewpoint to attain, that there are no monistic limits to the world; that everything, great or small, is a monad in the Midst, not of a universe but a pluriverse of centres having no circumference or comprehension. We regard this as the unquestionable fact; its denial results in metaphysical confusion. No one claims a limit to space, yet finite sophistication keeps limiting existence to an All, or a One, not considering how these notions antagonize such an unlimited space. Egoism must have all things under a central and personal control, a mental *comprehension* of an *admitted infinite!*

Certainly the cosmos is a problem of management;

the appearance of design is to be accounted for as best it may; but I shall show, on positively scientific grounds, that limited matter — as in a set or system of stars — is impossible under either physical or metaphysical gravitation.

The Midst

As in Aristotle nature and becoming are by the graduation of matter into form, or of being into knowing, the actual is ever at a turning point, the Midst. Our ordinary use of the word "universal" is for the inference of greatness; it is for telescopic rather than microscopic extension. But as we must see, in the demonstration of the relativity and ideality of size by the microscope, our determinations of size are limited by material agents; our ordinary Midst, or actuality, is contingent upon our inventional progress, variously with the telescope and the microscope.

(While our greatest telescopes still leave the fixed stars so far that the orb and its orbit are focused as but a motionless point, with the "infinite" still beyond, so the best microscope still raises the question whether in the infinitesimal direction, there is any creature so small but another creature lives upon it; does the infinite divisibility of matter carry the infinite divisibility of life and soul? On the other hand, does the illimitability of space exclude the possibility of personality as effacing the limits inseparable from One? As Truth, pursuing the infinite divisibility of matter, dives into Democritus' bottomless well, so, following the increasing length of the telescope, she diminishes the probability of

MONISM

intelligent and intelligible comprehension, and prompts all thought to fall back upon the actuality and practicality of the Midst as our only reality, holding with Parmenides, "that that which is should be infinite is not permitted." That All is One can be true only transcendentally, as a conjecture beyond all experience, either material or mental.)

Circular Monism

The monism of the circle, the recoil of compensation (with the waste and weariness and inconsequence of the whole process) is quaintly put by Emerson in his poem, "Uriel." He recalls ancient and pre-historic being, before the wild time was coined into calendar months and days, before there were orbs or orbits then, in the empyrean of pure thought, seemingly indifferent (in the poem) whether Nature was in fact or as yet in contemplation. The young gods were discussing necessary laws of form and measure, and resolving what exists and what seems, and Uriel "gave his sentiment divine, against the being of a line":

> *Line in nature is not found;*
> *Unit and universe are round.*
> *In vain produced, all rays return;*
> *Evil will bless, and ice will burn.*

"The rash word boded ill to all"; of what avail were ambition or temporal success, if an undiscriminating time could avenge and retrieve it all? "The stern old war gods shook their heads"; what mattered their victories or achievements? The red slayer but dreams that he slays. The balance-beam of fate is bent. Hell cannot hold its own. All glides into confusion and misuse. But

> *Straightway a forgetting wind*
> *Stole over the celestial kind,*
> *And their lips the secret kept,*
> *If in ashes-the fire-seed slept;*
> *But now and then truth-speaking things*
> *Shamed the angels' veiling wings;*
> *Out of the good of evil born*
> *Came Uriel's voice of cherub scorn,*
> *And a blush tinged the upper sky.*
> *And the gods shook, they knew not why.*

But the conjecture of an essentially centripetal or reverting element in thought, although we should not at all grudge it as implicating self-relation by process, fades before a more practical consideration, pertinent at once to metaphysic and common sense. The law or fact of gravitation renders monism scientifically impossible.

It is a matter of philosophical importance to determine the truth or falsity of this dictum, that "unit and universe are round"; that is, to know whether existence is a continuous democracy or a somewhat centered autocracy, for which space is wholly subjective, mere room or freedom from obstruction. This is no idle speculation. Any educated mechanic knows that his rules are perversions of scientific fact. He knows that his water-level is not the true tangent, which practically would bow up into the atmosphere, and that his plumb-lines converge at the bottom like the sides of a bell-crowned hat. It is of prime theological importance

MONISM

to know if intelligence has a centripetal or backlooking tendency, as has the flying foot of the compass, or the lost man in the woods, whose best leg brings him back to his starting point. For as before noticed, the fact, if such it may be, is no proof of self-relation, save as in the process of the Hegelian absolute — which ends nowhere and amounts to nothing.

We want a new or at least an additional critique of pure reason. Kant was thorough enough to see that man's limit of penetration and explanation is drawn in the plain "I think." But the liberty of transcendental speculation opens the field to very ambitious and pretentious thinking, and to the invention of new words; and at the same time, given the canon of reason as his own "I think," "*I feel*" must claim a large share in the matter of thinking. Hereby we get those exclamations of Herbart and Jacobi, and philosophy comes down to psychology — asking the opinion of the natural man and the unsophisticated child, appealing to the "heart" as well as to the mind, to sense as well as to understanding, to satisfy the obsession of Cause, or Why. Here the inarticulate divine gets utterance: Why not the same when a man, opposed or grieved or disappointed, growls of "God," or "damnation"? He gives the *heart* of reason, which has no profounder expression. We cannot go deeper than this for cause or explanation.

Needs there a deeper cause for the conception of a child than is experienced in the venereal heat, born of accidental contact and occasion? Shall we ascribe to primogeniture and succession the thousand seminal germs — active creatures under the microscope — of which but one or two are preserved and cherished? Why shall I doubt that my own need of contact or material company on a dangerous eminence *explains*, is the same as the gravitation of matter? It is not a highbrow explanation, but it shall serve if science can offer none more appealing to the something higher or deeper than science which Schelling declared he certainly did know. If philosophy ever succeeds it may have the discomfiture of finding its spectacles on its nose.

This consideration makes philosophy easier, or at least more hopeful. If we could discover some one thought or thing — whether form or matter or harmony or whatsoever — which, given time, could initiate and continue the results of nature in their variety and manyness, we would not so insist upon a superstitious primogeniture, but would give more credit to the mechanical impersonality of the environment. We are possibly too superstitious as to this primogeniture. We rightly assume, in general, that the oak comes from the acorn, and the acorn in turn from the oak, so telescoping the whole process out of a divine original, for which the environment seems merely negative and receptive. But the fact shows that this line of descent has no sacred integrity; there are organic wholes whose norm is to be credited to the environment alone, outside of the line of sacred heredity.

For example, here is a willow tree, a beautiful whole in æsthetic thought — root, stem and branches appealing to designing intelligence. We may regard it as of two parts, the roots and the apparent tree — a primogenital whole. But now as a fact of experience we may cut off a limb or a twig of the proper tree and plant it in the ground, and the environment will furnish it a root of its own, and make it a goodly organic whole; and if we sever the old top from the new root, the environment will furnish a new top from the remaining root — fulfilling a perfect organism outside the line of hereditary descent, and affording a complete break in the primogenitive succession, and so vacating any original intention of heredity in that instance.

A fact like this looms large in teleology, where we have to concur with M. Bergson, that however the positive activity appears in current life, the negative shores react and determine the course of the stream quite as much as they are worn and determined by it. The check is as potent in the result as is the ostensible intention, yet it gets credit for only a brute resistance or stolidity. So that modern philosophy, better affecting mechanism which it assumes to understand, is using in its explanation as little as possible of personality and metaphysics, preferring rather to ignore intention altogether than seek it in first principles, where it would be a mystery still and at last, and also lacking the familiarity and habitude of mechanical explanation — it being satisfied with science without speculating on the science of it. And given the fulcrum of Archimedes, and the hair trigger with which to let off M. Bergson's explosions of stored energy, a clever thinker can make a very plausible demonstration with matter and mechanism. He shall need only that his leading cornet finesse the high C.

Here then I invoke Kant's canon of pure reason, the plain "I think" of the cultivated man. This permits the entrance of the common sense, of the One of first principles, as well as the expert of the Many, who in his vast and labored complications may presume to determine such data as the parallaxes of fixed stars. There are certainties of sense below the threshold of relations, and there may be intimations of the first principle had in placing one's hand on the heart of Nature, or one's ear close to the ground — not as a great "reasoner" but with a simple faith — say of Herbart or Jacobi, or of Jesus, when he declared, "If any man will do His will he shall know of the doctrine." For it was thus that Plato conceived the first principle of being as the Good, the sense of *value* — not by an activity or equation (as Heraclitus made being inevitable in the equality of being and not being dialectically), and by a direct empirical appreciation of reality.

So I find gravitation a disproof of monism; and as no scientist assumes to account for gravitation as either an effect or a cause, I offer my insight of it as a heart experience, partly prompted by the ancient Scripture, the first afterthought of creation, "It is not good to be alone." Even God wants company in all the philosophies that I have read.

Gravitation, primarily, is not mere attraction to the earth, but a general principle, the affection of matter for its kind. A chip floating in a basin of water will draw up the motes beneath it; it would not float alone. Beasts and men alike want company. He who finds a prize is ill content therewith until he has found some one to share his admiration. A man at any high elevation must have contact with some material thing. When he has climbed the great pyramid and found himself in the empty heaven, on a square not wider than a bedroom, he may kneel toward the dear earth, "the ancient Mother, for some comfort yet." Is not this a gravitation that everywhere affects the local centres and prompts the thought of a one centre for the All, forgetting that such an All must be limitless and not one? Kant (inadvertantly doubtless) alluded to "the gravitation that holds the universe together"; he did not think of the gravitation which must hold the universe apart; for *any system or limited set of centres held in gravitation must finally all come together.*

It matters not what orbital independence, or what complication of alien forces may obtain within a limited set of stars; the uniform *togetherness* due to gravitation as a persistent whole would ultimately constrict their limited plurality to a central and motionless mass.

Under countenance of our idealism and monism we may now revert more familiarly to our original ground and purpose. It should be obvious that monism, or oneism in philosophy, is a vision through the lens of the human ego as a pattern on which its cosmos is designed. Disrupting the umbilical connection with his environment, no longer like a plant locally fixed and drawing sustenance from the earth, the man walks forth a more or less independent being, with a will and an intelligence of his own

— practically one on his own account. And when, condoning his parasital dependencies, he becomes a philosopher, a critic of complete and real independence and original principle, he forthright conjecttures the cosmos, the philosophical totality, as an ego like himself. It must be an independent Whole and One, a totality within its own comprehension, and known of itself, as he of himself affects to be. And herein was the latest triumph of his philosophy, the metaphysical insight that a totality must be an ego. For one is not one unless known as such, comprising in itself the limitation by which one is one, essentially combining as subject with the nonego requisite to an objective intelligence. It was the German Fichte who first authorized this position as a psychological "fact of consciousness."

Fichte was fully awake and sensitive to the logical contradiction of such a subject-object, while still insisting upon it, as not only a fact but the one fact without which philosophy is forever impossible; and to all objectors he had but one answer: "Ask not for the *how;* be satisfied with the fact." Our Professor Ladd, of Yale University, in his "Introduction to Philosophy" still insists, with the same trepidation and embarrassment, upon self-relation as the "prime fact of consciousness."

With the human ego thus regarded as the necessary model of the cosmos or theoretical world, we may understand how readily the later philosophers fell into the lines of the ancient cosmologies and their consequent theologies, in which unity and comprehension were the supreme and prevailing principles, while man and his destiny were the objects contemplated in their operation.

But what seems to us the greatest mistake in modern history, and that which is the main provocative of the present treatise, is the myopic and impudent assumption, not only that man is unique in nature, and that such a comparatively insignificant and incidental parasite can in any comprehensive sense represent the necessary qualities of the world, as his own best thought must conceive it, but that because a totality confessedly must be an ego *there must be any totality at all;* or again, that the stars, however many, must have a whole number, as so many and no more — this, although space will not be held to have limits, as possibly walled in or broken off, but must still extend, and presumptively carry an increment of stars.

This confusion as to number ignores the ideality of number itself — a very frequent mistake, such as is also the phrase "an infinite number," which cancels the explicit discretion for which number is intended. The slight "puzzle" which was mentioned in our Chapter I, wherein a new star, as one more than what are, must increase their number, and so prove that they have a whole number, so many and no more, will become "one more" by the addition of a new one, will depend upon the question whether they have already a number to be added to. Your "more" is a relative and comparative, and must have its *much* to begin with, and a definite limit which it may exceed; and such a factual limit is the very requirement at issue. If the stars go on and on, as an increment and occupancy of space, all thought of wholeness is excluded, and your "number" exhales as a merely subjective discrimination, or fanciful conjecture of addition by one, regardless of any sum resulting.

It is here that one needs most urgently the doctrine of idealism, that "consciousness posits this world," and that difference or distinction is mental, and not a property of "things in themselves." Our habits of thought have in many instances turned things inside out, so far as explanation is concerned. For instance, the ordinary notion of a volcano is of a huge tube that spouts lava and ashes; whereas in scientific fact the volcano proper is a cancerous hole in the earth, from which in time has been built up the mountain itself. So the civilized man is dreadfully weak and shameful without his clothes; your policeman feels most formidable in the buckram of his official overcoat, while your real fighter feels efficient only when he is naked.

Our most eminent thinkers seem to be still obsessed by the half-savage cosmologies which make man and his ego the centre of explanation. We cannot easily evade or positively deny the large field of thought in which all size is relative, to organic lenses; there are worlds within what some kind of sanity must still believe in as the real world. A modern man must indeed be tainted with one of Mr. Spencer's "insanities of idealism," to doubt that even if the earth were stripped of all living things and left barren and blasted as our moon appears — man and his philosophies and his histories and religions vanished into less than thin air — the glorious stars, among which by analogical reckoning his earth is but a speck, would still revolve as, theoretically at least, they have ever revolved, regardless of all impertinent sensitiveness to time or times.

It would seem that any rational contemplation of this scientific extensity and authentic endurance should obliterate the small prejudice of oneness and limitation, so obviously due to the subjective egotism in which it matriculates.

Yet it is not on the metaphysical necessities of the case that this essay mainly proceeds — at least not so much as upon the scientific and empirical induction that, whatever forces may be held to account for the local revolutions of the individual stars, the general impulse of *togetherness* (under which even their minor evolutions are performed) demands and assures an ever-external field of balance and compensation which excludes the possibility of wholeness and its limitation, lest the pluriversal Many, factually apparent, should become a conglomerate ball.

In brief then, monism is the general egotism which in idealism ends as pure solipsism. The worlds of idealism are home made; they are the microcosms of which monism is a macrocosm constricted to unity by its own egotistic limitation, founded, philosophically, upon faith in "self-consciousness." In monism, ego and non-ego culminate as God and the world.

Vulgar monism founds largely on the uncultured sentiment that there must be recognized an all and whole of the world that is other than the intelligent witness of it. Philosophical monism, assured of the metaphysical percept that comprehension and totality must include the being that comprehends, founds upon the hypothesis of self-relation as science of science, and confirms its position psychologically by the assumption of "self-consciousness" as empirical and unquestionable fact — however meritorious or unaccountable such fact may be.

Our position ignores (or at best condones) the subjective ideality of space, standing by the empirical commonsense in its inference of an element in existence that is opaque and objectively negative to knowledge, and is operated under laws as mysterious and as respectable as the laws prevailing over intelligence itself, as we exemplify it: that we have no science of science other than as the gift of an alien energy of which we have no comprehension or any such limitation as is requisite to the objective unity either of it or of ourselves. Restrained therefore from any other than the philosophy of fact, and confined to law as we empirically find it, we accept space as unlimited extensity; analogically carrying in it the sidereal increment which our science has revealed, and confirming our judgment of sideral continuity and innumerability: from the general law of togetherness, which, relaxing its force only according to the distance of its material, would ultimately tolerate no vacant space or room for orbital motion (by whatever cause) under any other condition than an extensity transcending all conception of centrality or unity, or such wholeness or comprehension as the word "universe" is obviously meant to infer.

To popularly establish this position — not as ultimate explanation — we now proceed to the consideration of cause or reason itself, and thence to a citation of the superior and most plausible judgments which have disqualified that notion of self-relation, or subject-object, which has been the staminal element of modern philosophy.

We are not to say that idealism and self-relation are not good philosophy — perhaps the best — but that philosophy at its best is not a satisfactory explanation.

CHAPTER IV

CAUSE

CAUSE, the insatiable Why of human curiosity and interest, is naturally the storm centre of philosophy. What is meant by cause depends almost wholly upon the culture of the one who means it. The curiosity deepens as the culture advances. The average thinker or student is content with referring any novel fact to an acknowledged class. One who should hold every thing or event to the arbitrament that he could produce it himself would be regarded as a thorough radical; yet such a thoroughbred would halt just where the ripe philosopher begins, for *his* most anxious question is, "Does Personality explain"? "Know thyself" is philosophy's most classic vocation; and possibly her keenest quest is as to whether one really knows himself when he thinks that he does. The definition of cause, or indeed of anything else, may depend upon the possibility of self-knowledge in a science of science.

All finite or parasitic reasoning is thrust out of rational propriety by the constant obsession of the reasoner's own beginning, so that its most strenuous theoretical curiosity or demand for explanation arraigns the cosmos itself for a foundation or a fertility beneath it, not reflecting that the notion of beginning is a shadow cast by his own fate upon a ground that is not necessarily subject to such a demand, a ground that cannot be referred to previous ground in a quest for explanation. Cosmic beginning is unthinkable, owing to the lack of marginal space and time in which to distinguish its advent: there is no canvas for such a picture, which can obtain only as a nominal conjecture.

Shadworth H. Hodgson, then president of the Aristotelian Society, of London, in an address, Nov. 7, 1887, on the reorganization of philosophy, spoke as follows:

"A cause is conceived as an absolute existent making something else to be or to become. When the inevitable question, 'How?' is put to one of these absolute existents or causes, a *progressus in indefinitum* is entered on, to cause beyond cause, which continues until it is arbitrarily arrested by assuming a First Cause, which being uncaused by anything else, is conceived as '*causi sui*' or self-existent . . . which combines the contrary characteristics of cause and effect in the same existent at the same time. . . . The term First Cause is therefore a contradiction which conceals ignorance, while at the same time it poses as an explanation. But such explanations are rapidly coming to be looked upon as not explanatory. The conception of cause seems to have been as unfruitful in science as it has been unthinkable in philosophy."

If one could identify cause in an alien world, it would appear as the satisfaction of interest and curiosity as concerning the contents of experience; but after a cause has served for perfunctory explanation for a thousand kinds of curiosity and interest, is becomes practically objective, and the subjective element in the situation is sublated and obscured; the lesson of idealism is ignored; the fact is forgotten that in some way, or in some sense, the reason of things is reason. In the whole fact or occurrence, as seen in the alien world, the reason or the reasonableness of cause should be in the interpretation of the fact to the curiosity and interest of the subjective element of the experience: be the fact as it may, the cause as explanation is what contents the intelligence concerned. Objective or factual cause therefore were absurd: only in the contentment of intelligence can it pose as cause or reason or explanation. Even if we knew the ground of the fact sought to be explained, the subject inquiring may not be included in the explanation.

Born and bred as we are to struggle for existence in the world of wonders, compelled to be satisfied at best with merely partial successes, habited to ignore a myriad of miracles, and admonished by urgent necessities to suppress any ambition transcending the claims of our finite nature — cuffed by the great Mother, as Emerson said, and admonished to "eat your victuals, children, and say no more of it," we realize betimes that even our curiosity is at fault, as to the limits and the meaning of our own discontent. "Pleased with a feather, tickled with a straw," men even glory in momentary achievements which should but emphasize their impotence and ignorance. It is only the highest culture that attains any appreciation of the mystery of being.

As for causes, we have, according to our conscientious thoroughness, various *grades* of explanation; for instance, here is an explosion of gunpowder; the mere scientist is content to observe, and proud to declare, that it is due to the release of certain gases latent in a composition of sulphur, nitre and carbon; the savant goes deeper and brings up his "elements," his electrons and what not; then comes the biologist with germs and cells and protoplasm; then the psychologist with his nerves, reactions, intuitions and instincts; then the metaphysician, questioning after reality and appearance; the idealist, determining all reality through subjective laws of the mind. And what next? If either of these experts shall plume himself with claims of radical explanation, he will but classify himself in an inferior culture; another expert shall warn him that his intelligence is but secondary and does not explain — that though he had himself made all things that are, as freely as he might write these words, his philosophy has yet to begin.

How philosophy grew, from the obsession of objective cause and natural necessity up to the conceit of self-relation; how it advanced from the savage superstition of controlling spirits in the air to elemental powers, as atoms and abstractions (such as heat and cold, love and hate) to the "nous" of Anaxagoras, and thence to the subjective skepticism of the sophists, in which every man was for himself the measure of all things, and the oracle of truth and justice; how Socrates as the chief of sophists made mind in general rather than man the individual the spokesman of reason, and made ideas the reality amid the illusions of sense; how the notion of principle, as prime fertility and power, mounted to the ego, first as the active demonstrator in a world of otherness, and then as surrepted (both the hammer and the anvil) into itself as self-related subject-object; how this psychological illusion of self-knowledge struggled for recognition for nearly a century (and has its defenders even now); how the disheartened professors shouted "Back to Kant!" how radical empiricism found matter-stuff as plausible as mind-stuff, so long as knowledge could not be essentially grounded in a science of science; how the post-Kantians (Schopenhauer, Hartman, Dühring, Lange, Bergson, *et al.*) exploited and glorified a de-personalized intelligence, and how Herr Eucken finally earned the Nobel prize by discounting the whole philosophical industry, and socially protesting, as to these latter-day protagonists, that "they do not exist!" — how all this came to pass makes a "very pretty quarrel as it stands." The only literary comment that we presently find appropriate is, that while the full and ripe expounder of "The Problem of Human Life," after graciously crediting all the original experts, merely deplores the "questions yet unanswered" and the "problems yet unsolved," and still fails to see, or at best neglects to explain that the one crux of all — the one solution through which philosophy could succeed and justify its long career — is Self-Relation, failing of which there remains for humanity but the Mystery, and possibly the ultimate surd.

The path from the naïve cognition of common sense and "free will" up to the position from which Schwegler announced "a certain existent unreason"

— or to that where Hodgson declares that "causality *per se,* has no philosophical or scientific justification," and that "search for cause has been replaced by search for phenomenal antecedents merely, under the recognition that realities answering to the terms 'cause' and 'causality' are impossible and non-existent," — is certainly a path of technical and scientific culture; yet the reader cannot know too soon, nor believe too cordially, that the mysterious glory and esoteric seclusion which have maintained the name philosophy as a headline of the literary program, and as well the pretensions that have emphasized the natural bewilderment of "the plain man," are utterly inconsequent. The Mystery remains, as somewhat not so badly hinted by the Philosophical Dude: "Something, you know, that puts you in mind of something you can't think of."

Said Eucken: "After all the weary work of many thousand years, we are to-day in a condition of painful uncertainty, a state of hopeless fluctuation, not merely with regard to individual questions, but also as to the general purpose and meaning of life. . . . The facts themselves are questioned; doubt arises as to whether they can readily be affirmed as facts at all. . . . The supremacy of man is now more and more disputed, and especially the assertion that his place among the creatures is unique. . . . The content of man's life is not the easy, unsought product of a natural process of historical development — not a necessarily proper process to or toward something really worth while."

Again he has said: "Scarcely anything repels so

much as the impertinence of representing the world as it is as a realm of reason." "God (in Christianity) has taken the burden of it upon Himself, and thereby sanctified it . . ." but "Evil remains a permanently insoluble mystery." . . . "An immediate consequence is the difficulty, indeed, the impossibility of an appropriate representation in thought and conception; every exposition remains a mere approximation, retains a symbolic character."

Kant says: "Our reason has this peculiar fate, that with reference to one class of our knowledge it is always troubled with questions which cannot be ignored (*because they spring from the very nature of reason*) and which cannot be answered because they transcend the powers of human reason."

As in idealism we were offered the alternative of regarding objects as either given to the mind from without or posited by consciousness from its own spontaneity, so, analogously, as to the question of cause, we may have acquired a habit of expecting to find only before our mental eye the ground of explanation, which can perhaps be found at least as plausibly behind it; in other words (as the philosophers say), cause may be only subjectively possible, and absurd when assumed as an object. And straightway we perceive, upon reflection, that any objective thing, taken as the cause of anything else, or of itself, would more obstreperously call for cause than does the thing to be explained; its presence would but double and complicate the problem; so that the reason of things must in some sense be

CAUSE

reason itself as knowing itself. In other words (again), since intelligence proper can only contemplate and reflect, and cannot create or produce, cause proper (for us) shall mediate or interpret, not between the void and the fact which it could not produce, but between the fact as given and our intelligence as really such. It is not *being* then that demands or can furnish or represent cause, for cause objectively taken must have being on its own account. Fact is the deepest reality.

For assume that a thing has had a cause; must the cause remain to sustain and keep it caused? Surely not; the cause shall have passed on and left the thing, possibly with a momentum which now by its presence demonstrates the sufficiency of being for itself; and since the thing may have been eternally, as well as may any objective or knowable cause, being as such does not call for cause, and must be originally presumed in any consideration of the problem of existence. Philosophy, or explanation, must begin with the recognition of some existence, and can succeed only as *the science of that science itself*.

Fact, otherwise being (not cause), is the "first principle" of dialectic, the original presumption from which explanation must begin: a pre-assumption in time, which cannot have begun, since beginning were possible only in a time presumed. Cause then can be only a witness or interpretation of fact to present intelligence, and as a "reason" can have only a historical ground, sufficiently announcing that "it is" — *because it is;* its authority in explanation founds no deeper than the authenticity of the fact.

It has always been too late for philosophy to factualize beginning or "first cause."

It has been held naïve or puerile, saying of anything "it is because it is," or "it goes because it is going." But consider a revolving wheel, still whirling by reason of its "momentum"; the belt may be off, and all the men gone home: there is no material difference in the wheel whether moving or motionless, yet it goes by a potentiality of mere fact that now has no relation to any present cause or explanation. In this case the fact is final, but it *became* so: it once had causes; but since it persists without them, the only ground of its present being is its fact, whose miracle exhales in the presumption of time.

This is the first principle of dialectic philosophy, true if being and time are necessary presumptions. Whether anything at all is necessary is a later question, for a newcomer in time.

Whether self-relation, in the being or the thought of it, is possible to a finite and secondary intelligence — to a parasite as commensurate with the cosmos — is partly a question of analogy and perspective, which, to say the least, imposes upon us a certain modesty and humility.

It is of prime importance to philosophical sanity, presumed as capable of due appreciation and perspective, that it should have such a right estimate of the worth and dignity of man as may forecast the *probability* of his being competent to the secret of the world. Advised upon one hand that man was made in God's image, and on another that nothing so becomes him as modest stillness and humility —

admonished by the divinest of his race that of himself he can do nothing, yet prompted by the genius of his art and poetry,

*Whose pulses, mounting through the pose of Ajax,
Confront the lurid blood of the high gods
As one therewith at last,*

the philosopher, who must hold by analogy, is admonished to regulate his pretensions and expectations by some contrast of his finite unity with any presumptive unity of the whole, or at least with the greatness of so much of it as he may apprehend in his brief career.

Measured under these lights, how pitiful indeed is the ephemeral parasite —

Without asking, hither hurried Whence?
And, without asking Whither *hurried hence.*

If philosophy *will*, like the green-eyed jealousy, still make a meat to feed upon, it should, in decency if not in reverence, consider its trivial measures as contrasted with merely the measurable — postponing for the moment the unlikelihood that the hymnic Mystery of the cosmos should be vocal to it puny and infantile ears. Even if he could learn the tune of it he cannot stay to enjoy it.

The authentic duration of time, with its inconsequent and seemingly purposeless destruction of organic and ambitious successes, and the violent disruptions of the strata which show that our planet was once symmetrical with water levels, discourage any conclusions or fanciful conjectures of progress toward a scientific resolution of the mystery or fate of being as a purpose of eternity. The whole conception of a development to some unthinkable result is alien to the ineluctable concession of eternity. We have authentic history which revered an antiquity long before it, which yet witnessed Assyria trampling down the nations and gathering their treasure "as one gathereth eggs that were forsaken," and saw her in turn fall, exalting over the overthrow of Nineveh. It saw the second rise of Babylon under Nebuchadnezzar, and lived in the midst of its splendors, and beheld them all pass away. "Then came down midnight." So utterly had the local habitation and the name of these great cities vanished from the memory of man that 400 years before the birth of Christ, when Xenophon and the Ten Thousand marched through the land after the battle of Cunaxa, they passed the site of Nineveh and never knew of it, and camped before the ruins of Kalah, another of the cities of Assyria, and recalled them as of an "ancient city called Larissa."

But we foreshorten and localize history, to make ourselves the special pets of Providence — children of God — the seed of Abraham or David, people of but six or seven thousand years ago, while as literal and secular fact we have in our institutions the unquestionable records of civilization in France a hundred thousand years ago. The excavations of Nineveh and Babylon have brought to light records which show Moses and Abraham as characters in the modern fringe of an antiquity that worked in bronze and silver and gold, and wrote laws and history and "literature" with diamond-pointed tools.

And before these run the sure records of geology,

which like the stellar distances have to change the units of measurement, using millenniums as moments, to bring their expression within the compass of human calculation.

Said Kant: "From something that happens as an effect to infer a cause, is a principle of nature, though not of speculative knowledge. There does not remain the smallest justification of a synthetic proposition, showing how, from something which is, there can be a transition to something totally different which we call cause. . . . The principle of causality, which is valid within the field of experience (natural law), is utterly useless, nay, even meaningless, outside it."

Hegel, in his logic of "essence," drops the remark, "There is no such thing as a true causality." . . . "In the case of cause and effect, the same matter is twice put" . . . "reciprocity is a higher relation than causality."

It is impossible in logic that one thing should really produce another; at best it could be only on reciprocal or convertible terms: that is to say, logically each is cause or necessity of the other, as neither can be complete without the other. Cause proved as such, and emptied of its effect, would have ceased to objectively be.

It seems the best way to set this matter of causation right in popular apprehension to exploit the positions and relations of Kant and Hume in regard to it.

David Hume was a philosopher whose vocation was not so much to radical explanation as to the vacation of a popular and even a scientific preposession in regard to it — *i. e.*, to the relation of reason to causality as a necessity in the nature of things. Kant was a philosopher only incidentally and by a necessary implication: he did not pose as an expert in fundamental explanation, nor in the enlargement of knowledge, but rather as a critic of the form and method of knowledge, regardless alike of the contents of the objects of knowledge and of the source of our power to know them. His metaphysics advisedly cut off philosophy and psychology at both ends of it. The power to think was by him attributed outright to "spontaneity" in the understanding — cutting off all debate so far as radical explanation was concerned — while on the other hand he ignored whatever matter might be found as a property of things in themselves. Between these two ignavias he proposed to criticise the form and method of thought, untroubled by either its origin or its results.

In his "Transcendental Analytic" he said: "I do not intend to burden my critical task, which concerns only the forms of synthetical knowledge *a priori*, with analytical processes which aim at the explanation of our concepts. I leave a fuller treatment of these to a future system of pure reason."

"Pure logic takes no account of the contents of the knowledge of the understanding, nor of the difference of its objects. It treats of nothing but the pure forms of thought.

"Pure logic has nothing to do with empirical principles, and borrows nothing from psychology (as some have supposed). Psychology has no influence whatever on the canon of the understanding; everything in it must be completely *a priori*."

"The Critique of Pure Reason," in its scientific and only valuable content, was an inconsequent diversion, in academic rivalry with its predecessors, charging them with a haphazard procedure, instead of following the "sure method of a science." This procedure he held at fault mainly in its assuming as realities mere conceptions, mere linguistic expressions (here following Bacon), which had no perceptive experience to corroborate them. In this unwarranted habit there had been pretentious demonstrations of God, and of freedom and immortality, which properly admitted of no such proof in any sure method of science that demands a foundation in an experience whose matter should staminate the logical form of thought.

This sure method of science Kant borrowed from Aristotle, who held Nature as the graduation of matter up to form, of being up to thought. These two items of matter and form Kant substituted with sense and understanding. Taking human cognition as his logical problem, he divided our mental equipment as of two stems from an unknown root, one stem, sense, having a receptive capacity to which objects are given, the other, understanding, being active, spontaneous, whereby objects are thought. These two faculties were in practice united, pervading each other, and considerable separately only for analytical results. Neither could be preferred to the other as an authority on truth or reality; they render a joint verdict, and every whole utterance of thought must have both their voices. Percepts of sense are blind without concepts of thought, and without the matter of sensibility concepts are wholly empty. The interpervasion of the two faculties is so thorough and essential that in their utmost distinction each shows a trace of the other: there is no sense so dull but it has a scintil of intelligence, and there is no conception so fine but it is haunted by the shadow of "a certain existent unreason."

This unity of sense and understanding Kant seems to have mentally likened to a stream as of water that was ostensibly pure, yet carrying a sediment at its veriest surface, while the grossest matter at the bottom was not hopelessly opaque. Or he might have regarded the joint faculties as of a pencil, sharp at one end for punctual and explicit delineation, the other end being dull or blunt, for surfaces and gradations.

But we may see at once that he did not contemplate radical *explanation* in the union of these so different faculties, one wholly passive and receptive, the other spontaneous and autonomous; for while we may easily understand, how to the senses objects are "given" from without, we have still to wonder at the origin of thought, why that also is not "given." In spite of his disqualification of all "empirical principles," he jumbles cause, psychology and God in one monstrous fetich of "spontaneity."

Lost amid the barren logomachies of the past, the weary spirit of philosophy has latterly paused in a certain resentful self-respect, as if she had gone too far afield, or looked too high, for a sufficient explanation. A man sometimes has moments when, if he were a divine psychologist, he might respect himself as original, as elemental, pure cause. When the boy is called down for the motive of his action, and shouts " 'Cause!" he claims the heart and truth of being. When a man, thwarted, baffled in his most desperate endeavor, growls through set teeth his fervent "God damn!" he is for once a reality; he gives assurance that out of the heart of Nature rolled the burden of the Bible old; that the canticles of love and woe came from the burning core below; that genius builds better than he knows.

I saw a plainsman involved with a corral of wild horses. Like a panther he encountered a huge stallion. Seizing his mane with the left hand he grasped the nose of the beast with the right, and was borne along, pounded from below by the knees of the creature as he reared and plunged, but the cowboy kept his hold, and with ever-shortening breath protested, "Die here! die here!"

The light, the vehemence that comes from beneath the threshold of articulate thought, or the venereal orgasm of the love that makes the world go round, is it not heat enough for cause? Should not something come of it? When we reach these depths of feeling do we not touch bottom? Are they not "sufficient reason"?

But now Citizen Kant had not the nerve to leave reason, our highest attribute and sublimest essence, at such an anomalous outcome as this; he had neither the courage nor the patience to appear the subtle agnostic genius that he really was. There was no sustaining audience for the most expert metaphysician in mental history. The Prussian bureaucracy and the Lutheran orthodoxy overshadowed his individual prestige. What then? What but a further demonstration of his skill, by showing that there is a counterpoising answer to all his charges against pure reason, a "moral" answer, complacent to the religion of his nation (which Hume made light of), to be won out of the heart and conscience of the people — a practical as against a theoretical judgment! What then but a rank stultification of the very reason that proposed it — a relief from the agonism of intelligence for a true vision of itself, by a cringing faith in a superstitious authority? Thus as a benevolent hypocrite ("corrupt," as Schopenhauer characterized him, showing that in his revoke Kant had repressed some fifty-seven of the most liberal pages of his work), he exploited the sense of "duty," the subservience forced upon human weakness by an overpowering environment, as a "categorical imperative": "thou shalt," and "thou canst because thou oughtst" — this although Luther himself had well said before, "There is no logical connection between *can* and *ought*." But our apologist would hold no controversy as to how this sense of duty and the "ought" originated: it was there, and there was the end.

Though there truly were such a humiliating sense of subserviency it should be regarded only as an unfortunate handicap, indefensibly embarrassing explanatory thought. And while urging this moral sense of duty, obviously and undoubtedly in behalf of the prevailing view of Christianity, he seemed as having never heard the name of Jesus, who of all the race was the most distinguishably first to deny the self-sufficiency, the essential self-groundedness by which alone knowledge, as the science of science, would be philosophically possible. [If the name of Jesus appears in the 800 pages of the "Critique of Pure Reason" I have overlooked it.]

That Kant was weak, if not quite disingenuous in his *quasi* conformity, appears in an inconsistency too rank to pass for mere inadvertence in so clear a mind. There can be duty only as to acknowledged superiority; but Kant's "reason," despite his fling at it as in conflict with itself, was as spontaneous and autonomous in his account of knowledge, the dogmatic primate of first principles, the unconditioned referee of all metaphysical controversy, who should impose all duties and defer to none. The supreme may not subserve; so that his "categorical imperative" can be recognized only by an intelligence either incompetent or stultified; it should as well determine justice as cognition in its own case. Only his arrant slave should feel a sense of duty; the great man's "ought" should be divinely his own, if reason is the true first principle.

It will appear in our notice of self-relation that Kant utterly disqualified the psychological illusion of "self-consciousness" from which popular theology infers its notion of "free will" — the same which Kant invoked for his "thou canst because thou oughtst." But it is relevant here to recall from history and poetry instances of the divine "imperative" and the higher law, where great spirits have taken fate in their own hands, and assumed the judgment of justice itself, and law. For the law says well, "Thou shalt not kill"; but where was law, or justice, or any exoteric imperative, when Virginius drove home the flesher's knife into the bosom of his daughter, and the flow of her young blood renewed pulsation in the stagnant heart of Rome? Or when sad Andronicus enacted the same tragedy with his daughter Lavinia? We recognize here the autonomous first principle, the dogmatic imperative of the theoretical reason, but the "ought" that shall subserve any alien category has sunk to insignificance. What shall impose a duty on the divine and highest? Shall he not do as he will with his own — even with his life?

We had an eminent literary recognition of divine independence in an obviously second thought of Tennyson, as correcting his poem "Lucretius" — not only in the hero's taking his own life, but in his resentment of any imposition of duty upon his action. As first published the final paragraph of "Lucretius" read as follows:

With that he drove the knife into his side.
She heard him raging, heard him fall — ran in,
Beat breast, tore hair, cried out upon herself
As having failed in duty to him — shrieked
That she but meant to win him back — fell on him,
Clasped, kissed him, wailed; he answered: "Care not
    thou.
What matters? All is over. Fare thee well."

I could not resist the impulse to congratulate the distinguished poet on this amendment, and his lordship graciously responded: "In 'Lucretius,' 'What is duty?' was the first reading; it was changed because I could not find that Lucretius had anywhere used the word 'duty' in that sense; but it stands now as at first."

[An anecdote of Dr. Stirling.]

I have to recall an incident of the life of Dr. Stirling as having philosophical interest, in that it seems to demonstrate the psychological effect of the habit of transcendental thought upon practical affairs.

The learned doctor was very good to me in his day, corresponding freely and sending me his works, and indeed in his last book, "What Is Thought?" over-crediting me as "the authority" upon modern mysticism. He had achieved a considerable success through his literary ventures, especially his "Secret of Hegel" and his translation of Schwegler's "History of Philosophy," and it happened that he had on his hands some £4,000 which he desired to profitably invest.

Now here begins our moral. Of course the business world has developed a general conception of investment, which involves the agency of a professional broker — such is the conventional method, and so far well; so he placed his £4,000 in the hands of a broker. And conceptually a broker is a broker; as concepts there is no difference between brokers. But a canny Scot, even an LL.D. in metaphysics, should have been supposed to be alert to the perceptual and pragmatic difference underlying the transcendental concept, broker; unfortunately in this case the broker was a rascal, who abused the confidence unavoidable in his profession by misplacing the money, undoubtedly through a collusion intended for his own ultimate advantage.

Still untaught by this too frequent experience, our transcendental dabbler in "business" resorted to the next conventional method of righting a wrong: he employed a lawyer to make application to the courts. But the concept "lawyer" is not less general than the concept "broker." Any honest expert would have told him that a breach of confidence is fatal, and that he had "lost" his money; but he persisted, still sending good money after bad, until, in spirit at least, he was nearly a broken man.

He sent a laborious account of the proceedings in the trial, still arguing against the errors of even the Court himself. I responded with encouragement, not indeed for the lost cause, but as contemplating for him a series of lectures in America, assuring him that our people loved a foreign celebrity quite as clearly as a Briton loves a lord. At first he seriously considered the undertaking, but I suspect that his keenness and his discomfiture alike were soothed to inactivity by reflections upon the good company in which I took pains to place him and his misfortunes. Had not Sir Walter Scott embarrassed himself and recovered? Had not Mark Twain retreived a fortune lost in attempting pilotage through currents wholly strange to him? And as for being done out of his money, he had but to think of our General Grant: credited with the conquest of the great Rebellion, given a warship in which to junket around the globe, as the nation's ambassador and the honored guest at every foreign court, he returned only to show his transcendental unfitness to the working world. He entrusted to a rascal the use of his signature, and became involved

for ten times your £4,000, and then, with a virulent cancer gnawing at his throat, he put the last of his indomitable energy into a book that cancelled all his obligations, so fraudulently imposed, and scored his untarnished signature among the few, the immortal names that were not born to die.

I heard no more of the lecture course, but in the last of his letters, after a humorous protest at having to pay extra postage on my last advice, he woulded to God that he might again get so much consideration at any price.

CHAPTER V

SELF-RELATION

WE have seen Kant, ignoring the value of things in themselves, with equal disregard tossing the cause of them to an irresponsible and libertine spontaneity. He was but a Phaenarete, an accoucheur, whose vocation was to insure the proper delivery of conceptions. But his ingenuity and success, especially at a time when philosophy had outworn its welcome in esoteric circles, roused in more ardent spirits a curiosity, not only as to things in themselves but as to the origin of the principle of knowledge itself, of which Kant had so cleverly delineated the logical form. They revived the ancient interest in the relation of thought and being, and in subjective cause.

The quest of these aspirants was the meaning of absolute principle; not so specially of a supreme principle, but of any rational principle. Theretofore thought had affected objective principle, or cause; it had looked only outward; it had no resource but to an Other; and the other called for still another indefinitely. A crisis came in the conviction that principle, in the absolute, must be its own other, in itself and for itself at once, a self-relation — if such were possible.

SELF-RELATION

We stay our leading for a moment here to say that self-relation is the Ultima Thule of philosophy — a land that should be, by the legends, but which, by the bearings of the compass, has not been charted yet.

The reader who has been thwarted and confused in his commendable ambition to understand German philosophy shall be advised that the main cause of his discomfiture was the expert presumption of self-relation; and the hope is here indulged that as a consequence of this treatise he may well throw down and disregard any work that proceeds upon its admission — either as self-consciousness, self-knowledge, self-sustenance, self-cause, or any other relation to self. The fact shall appear, in citation of the most approved of thinkers, ancient and modern, that there is no such possibility as a self-relation.

The leanest metaphysician who ever entertained the conception of a whole, and the clumsiest mechanic who ever built a machine that would "work," will concur upon four necessary requisites of totality: there is no other outside it; its comprehension shall include that which comprehends; if it is known, or determined, or sustained, all these effects it must produce for itself; if it has or ever had a cause it is and was "*causa sui*."

The whole cannot have become, for various reasons: for one, becoming is a process, and the whole could not partly be; for another, even as time, to begin, assumes as already a time in which to begin, so a concrete world as becoming requires an ideal void, a space-world to receive it.

If self-relation were the first principle it should

seem that men, who have somehow the good fortune to live, would only voluntarily die. But so far is this from the fact of man's condition that a cartoonist might cleverly depict him as one of those gyroscopic toys that we have seen attached to a stovepipe, in which a manikin model appears as mightily cranking the wheel above, which in fact is actuating him. Indeed, the materialist might cartoon the idealist as functioning in a similar delusion — seeming to posit the world that sustains him, or to furnish through a bellows the breath that inspires him. Men, and not the worst of men at that, have been so conventionalized by social necessities as to feel that it is one's handkerchief that blows one's nose. Why not, since nothing is something in the professional necessity of discourse?

It will be seen in a criticism of "truth" that the baffling obduracy of the philosophical problem lies in the coincident necessity and impossibility of self-relation.

Truth should be what it never is. It must be of knowledge, and knowledge of somewhat that is; it is not itself ostensibly that somewhat, nor a property of it, but it guarantees a claim that somewhat (as knowledge, or copy, or statement) represents it. Now to represent the somewhat fairly, in a copy, were very well, very practical and plausible; but "very well" will not serve; a fair copy is admissible as such, but your "truth" is precisely what any copy lacks of the original; for thus the original is made no better than an imitation; original merit, that may be unique, is disqualified by a pretended re-presentation.

SELF-RELATION

Truth requires that knowledge shall be equal to reality — which it cannot be, save as identical with it — and then there is no relation between the knower and the known (there is no truth where there is no knowledge); no truth unless the identical knows itself.

It is very obvious that the notion of truth grew out of the failure, or at least the suspicion of knowledge. Making many mistakes himself, and misled by the machinations of others — waking and sleeping and forgetting, all involuntarily — a man is entitled to question his facts not only, but his intelligence itself. Such questioning in due time evolved the abstraction, truth, as challenging all pretensions of knowledge; and thus came philosophy, with all its complications of being and knowing, reality and appearance, etc.

It were a natural thought, that there is no call to make difficulties, or to find problems or puzzles in this simple fact of knowing, or to make criterions and distinctions in knowing; but we find that there are difficulties in the way of absolute definition and distinction. Things will not lie still and be identified. Each is for all; "nothing is fair or good alone."

This fatality is instantly detected when the professors set out to tell off-hand, in a popular way, the meanings of words. Webster's Dictionary was begun in 1828, and has since been enlarged under the vigilance and assiduity of more than fifty distinguished scholars, all eager, doubtless, to tell the truth; but the reader shall judge, from what should be one of their capital definitions, how little care or sympathy these scholars had for the problem which haunts our troublesome essay. We quote their definition of truth:

"TRUTH. — The quality of being true; as (a) conformity to fact or reality; exact accordance with that which is, has been, or shall be."

How happy the philosopher might be if the world-secret could be adroitly told with the dash and abandon of this forthright deliverance!

Does conformity embrace all the possible truth and essence of fact and reality? Has all their matter gone up into form, and left no *substance* to be identified, realized and lived? Fact and reality cover being alone; they leave out thought and relation and difference, which are not properties of factual things, any more than are illusions and negations and nonentities. It might seem a better definition of truth to call it, not conformity, but identity with fact and reality; but when we turn to their definition of identity we receive a slap from Sir William Hamilton: "Identity is a relation between our cognitions of things, not between things themselves." But in any explanation, are not these cognitions to be things of themselves, even if mere spectres? The fact is that philosophers as a class give truth a sinister fling in quotation marks, as a word for the people, and not for the elect. The reason for this is that they find knowledge a gift that has no confirmation of its pretensions — especially none from itself, its only possible critic. It tries, but fails, to focus its faculties upon itself. In identity it finds at best the same, and the same is another: there needs two for sameness. And when all is said, difference has as good an identity as sameness, and sameness has "all the difference in the world" from difference.

Then as to truth being "accordance to that which is, has been, or shall be," does it accord in these vital respects, that it has been, or shall be, as really as it is now? And what shall accord to what is — to all that is? Unless all that is can accord to itself in that self-relation which our authorities shall keenly resent. And again as to "accordance to what is, has been or shall be," we might suggest a few things that *ought* to be, at least in definition of truth. Hegel, in his definition of truth, held frankly to the self-relation: "Science does not seek truth: it is *in* truth; it *is* the truth."

That there is such a possibility as rational self-relation is a notion taken from popular psychology, assumed from empirical "self-consciousness," so called. Plato, as I will notice, had no serious use for this conception of the "self-moved," except as a tentative prop for the doctrine of the immortality of the soul; for recalling in his "Phædrus" the same notion (the self-moved) he cast it aside with something less than approval, saying wearily: "Enough of the immortality of the soul!" He had probably no conviction in regard to it; and when the topic of mental self-relation came specifically before him, as where in "Charmides" he raised the question of a "science of science," otherwise "self-consciousness," he made it ridiculous, as I will amply show. I will show also how Kant, Hume and others have utterly disqualified it. Before we come to that citation, however, we must appreciate the agonism of controversy which self-relation, as subject-object, has occasioned.

We must first more clearly define self-relation. There is a wide though illusive difference between anything regarded as moving itself and as moving *of* itself — which last, as his whole context shows, was Plato's intention. Any principle must move of itself as excluding all outside influence; and why the principle, as objectively regarded, so moves, is left by all philosophy as the secret of the divine nature or power of the world—at least, no explanation of it is technically proposed. But in the proposition that it "moves itself," not only is outside assistance excluded, but the principle is actively a divinity in and for itself.

Now as we have the ineluctable fact of the world, to be acknowledged and accounted for as best it may, and as reason is our only recourse, and as God and man are the only intelligences to which we may hopefully resort, we have the alternative of preferring either, or of dividing the onus of the Mystery between them — *i. e.*, between the monads of the Many and the supremacy of the One.

Jesus said, "As the Father hath life in himself, so hath he given to the Son to have life in himself." — "To them gave he power to become sons of God, even they who believe on his name."

And here I must profess a certain indifference, so far as explanation is concerned. There is a very gratuitous skepticism of "miracles," as arising among powers or creatures unwarrantably condemned as of course secondary and barren. With the great miracle or mystery of the whole freely and generally acknowledged, I am so much the pluralist as to see no fatal discrepancy in a participation of it by the parts; and this indeed seems ostensibly admitted in any doctrine of responsible free wills. My philosophy balks at self-relation either as divine or human. And German philosophy, too practical to insist that any entity can lift itself by the straps of its own boots, has overborne the human ego and its determining organization, and advanced to the presumption of a "universal" ego as subject-object — rather an institution or an atmosphere than a normal personality, in a purely transcendental field, a conception of mere language and logic, as we shall find, having no authentic ground in perceptual experience — a field which Kant had spent his best efforts in disqualifying by "the sure method of a science." The fatal fault of the whole dialectic industry is the obsession that besides all fact there is an explanation, a self-relation, that shall satisfy our finitude in the cosmos, however contradictory its expression may appear. The extravagance, the willful blindness with which post-Kantian philosophy exalted this universal self-related ego above all empirical mechanism and common sense evolved and published expressions almost outrageous. Witness the following sentence from Hegel's private outline of his lectures at Nürnberg in 1808–11: "But the Mind, *according to its self-activity within itself in relation to itself independent of all relation to others*, is considered in the Science of Mind proper, or 'Psychology.'"

In his practice Hegel rather avoided responsibility for that instant and constant self-relation which a mechanic would scout, and rather, as in his "Phenomenology of Spirit," made the soul take up its various attributes successively as partial phases, "until finally" all difference between subject and object is eliminated. This doing by pieces the problem of the absorption of an entity by itself only postponed the whole difficulty of the original problem to the last phase, which for its own part had no piece but itself to work upon, and so the "finality" satisfied the whole inconsequent process. But Hegel knew that the endless future will never test his finality! We may see how clumsily, and all-but cavalierly, he treated self-relation in his "Logic," when defining "truth":

"In common life we call truth the agreement between an object and our conception of the object. We thus presuppose an object to which our conception must conform. In the philosophical sense of the word, on the other hand, truth may be described, in a general an done-sided way (!), as the agreement of the subject matter of thought with itself." He says elsewhere: "Science does not seek truth, but is in the truth, and is the truth itself."

(Kant himself had forecast a countenance for this maladroit proceeding by a doubtless inadvertent proposition — in "intensive quantity" — that reality could fade to zero "by degrees." The practical mind must see that the last degree, be it ever so minute, reserves in its wholeness all the degrees of infinite divisibility. Any perceptible degree must carry a gross bulk under the metaphysical microscope.)

The Johannine proem ("In the beginning was the

Word," etc.), which, except the question of Pilate, "What is truth?" Fichte valued as the text of the Christian Scriptures having the most special philosophical appeal, is indeed a most affirmative counterpart of Aristotle's doctrine of matter and form, later repeated in Kant's exposition of sense and understanding. As was *Dasein* to *Sein* (for Fichte), thought to being, form to matter, difference to identity, so for John (as for Swedenborg) was the Word, the *logos*, the manifestation and presence, to the divine essence. All things were made, or are such, through and by this *expression*; this is the light of the world, by reason of which identity attains distinction, or God, whom otherwise no man hath seen at any time, is manifested in flesh and spirit.

It is wonderfully suggestive of the homogeneity of intelligence, to observe how this fine conception of the existence of inherent or latent being, through its manifestation in form, or knowledge, has come to men of genius regardless of each other. Fichte gave no credit to Aristotle's explanation of nature as matter grading up to form; and in noticing St. John's doctrine of all things becoming through the Word he made no mention of Swedenborg on the same lines, but claimed (as he doubtless believed) that his doctrine was "now for the first time scientifically set forth."

The truth is that Swedenborg's exegesis, whether from insight or inspiration, was at once the clearest and profoundest of them all. He explains that *by definition things become*, and that definition is a mental act. It is by definition as the Word that things come out of latent being, into existence as knowledge and form. It is through definition by the Word that the One, whom none hath seen at any time, becomes the Many of things and souls.

But our instant concern with Fichte is that perversion of consciousness into self-relation which distinguished him as the primate of that absolute idealism which staggered the sanity of his generation, exhausted his own patience if not his mental force, and humiliated his imperious spirit to the faith and docility of the natural man.

This implicit emphasis of self-relation as science of science began with Fichte in his "Vocation of Man" as self-conscious:

"Thou seest, thou hearest, thou feelest; also thou thinkest. Thou hast also a *consciousness of* thy seeing, hearing, feeling and thinking, and thereby thou perceivest an object. Thou couldst not perceive it without this consciousness. Thou canst not recognize an object by sight or hearing or feeling, without *knowing that* thou seest, or hearest, or feelest it. The immediate consciousness of thyself is therefore the imperative *condition* of all other consciousness, and thou knowest a thing only in that and so far as thou knowest that thou knowest it; no element can enter the former cognition that is not contained in the latter. Thou canst not know anything save as knowing that thou knowest it."

This subtle and plausible appeal to unsophisticated experience, whereby cognition (a miracle in itself) is doubled and meretriciously explained as *re*-cognition, is the entering wedge of absolute idealism, disrupting Kant's "unknown root," flippantly thrusting into the ego of common consciousness the mystery that can be thought only as the Supreme, and thenceforth exalting speculation from the empirical ego to an ego universal — and transcendental. But the sure method of Kant, that will not permit this light-winged concept to rise without the empirical percept of given experience (and thus to sunder the twin stems of sense and understanding), drags it back under the insuperable criticism of the present tense, and arrests this arrogant self-relation with the question whether it is indeed instantly such, and whether this "knowing that it knows" is not rather a quick *remembering that it knew*. Science and speculation cannot overbear the rational necessities of a present tense. Assume as we may that the past is gone and the future has yet to come, and that only the present instant is real, we have to compromise the static and dynamic viewpoints — to draw upon both the past and the future, to get a foothold for reality at all.

Our most careful metaphysicians have agreed that for us there is no being or thinking without the *lapse*, the Heraclitic flux. The present tense, which presumptively carries all reality, is mused of as a platform loaded with the increment of the process of becoming and a residuum of the process of departing — a platform on which the serpent truth has ample room and verge enough to take its tail in its mouth and do the acrobatic stunt of swallowing itself without disappearing. But reflection, second thought, will have all that is sensible also divisible. Your non-existent past and future demand, what is between us? How do we have names, if we have no part in reality? Your present, if substantial and sensible, has its older and younger sides, and only an ideal line or division between them can be strictly real, in the infinite divisibility of the material. The present, as real, is to be sought down the bottomless well of Democritus. How then does the present sustain itself? How does truth climb out of this bottomless well? . . . It must be by some art of livelihood; it is the trick of the chimney-sweep, who has neither foothold nor handhold, but climbs by the lateral impact of his elbows and his knees.[1]

It should be obvious that the attempt to construe self-relation in the instant present tense, as an essentiality without lapse or passage of time, is a failure, and that "self-consciousness," as a knowing that you know, is an implication of memory and anticipation. The language of the proposition stultifies it. Why, in knowing, know that you know? Is not simple knowing sufficiently wonderful, without invoking its second power? or why not invoke the third power, and say that we *know* that in knowing we know that we know? This reiteration neither adds to nor accounts for the simple gift of knowledge.

This is the central crux of all philosophy, and of religion as well, that knowledge and will are secondary, and not essentially grounded; and although Jesus was the first to utilize the insight for the relief of human conscience, Plato had exhausted the topic metaphysically some 400 years before Jesus was born.

The divine Greek, in his "Charmides," treated the problem of self-relation as it is involved in the

[1] See further in our Chapter IX, on "Ancillary Unity."

SELF-RELATION 123

proposition of a science of science, or popularly, self-consciousness. He covered it both mathematically and pragmatically. To test the vulgar illusion of a man's knowing himself he exchanged the word *knowing* for *excelling* — a concept of the same order, whose percept may have a tangible quality and quantity which consciousness lacks — and then argued that anything instantly excelling itself would be at once greater and less than itself, and so mathematically impossible.

Our English Jowett, translator of Plato, emphasizes with a footnote this very palpable hit.

Plato then subjects the topic to his usual Socratic method. Self-consciousness will infer a science of science itself. Now every science can be taught, and its interest will assure and benefit professors. The physician knows and lives by the science of healing, the cobbler by the science or art of mending; but a professor of the science would have no call; however knowing, he knows only that he knows, and would be as useless as a windmill for grinding the wind that drives it.

It is not a natural but a wholly artificial ingenuity that deduces self-determination from the common consciousness, which indeed thinks nothing at all about it. I recall that Jonathan Edwards — who had but the natural wit where dialectic was concerned — in his treatise on the "Freedom of the Will" said he would not make so light of the discretion of "even an Arminian" as to assume that by self-determination (of the will) he meant an activity of causing it to act (*i. e.*, by a self-relation), but consented that he should intend an originating independent principle; for he would credit his opponents with knowing the fling of Thomas Hobbes, which was as follows:

"The question is not whether a man be a free agent, that is to say, whether he can write or forbear, speak or be silent, according to his will; but whether the will to write and the will to forbear come upon him according to his will, or according to anything else in his own power. I acknowledge this liberty, that I can *do* if I *will*; but to say, I can will if I will, I take to be an absurd speech. . . . A man hath freedom to do if he will, but whether he hath freedom to will (*i. e.* is an original rather than a given power) is a question which it seems neither the bishop nor they ever thought on."

Edwards did shrewdly arraign self-relation in the Calvinistic interest making man wholly subject to the grace of God; but all his arguments against human originality are equally cogent against original principle in any case, even that of God. And the only policy or "plan of salvation" in which man's dependent quality was useful to free him from the exceeding sinfulness of sin, to be borne rather by its original author in the sole vocation of Jesus as a divine substitute, seems to have never occurred to him.

In attacking the problem of self-knowledge Professor Ladd first staunches his nerve with a backward glance at idealism and its doctrine that objects are determined by (or through) the subjective organs (as lenses, or functions or what not), and then states his general proposition thus:

"In opposition to all views like the foregoing, we

SELF-RELATION 125

desire to maintain the identity of knowledge and being-as-known. . . . What is first of all, really and indubitably existent, is this fact of knowledge. . . . Self-consciousness is; it is an actual datum; and the very attempt to be skeptical thereupon does but lead to confirmation by repetition of this fact of reality. . . . It is not a conclusion drawn in the region of mere thinking; it is rather a rational conviction respecting the envisaged reality which all knowledge involves. . . . It is the inevitable product of the attempt to represent in terms of sensation that which is known to be implicated in sense perception, but is not to be given to thought in terms of sensation. . . . We never envisage or otherwise know, in its naked simplicity, this substance of the states (self), whether physical or psychical. It can only be said to be known as necessarily implicated to reason, present and actually existing. . . . Neither can it be said to be known as the result of reasoning alone. Knowledge of the really existent follows upon processes of analysis and synthesis which we may feel obliged to describe as involving instinctive inference.

"In every act of knowledge through self-consciousness the subject knowing is regarded as having become the object of knowledge to itself. The very essence of 'self-consciousness' is that the subject knowing and the object known are one and the same being.

"We may be unable to psychologically explain the fact of self-consciousness. We may represent the case as though the mind could never so far catch up with itself as not to be at least one step behind the act of self-realization in the unity of self-consciousness. But neither in this nor in any other way can we invalidate the primary fact of knowledge, with all the conviction of being really existent which it involves.

"We may doubt whether the being that now knows is the same being as that which knew a moment since; but that the being which, as subject, knows in the self-consciousness act, is really one and the same with the being known, as object in the selfsame act, is a known reality which it is impossible to doubt."

Mr. Ladd has, it will be seen, committed himself to the infallibility of a controversial notion not nearly so plausible as the vulgar intuition that the sun goes around the earth, and one moreover which the history of speculation so eminently confutes. As for the impossibility of doubting the factual reality of self-relation, the following citations from Kant, Hume and others should rather show it impossible, at least for a scholar, to believe in it. Professor Ladd's own halting reservations signalize it as merely a *modus vivendi* for philosophy, and we do not see the necessity for that. In fact Prof. Ladd discounts all that he says above:

"The mind in its highest and wildest flights of self-consciousness never knows by envisaging, as it were (?), its own simplicity of reality; or by rationally attaching to any particular conception which it forms of itself the unquestionable faith of intuitive self-knowledge."

[This is to say that the transcendental concept of a self-knowledge has no percept in experience.]

"Strictly speaking, knowledge cannot be defined."

SELF-RELATION

[And yet it is self-known?] "The true definition of knowledge would be a highly complicated instance of that which in its simplicity we seek to define." This is the crux precisely — the ultimate surd.[1]

It seems hardly necessary here, in passing, to confess what there really is in the conceit of self-knowledge. Of course a man knows himself superficially. He bears in memory the record and attestation of his normal quality. His past experience culminates in a sense of more or less definite individuality; he knows in a general way his natural ability, his courage, and his impulses, and he has reliable conviction as to what he is, and what he would be and do in any given contingency. He knows, too, his civil and social responsibility in the state. And he

---

[1] From Prof. Ladd's "Secret of Personality": "The conception of what it is to be a Self, and equally the conception of my own particular Self, is not a matter for immediate Knowledge, or for mental envisagement, in a single mental act. It is formed by intellectual processes. . . . The Knowledge which is of Self differs from the Knowledge which sense-perception brings. . . . The sensuous elements of consciousness, especially those of the most definitely localized and clearly projected sort, are relatively suppressed. In predominating states of self-consciousness, the sensations are of the vague unlocalized order which are attributable to myself as a sentient organism, rather than to any objective thing . . . by the influence of feeling over attention *one often passes back and forth between the objective and the subjective aspects of the same experience.*" "But the sanest activities of the same intellect compel it to conceive of the Self as having qualities that cannot be ascribed to any Thing."

This making a static identity of a process, and then passing it back and forth (fully identified) between the two factors (subject and object) which compose it, is about the most pitiable infatuation that any scholar has ever exemplified. And then the smug composure of it all!

may well have had moments of reflection upon his relations to his inner as well as to his outer world; he may have become even a professor of philosophy, and yet have never clearly discriminated between the philosophical requirements of an original as distinguished from a secondary and given principle. For example, he may have never contemplated any supposable difference between his accountability to his fellow creatures and his standing before his Creator, as the source of his sustenance and inspiration. In a word, he may have never been concerned in fundamental explanation. Against Prof. Ladd's naïve and over-confident dictum, let us cite the good-natured comment of Hume:

"There are some philosophers who imagine we are every moment intimately conscious of what we call our 'self.' For my part, when I enter most intimately into what I call myself, I always stumble upon some particular perception, heat or cold, light or shade, love or hatred, pain or pleasure. I never catch myself at any time without a perception, and never can observe anything but the perception."

Said Plotinus: "We feel distinctly only what is alien, not ourselves, not our own inmost being. It is impossible that consciousness should be the essence of the inner life and the source of truth; the fountain-head must be a world behind consciousness.

"In order to seek for reason we must already possess reason." In a word, The Hound of Heaven is on his own trail and what he seeks is nothing else than a foregone conclusion. . . .

The acute discrimination of Kant invites special attention: "Reason imposes upon us an apparent knowledge only, by representing the constant *logical* subject of thought as the knowledge of the *real* subject in which that knowledge inheres. Of that subject, however, we have not and cannot have the slightest knowledge."

"In what we call soul there is a continuous flux, and nothing permanent, except it may be (if people will have it so) the simple I, so simple because this representation has no contents. . . . But this I is neither an intuition nor a concept of any object."

"The reason why that being which thinks within us imagines that it knows itself by means of pure categories, and especially by that which expresses absolute unity under each head, is . . . it does not *know itself* through the categories, but knows the categories only. It appears self-evidently that I cannot know as an object that which is presupposed in order to enable me to know an object, and that the determining self (thought) differs from the self that is to be determined, as knowledge from its object. Nevertheless nothing is more natural, or at least more tempting, than the illusion which makes us look upon the *unity in the synthesis of thoughts* as a perceived unity in the *subject* of the thoughts. One might call it the surreptitious admission of a hypostatized consciousness."

"What I maintain is, that all the difficulties which we imagine to exist in these questions, and with which, as dogmatical objections, people wish to give themselves an air of deeper insight than the common understanding can claim, rests on a mere illusion, which leads us to hypostatize what exists in thought only as a real object outside the thinking subject."

(The reader should forecast from this notion of hypostatizing a thing outside itself — like Fichte's "being out of its being" — the struggles for *causa sui*, and the Heraclitic and Hegelian claims of something from nothing, the inevitable, etc.)

"Such a concept is necessary for practical purposes, and sufficient, but we can never pride ourselves on it as helping to expand our knowledge of ourself by means of pure reason. . . that concept is only constantly turning around itself in a circle, and does not help us with respect to any question which aims at synthetical knowledge."

"I put my concept and its unity in the place of the qualities that belong to me as an object, and thus really take for granted what was wished to be known."

"The internal sense by means of which the mind perceives itself or its internal state does not give an intuition of the soul itself, as an object." "Besides this logical meaning of the 'I' we have no knowledge of the subject in itself, which forms the substratum and foundation of it (consciousness) and of all our thoughts . . . it signifies a substance in idea only, and not in reality."

"The subjective I can never be divided and distributed; and it is this I which we presuppose in every thought."

"Although the whole of a thought may be divided and distributed under many objects, the subjective I can never be divided and distributed; and it is this I which we presuppose in every thought . . . but that concept, or that proposition, teaches us nothing at all with reference to myself, as an object of experience, because the concept of substance itself is used as a function of synthesis only, *without any intuition to rest on,* and therefore without any object — valid with reference to the *condition of our knowledge* but not with reference to any object of it."

By this **I**, or *he*, or *it* (the thing) which thinks, nothing is represented beyond a transcendental subject of thought $= x$, which is known only through the thoughts (remembered?) that are its predicates, and of which, apart from them, we can never have the slightest concept — so that we are really turning round it in a perpetual circle, having already to use its representation, before we can have any judgment about it."

"Though the **I** exists in all thoughts, not the slightest intuition is connected with that representation by which it might be distinguished from other objects of intuition. . . . The internal sensuous intuition of our mind (as an object of consciousness) which is represented as determined by the succession of different states in time, is not a real self, as it exists by itself, or what is called the transcendental subject, but a phenomenon only, given to the sensibility of this to us unknown being."

"The non-sensuous cause of these representations is entirely unknown to us, and we can never perceive it as an object."

"The whole representation is nothing but the idea of a possible experience."

Schwegler subsumes the whole matter thus: "In the traditional psychology the soul was regarded as a psychical thing, a simple substance — an intellectual, numerically identical substance with the predicate of personality. All these statements are subreptitious, *petitiones principii*, derived from the simple 'I think' which is neither perception nor notion, but a mere consciousness, an act of the mind. This act of thought is falsely converted into a thing; for the existence of the ego as subject, the existence of the ego as object, as soul, is substituted. That the ego might be treated as an object and apply categories in its regard, it would have required to have been empirically given in a perception, which is impossible." (No one ever saw such a thing, or dreamed of such an experience.) "There is no rational psychology which might procure us an additional knowledge of ourselves, but only a discipline which sets insurmountable bounds to speculative reason in this field. We may view this discipline, too, as admonishing us to confess the refusal of reason perfectly to satisfy the curious in reference to questions that transcend this life."

In contrast with these clean-cut sentences, which appeal to the plainest common sense, the reader shall have a specimen of the mental contortion which, assuming that philosophy must of course succeed, has exploited the opposite position: he shall see how haltingly the explorer sets his feet upon the quaking ground. Observe first the hopeless entanglement of the dialectic in this concession of the preface to "The Secret of Hegel":

"There is no concrete which consists not of two antagonistic characters, where, at the same time, strangely somehow, the one is not only through the other, but actually is the other."

SELF-RELATION 133

In his last book, entitled "What Is Thought?" Dr. Stirling has this, of self-relation:

"I as I is the subject, and Me as Me is the object; but both are identically the same. This is the primitive relation — the unit of what is, the unit of what it is to think, and the unit of what it is to be."

To countenance this doctrine he quotes as follows from his "Secret of Hegel": (The reader may safely skip the entire quotation.)

"The idea is Thought, self-identical Thinking; self-identical because in its own nature the Idea is two-sided — an objective side is, as it were, exposed and offered to a subjective side, and the result is the return, so to speak, of the Idea from its other, which is the objective side, into its self or subjective side, as satisfied, gratified, and contented knowledge."

"*Cogito ergo sum.* That is, Thought is; it has come to be, it simply is — as yet, however, only in itself: there is as yet only blank self-identity — it can only say *is*, rather than *am*, of itself, or to itself."

"This is just a description *in abstracto* of self-consciousness. The Ego is first unal simplicity — that is unal or simple negativity; but just, as it were, for this very reason (that is, to know itself and be no longer negative, or because it finds itself in a state of negativity) it becomes self-separated into duality — it becomes a duplication, a duad, the units of which confront each other, in the forms of Ego-subject and Ego-object; and then, again, this very self-separation, this very self-duplication, becomes its own negation — the negation of the duality, inasmuch as its confronting units are seen to be identical, and the antithesis is reduced, the antagonism vanishes. This process of self-consciousness has just to be transferred to the All, the Absolute, the Substance, to enable us to form a conception of unal negativity of Spirit passing into the alienation of external nature, finally to return reconciled, harmonious, and free into its own self."

Opposing this we quote a few sentences from Bradley's "Appearance and Reality":

"It is not only possible but most probable that in every man there are elements in the internal felt core which are never made objects, and which practically cannot be." "Metaphysics pays no regard to the origin of our ideas." (In a logical conflict you may use vacuums for balls. In all efforts at self-knowledge the subject still is such, still retains the observant and superior side, and cannot forfeit it.) "It is not known, and never as a whole can be known, in such a sense that knowledge would be the same as experience or reality." "There can be really no such science as a theory of cognition." "Every soul has existed as a not-self." "The self is one of the results gained by transcending the first imperfect form of experience." "A complete state of existence as a whole is at any one moment utterly impossible."

"There is no self-consciousness in which the object is the same as the subject, none in which what is perceived exhausts the whole self. In self-consciousness a part or element, or again a general aspect or character, becomes distinct from the whole mass, and stands over against the felt background.

But the background is never exhausted by this object, and it never could be so. An experiment should convince any man that in self-consciousness what he feels cannot wholly come before him. It can be exhausted, if at all, only by a long series of observations; and the summed result of these observations cannot be experienced as a fact. Such a result cannot be verified as quite true at any particular given moment. . . . If self-consciousness is appealed to, it is evident that at any moment I am more than the self which I can think of. . . . In thinking, the subject that thinks is more than thought." "In practice, thought always is found with, and appears to demand, an Other." "The emotion we attend to is, taken strictly, never precisely the same as the emotion which we feel . . . it has become a factor in a new felt totality. . . . Our experience is always from time to time a unity which, as such, is destroyed in becoming an object. . . . The Other which it asserts is found on inquiry to be no other. . . . If I attempt to elaborate this point I should perhaps obscure it."

"Truth made adequate to reality would have become something else, for us unattainable." (A relation must have terms, which it relates, or connects, as by a line between them. What are the terms of a self-relation? If a thing knows itself it is known by itself; the terms are identical, or else doubled in defiance of the unity assumed.)

"To say of any temporal process whatever that it is in the end self-intelligible, is, so far as I can perceive, a mistake. There is a difference unremoved between the subject and the predicate which shows a failure in thought" (surd?) "but which, *if* removed, would wholly destroy the special essence of thinking." "There is no idea which as such contains its own existence." "A relation which can get on somehow without (different) terms, and with no difference beyond the mere ends of a line of connection, is really a phrase without meaning." "Self-relation has a double character as both supporting and *being made by the relation.* It is a false abstraction, a thing that loudly contradicts itself." "Without entering into psychological refinements and difficulties we may be sure of this main result: The actual subject is never, in any state of mind, brought before itself as an object. . . . The actual subject never feels that it is out there in its object, that there is nothing more left within, and that the difference has disappeared."

"I stand on this: Present your doctrine (whatever it is) in a form which will bear criticism, and enable me to understand this confused mass of facts; do this and I will follow you, and I will worship the source of such a true revelation; but I will not accept nonsense for reality though it be vouched for by a miracle, or proceed from the mouth of a psychological monster."

Late as it is, I muse that the consciousness of Hegel has never been reflected; at least I have not recognized it in literature. As not only a teacher but the highest authority in a *quasi* State-philosophy, it was not his cue to emphasize the Socratic concession, "We do not know"; the right German retort would have relegated the whole profession to

SELF-RELATION 137

innocuous desuetude, since one man's ignorance can hardly be more relevant than another's. But the problem is ever pressing, and by dexterously alternating the static and dynamic viewpoints — one the eleatic Sufficient Intelligence, in which all things always are, and the other the process and novelty of Nature, which it were suicidal to deny — he knew that only a superhuman detective could impeach his profession. The philosophical position is unique. Let one boldly declare, and who shall ask him to explain? or to explain what? for, this is the problem of the world: to know by self-relation the nature of knowledge itself — the curiosity that would turn upon and envisage itself (which "of itself can do nothing").

Well assured of the futility of Fichte's endeavor to embrace ego and non-ego in an immediate self-related unit, and for his own part so far compromising the régime of self-knowing as to assume the man gradually analysing his composite faculties one at a time (still postponing the real problem *to a last with which futurity could never confront him*), he determined the Absolute as the *process* of the in-itself to for-itself, and disingenuously allowed the practical process of Nature to countenance a meretricious violence to logical pure reason.

But this was only one of the "moments" of his strenuous and prodigious versatility, which doubtless realized the utmost agonism of mortal speculation. Thought long ago transcended the dilemma, "to be or not to be," and proffered the duplexity of being and not-being at once — not consecutively, but jointly and essentially. If there is no self-relation of Something, the key to sufficiency is either nowhere or else in Nothing as logically construed.

As another instance of the delusive presumption of self-relation I will recall an elaborate attempt of Stephen Pearl Andrews to reorganize philosophy under the ambitious title of "Universology" — a book of 764 pages, published by Dion Thomas (New York, 1872).

I shall not offer any sketch of his endeavor, except as explaining that he subsumed all explanation under the three categories, Unism, Duism, and Trinism. It will serve our immediate purpose to indicate the necessity that, as a universologist, he had to assume a transcendental viewpoint — *i. e.* to oversee the universe; so that he naturally fell into the method of assuming a "wholeness aspect" and a "partness aspect" of being. Taking occasion to remind him that an aspect presupposed an observer, I addressed to him the unsophisticated but surely pertinent question, "To *whom* is the wholeness aspect of being?" He answered:

"Your question seems to read: 'To whom is "the wholeness aspect of being" '?

"I confess that your question is as blind to me as Trinism, or all beyond Unism and Duism, is to you. The wholeness aspect of being is the antithet or counterpart of the partness aspect, of the same being, of whatsoever being, and to any beholder or contemplator. It is the Unism contrasted with the Duism — the two combined being the Trinism. But there is no good in letter-writing. Come and see me and I will tell you all about it. N. E. corner

54th Street and Fifth Avenue, up two flights — a houseful of splendid fellows, male and female, the incipient Pantarchy."

To sum up: Starting from the naïve position that the being that knows, in what is called "self-consciousness," is the same being that is known (*i. e.* that the subject and the object, by whatever authority separately named, are instantly and identically one — miraculously, as held by Fichte, without help or compromise from the "process" of Hegel, wherein the in-itself *becomes* for-itself by being taken up piecemeal, and so avoiding the charge of absolute and immediate self-relation), we have laboriously arrayed against that merely popular and psychological notion the profounder insights of Plato, Jesus, Swedenborg, Plotinus, Berkeley, Hume, Kant, Schwegler, Jowett, Bradley, Hodgson, Emerson, and Eucken.

At the same time we have had to endure the weak defection of Kant, in view of his orthodox popularity, by assuming as a categorical imperative the uncultured consciousness of "the plain man," so stultifying all his metaphysical excellence and industry.

It behooves us to see more clearly the proper use and philosophical importance of the doctrine for or against the claim of self-relation. Is the want of it fatal to philosophy? *With this granted would the problem be solved?* Many presumptive experts have claimed in the notion of Hegel the plausibility of self-relation by the process of in-itself to for-itself as "finally" self-knowledge. Notwithstanding all the admonitions that self-knowledge is but a whim of words, is but a transcendental concept which no perception ever corroborated; that no man ever saw a self or a soul; that the subject would forfeit its whole supremacy in becoming an object and cease being a subject at all; that the gun cannot shoot into its own muzzle; that "truth" is precisely what every representation or pretence of knowledge without identity must lack, etc. and etc. — the claim still seems to hold that in a man's taking himself or his faculties up piecemeal, or by degrees, he should exhaust his entire contents, and leave no such wonderful "secret" undiscovered. For example, he would visualize his courage, or his conscience, or his memory. None of these, as abstracted from his subjective totality and made an object, should very seriously cripple his critical judgment, so what recondite element of his "self" should escape the inventory? Have you not seen "the nation" if you have seen all the people? do not the parts comprise the entire contents of a whole? What is the crux, the mystery, which our long catalogue of authorities grudges to the claim of "self-relation"? Or, allowing the claim, as it is endorsed by the popular psychology, does philosophy succeed as explanation? In brief, *why do we cite these authorities against the very natural notion that personality explains, and that the world in itself becomes rational in and only in the presence of God? The grudge of science as against the pretence of self-relation is that our highest claim and achievement namely, knowledge, is therein made to countenance with its full authority and significance a claim to have attained the comprehension and*

SELF-RELATION 141

mastery of that which halts our curiosity, controls our interest, and occasions our discontent, while in fact it does not fundamentally understand the least and simplest thing in the world. Our consciousness, even as it glows, is a helpless projection from an alien energy, bottomless in its own regard, utterly unqualified to declare or to determine anything as necessary, and therefore wholly incompetent to radical explanation.

It is its insult to rational principle and real power that condemns self-relation, for those who question reality as dependent upon conventional terms. And as mere self-*knowledge* it is still hopeless of being and of power, all-requisite to the pose of the universal — the Supreme.

Supplementary Note on the "Speculative Philosophy" of W. T. Harris.

Speculative knowledge, or knowing, is for its professors a grade beyond the transcendental, and would be inadmissible by Kant, as being what he would call transcendent, or beyond the mental purview — in fact out of the world. Transcendentalism uses the pure forms of the mind, indifferent as to their contents (*i. e.* it is concerned with pure thinking, regardless of what it is about); and to pure formality only contradiction can be fatal. Although the topic of its thought has no element of perceptual experience, and is of concepts wholly, the transcendental must still have consistent forms, capable of logical expression. Borne on the current of pure logic, it may think what it shall not really know, as lacking the perceptual and corroborating ground of experience.

(I have before instanced the converse of this last position, in the fact that we may know what we cannot think — as appears in the failure of mathematics to articulate in its digits the side of the double square, or of $\sqrt{2}$ or $\sqrt{8}$.)

But the speculative will not be withheld from truth by the impossibility of its appearance in either imaginable or logically conceptual form, nor will it allow truth to be discredited by its practically necessary appearance in the form of contradiction. Its claim is to "the unpicturable notions of intelligence"; and these notions are not amenable to immediate or direct knowing, but are to be achieved by method and system, in a mediate or roundabout process, which must defer the student's conclusion until he has learned to think properly.

And this delay is in any event advisable; for there are various cases in which immediate conclusion and forthright expression may result in utter confusion. Truth is largely amenable to its viewpoint; and there appear various overt contradictions in the countenance of half-truths used as whole ones, affording expression in contradictions which necessitate no antagonism in reality.

Two observers, of but partial experience, may truthfully declare, one that a given shield is concave, the other that it is convex; the result, as a matter of evidence, can be assured only methodically, by a duodiction, or a uniting of the two assertions. An honest man may swear that the sun goes around the earth; an astronomer may swear, by the light of his science, that the earth goes around the sun; the truth of the matter, if it is a single or toto-truth, is determinable only upon considerations which neither of the two witnesses can have ever exploited — to wit, whether the "universe" is one or many, or both, or neither. And the two assertions, although different, are not contradictory. Neither says that the other is not true.

From the speculative viewpoint the ultimate truth is a methodical deduction, to be entertained only under a trained and scientific vision, which can conclude esoterically in spite of, and without the assistance of either language or imagination, both of which, though necessarily to be used in *declaring* the speculative insight, are used under protest, as handicapping the true meaning. At least its advocates will not balk at the assertion that all reality is the cause of itself.

The Journal of Speculative Philosophy, edited and published by William T. Harris, superintendent of the schools of St. Louis, first appeared in 1867, and continued quarterly until 1899, when Mr. Harris was appointed by President McKinley as U. S. Commissioner of Education. The initial and constant inspiration of the magazine was "*causa sui*," or self-determination, as the philosophical first principle of thought and being, and the only fundamental basis of explanation. With the first number the editor began an elaborate "Introduction to Philosophy," which was rather, as is usual in such cases, an introduction to the reader of what philosophy the author knew. All such introductions are but reveries as to what the problem really is — or how to state it.

This "Introduction's" chief appeal to the reader was the alleged inconsequence of objective or historical cause as preceding effect — a first cause as originating all effects in a succession of dependent beings — while no dependent being could have any causality to spare — whence first cause (whether first in history or in the order of reason) must be independent, having all causality in, for and of itself.

This very cheap and very peremptory assertion seems to ignore the clôture imminent in the previous question, whether there is or must be any cause at all — or who shall determine the sufficiency of anything alleged as a cause — and whether in fact a cause is objective or subjective. One does not need much logic to perceive that even the admission of the claim (that self-cause is the only possible cause) gives cause no standing as yet in any court.

Now Doctor Harris knew as well as any other man (and far better than most men) the logical impossibility of self-relation as we have sufficiently exposed it; but encouraged by the vulgar psychology of "self-consciousness," and by the propriety of certain systematic conclusions which outface immediate knowledge although handicapped by contradiction, he called in the assistance of an inadvertent remark of Kant that space is "an infinite quantity" — whence, since quantity founds upon quality, space could be regarded as objective. And now, before citing the use that Prof. Harris made of this inadvertence of Kant, it is highly important that we have a correct definition of space, even as Kant himself more carefully defined it.

Space is purely ideal — that is to say, vernacularly, it is nothing save as it is made a topic by thinking of it. Space is a contemplation, a subjective concession or informal judgment, implying absolute freedom, room or opportunity for any mental project of either adventure or conjecture — *i. e.* there is in space no hindrance or objection to any proposition. Space does not in itself imply extensity, but means liberty to extend.

Space taken objectively, as a quantity, would infer a field of thought which its proprietor might sublet by the yard or the acre, and guarantee it from trespass or interference — there being just so much of it on record and no more. On the contrary the occupancy of space is infinitely heterogeneous and doubled up. Taken as mere extension, there is double space here in the street, where the mirror on the wall shows my room projected several feet over the pavement, including color and form as real as such can be. In the room itself are heat and light in the same space; there is appreciation and speculation, and there is certainly room for improvement.

Kant's scientific definition of space is as follows:

"Space, as prior to all things which determine it (fill or limit it) is nothing but the mere *possibility* of external phenomena, so far as they exist already, or can be added to phenomena given."

This argues something very different from "an infinite quantity."

Now returning to Harris's different kinds of knowing, the reader may grudge the space required here, but he should know the quality of what for twenty years passed as the best thought of America, and was carefully reflected in various European publications.

[From Harris's "Introduction to Philosophy":]

"It is a mistake, to attempt to introduce the beginner of philosophy at once into the dialectic. The content of philosophy must be first presented under its sensuous and reflective forms, and a gradual progress established. In this chapter an attempt will be made to approach again the ultimate principle which we have hitherto fixed only in a general manner as *Mind*. We will use the method of external reflection, and demonstrate three propositions: 1. There is an independent being; 2. That being is self-determined; 3. Self-determined being is in the form of personality, *i. e.* is an *ego*.

"1. — *a*. Dependent being, implying its complement upon which it depends, cannot be explained through itself, but through that upon which it depends.

"*b*. This being upon which it depends cannot be also a dependent being, for the dependent being has no support of its own to lend to another; all that it has is borrowed. A chain of dependent beings collapses into one dependent being. Dependence is not converted into independence by mere multiplication.

"*c*. The dependent, therefore, depends upon the independent and has its *explanation* in it. Since all being is of one kind or the other, it follows that all being is independent, or a complemental element of it. Reciprocal dependence makes an independent including whole, which is the *negative unity*.

"*Definition.* — One of the most important implements of the thinker is the comprehension of "negative unity." It is a unity resulting from the reciprocal cancelling of elements; *e. g.*, *salt* is the negative unity of *acid* and *alkali*. It is called *negative* because it negates the independence of the elements within it. In the negative unity *water*, the elements oxygen and hydrogen have their independence negated.

"2 — *a*. The independent being cannot exist without determinations. Without these, it could not distinguish itself or be distinguished from nought.

"*b*. Nor can the independent being be determined (*i. e.* limited or modified in any way) from without, or through another. For all that is determined through another is a dependent somewhat.

"*c*. Hence the independent being can be only a self-determined. If self-determined, it can exist through itself.

"3. — *a*. Self-determination implies that the *constitution* or *nature* be self-originated. There is nothing about a self-determined that is created by anything without.

"*b*. Thus self-determined being exists dually — it is (*a*) as *determining*, and (*b*) as *determined*. (*a*) As determining, it is the active, which contains merely the possibility of determinations; (*b*) as determined, it is the passive result — the matter upon which the subject acts.

"*c*. But since both are the same being, each side returns into itself: (*a*) as determining or active, it acts only upon its own determining, and (*b*) as passive or determined, it is, as result of the former, the selfsame active itself. Hence its movement is a movement of self-recognition — a posting of distinction which is cancelled in the same act. (In self-recognition something is made an object, and identified with the subject in the same act.) Moreover, the determiner, on account of its pure generality (*i. e.* its having no concrete determinations as yet), can only be *ideal* — can only exist as the *ego* exists, in thought; not as a thing, but as a *generic* entity. The passive side can exist only as the self exists in consciousness — as that which is in opposition and yet in identity at the same time. No finite existence could endure this contradiction, for all such must possess a *nature* or *constitution* which is self-determined; if not, each finite could negate all its properties and qualities, and yet remain itself — just as the person does when he makes abstraction of all, in thinking of the *ego* or pure self.

"Thus we find again our former conclusion: — All finite or dependent things must originate in and depend upon independent or absolute being, which must be an *ego*. The *ego* has the form of infinitude (see Chap. 2 — "The Infinite is its own Other").

"We hope to see those necessities of thought which underlie all philosophical systems.

"Many of the 'impossibilities' of thought are easily shown to rest upon ignorance of psychological appliances. The person is not able because he does not know *how* — just as in other things. We must take care that we do not confound the incapacity of ignorance with the necessity of thought.

"Among the first distinctions to be learned by the student in philosophy is that between the imaginative form of thinking and *pure* thinking. The former is a sensuous grade of thinking which uses *images*, while the latter is a more developed stage, and is able to think objects in and for themselves (*i. e.*, as 'unpicturable').

"At first one might suppose that when finite things are the subject of thought, it would make little difference whether the first or second form of thinking is employed. This is, however, a great error. The Philosopher must always 'think things under the form of eternity' if he would think the truth.

"Imagination *pictures* objects. It represents to itself only the bounded. If it tries to realize the conception of infinitude, it represents a limited somewhat, and then Reflection or the Understanding (a form of thought lying between Imagination and Reason) passes beyond the limits and annuls them. This process may be continued indefinitely, or until Reason (or pure thinking) comes in and solves the dilemma. Thus we have a dialogue resultant somewhat as follows:

"Imagination: Come and see the Infinite, just as I have pictured it.

"Understanding (peeping cautiously about it): Where is your frame? Ah! I see it now clearly. How is this? Your frame does not include all. There is a 'beyond' to your picture. I cannot tell whether you intend the inside or outside for your picture of the Infinite; I see it on both.

"Imagination (tries to extend the frame, but with the same result as before): I believe you are right. I am well nigh exhausted by my efforts to include the unlimited.

"Understanding: Ah! you see, the Infinite is

merely the negative of the finite or positive. It is the negative of those conditions which you place there in order to have any representation at all.

"While Understanding proceeds to deliver a course of wise saws and moral reflections on the inability of the Finite to grasp the Infinite, sitting apart upon its bipod — for tripod it has none, one of the legs being broken — it self-complacently and oracularly admonishes the human mind to cultivate humility. Imagination drops her brush and pencil in confusion at these words. Very opportunely Reason steps in and takes an impartial survey of the scene.)

"Reason: Did you say that the Infinite is unknowable?

"Understanding: Yes. To think is to limit, and hence to think the Infinite is to limit it, and thus to destroy it.

"Reason: Apply your remarks to space. Is not space infinite?

"Understanding: If I attempt to realize space I conceive a bounded, but I at once perceive that I have placed my limits *within* Space, and hence my realization is inadequate. The Infinite, therefore, seems to be a beyond to my clear conception.

"Reason: Indeed! When you reflect on Space, do you not perceive that it is of such a nature that it can be *limited only by itself?* Do not all its limits imply Space to exist in?

"Understanding: Yes, that is the difficulty.

"Reason: I do not see the 'difficulty.' If Space can be limited only by itself, its limit continues it instead of bounding it. Hence it is universally continuous or infinite.

SELF-RELATION

"Understanding: But a mere negative.

"Reason: No, not a mere negative, but the negative of all negation, and hence truly affirmative. It is the exhibition of the utter impossibility of any negative to it. All attempts to limit it, continue it. It is its own other. Its negative is itself. Here, then, we have a truly affirmative infinite in contradistinction to the *negative* infinite — the 'infinite progress' that you and Imagination were engaged upon when I came in.

"Understanding: What you say seems to me a distinction in words merely.

"Reason: Doubtless. All distinctions are merely in words until one has *learned to see them independent of words*. But you must go and mend that bipod on which you are sitting; for how can one think at ease and exhaustively, when he is all the time propping up his basis from without?

"Understanding: I cannot understand you. (*Exit.*) "

I think that the reader who has gone over our previous ground may be trusted to sympathize with poor "Understanding," who plays the rôle of common-sense in the above colloquy. He should detect both the misuse of the notion of objective space as a quantity, and the distortion of the negative into a positive quality in a merely logical field.

How can space, in the mere fact of its being continuous, be held as "limiting itself" because, forsooth, it can have no *other* limit? How does the word *limit* get into the discussion at all? One may have said in an unnecessary criticism that space is unlimited — unnecessary and impertinent because the very constitution or nature or meaning of space would, if called upon, exclude limit — but why should it be called upon to reject an idle qualification, to touch a pitch that would defile it? It is no more unlimited than it is unpainted, or uneducated; the *un* excludes all qualification; yet by mere verbal mention in the same connection a logical expression soils the pure reality.

It is as if a crier should go through the streets proclaiming that Cæsar's wife is *not* unchaste; the announcement may be true, and is surely commendatory, but the parties in interest would hardly be grateful for it. It was held as slanderous in our courts, that one man had said to another, "*You* never stole a sheep, oh, no!"

The aggravation is still heavier when the fact (that any space as given or contemplated can be regarded as limited only by more of the same) is construed as rendering space self-limited, and as countenancing various other claims of self-relation: especially that of the ego, which, although confessed as an "impossibility" for understanding and imagination, is speculative fact. It is Harris's illusion that the unlimited gets unity and limit from its mention as *the* or *this* — a nominal concept — as if the unknowable were really *known* as such. This is the sphinx riddle: he who knows the universe shall be swallowed by it. There is no such knowledge, nor any such object for knowledge.

Especially Harris labored under the Hegelian obsession that negation is determination, always positive in its results; that all assertion is affirma-

SELF-RELATION 153

tive, the negation of negation; that destruction is logically impossible. If the red slayer thinks he slays, he makes the mistake of his life; he knows not of the cunning ways in which the dialectic can pass and turn again. That a thing has no quality — is not *that* a quality? The unknowable — is it not *known* as such? Does not the breath that would vacate it come back into your own face? Not being? well, since you mention it, is it not one kind of being? Nothing — if it is not something, how can you think of it? or the ego — if not self-known, how does it think of itself?

But Kant said well, you *do not* think of it; you merely *talk* about it. The Kantian yataghan cuts the props from under these dialectic constructions — these verbal concepts which no percepts, which no experience may confirm. Negation that does not vacate and destroy is but a scrap of paper. What is *meant* by nothing does not get into thought, nor into print. Non-being is *flatus vocis* — a mist that rises in our dreams from the compost of decay and death. With Parmenides behind us we shall hardly countenance a not-being which can be only in a delusive array of words.

The solution of all this dialectic confusion, in which the plain man's understanding is insulted, and truth is stultified as impossible or contradictory, lies in the fact that its propagators have not sufficient dignity or self-respect to question what has unfortunately become conventional — to discern that many words are misused, and that many have no meaning whatsoever. The greatest mistake of all is that the world *must be rational,* and that there *must* be possible a true statement and explanation of it, commensurate with our finite capacity. How puerile, or at least how inexpert, is this argument that since the whole can have no *other* cause it must be the cause of itself — even though the doctrine shall revolt our understanding, and pretend that words need no basis in empirical reality — boasting with Novalis, that "although Philosophy can bake no bread she can give us God, freedom and immortality" — three words of wholly problematical meaning. A cause that would really explain should hardly fail us for daily bread; it might even afford an occasional pot of beer.

It will be perceived, as regards Mr. Harris's recognition of the psychological embarrassment in thinking self-relation — which he like the majority of thinkers, has to confess as mechanically contradictory — his main assurance as to first cause being *"causa sui,"* is that it is the *only possible* cause or reason that can be used as explanation. He would be well disposed to say with Fichte, "Ask not for the how — be satisfied with the fact." He would join heartily with Prof. Ladd in boundless reverence for the unaccountable "prime fact of knowledge." But if one shall say to them, Have it your own way: there can be no other first cause than *"causa sui":* yet how if there is no cause at all, in the sense of radical explanation to us or to reason? The merely formal phrase, *"causa sui,"* will not come down to the relief of mechanical sense, or of imagination endeavoring to picture the self-swallowing stunt, or of a thing's being its own creator before it is born. Admit that *"causa sui"* is the only logical state-

SELF-RELATION

ment of the problem; that or any other statement may be worthless for explanation — which will require a certain treatment of the time element —which they have not yet achieved. Every active relation implies a lapse of time, which divides the instant integrity of any hypothetic self-relation. This is the difficulty with all self-relation, as a principle, or a fertility, that the miracle which it is to perform by its *activity* is already pre-supposed as accomplished in its divine nature or essence.

It recalls the juggler, Katerfelte, "with his hair on end at his own wonders — wondering for his bread."

CHAPTER VI

THE NEGATIVE

SINCE we find that the only plausible reason of things is reason as a reason for itself by self-relation — and that this is impossible logically, and considerable only as seeming a psychological fact in empirical "self-consciousness" — and that this seeming fact (self-consciousness) is by our highest authorities determined as an illusion; and since we find, in the problem of causation, that no being can be held to contain potentially another being, neither to empirically produce another being; there remains only, to account for existence, the presumption of its eternity as matter of fact, whose only ground of being, in either fact or observation, is the void, conceivable as in lieu of all content, and named, for speculative purposes, the negative.

It may be admitted (at least by us, who live only to surely die) that a *real* void (however may be the case of a logical one) would vacate all being and distinction; but since being in general persists in spite of our solipsistic failure, the question remains, as to being in general, whether there is a principle of necessity which eternally holds and held it positive in fact — not antagonized but rather sustained and emphasized by the void, which should prove only a suggestion or shadow of our own finite fate

THE NEGATIVE 157

and limitation, against the ever-living truth and fact that being must be.

Parmenides argued earnestly that "not-being" is only a play upon words, with no thought behind them.

Hegel argued, quite as earnestly, that in the world of pure thought, where the matter should be determined, the vitality of the negative is essentially the life of being, and that negation is "positive in its result."

In the same spirit Heracleitus made opposition the basis of distinction, and strife the father of things. Said Parmenides:

"Listen and I will instruct thee, what are the two only paths of research open to thinking. One path is: That Being doth be, and Non-Being is not: this is the way of Conviction, for Truth follows hard in her footsteps. The other path is: That Being is not (All) and Non-Being must be. This one, I tell thee in truth, is an all-incredible pathway; for thou never canst know what is not (for none can conceive it) nor canst thou give it expression, for one thing are Thinking and Being.

"Never I ween shalt thou learn that Being can be of what is not. For IS is of Being; Nothing must needs not be.

"What is is birthless and deathless, whole and moveless and ever enduring. Never it was or shall be, but the ALL simultaneously now is, one continuous one.

"How or whence it hath sprung I shall not permit thee to tell me; neither to think 'of what is not'; for none can say or imagine how Not-Is becomes

Is, or, what should have stirred it, after or before its beginning, to issue from nothing?

"Men have set up for themselves twin shapes to be named by Opinion (ONE they cannot set up, and herein they wander in error), and they have made them distinct in their natures, and marked them with tokens. . . . All things now being marked with the names of Light and of Darkness — yea, set apart by the powers of One or the Other, *so that the All is at once full of light* and *invisible darkness, both being equal, and naught being common to one with the other.*"

As unfalteringly as he defined idealism against the face of experience, so Hegel thus announced the positive negative, with its essential contradiction, as the logical necessity of reason, and the only possibility of philosophy:

"The only thing (!) essentially necessary to an insight of the method of scientific evolution is a knowledge of the logical nature of the negative: that it is positive in its results. . . . Its self-contradiction does not result in zero, or the abstract nothing, but rather in the subversion of its special content (or topic) only. . . . In the result is preserved essentially that from which it resulted."

This, then, is philosophy: what is not, and cost nothing, is the matrix and the mother of what is; yon mist that rises from the rotting compost heap — it is the breath of life. . . . THE secret then, the problem, the Mystery, the Veil, and what is behind it? — The VOICE is "dialectic" — the Vision is of a fig-leaf on the occult genitals of Death.

Dialectic, which for Plato meant conversation, as

THE NEGATIVE 159

rendering opposite sides, is an esoteric diversion, in which the negative has been exploited as a *quasi* positive. Whether seriously or otherwise, Democritus is credited or discredited with the saying, "Being is by nothing more real than not-being." Equivalently he might have said, "Visible and material body is no more real than invisible and formal mind" — and then added, "Logical concepts are as real as rational percepts; and but for Aristotle, and especially but for Kant, the notion might still be tolerated." The whim is as old as Lucifer, and as man's fall through knowledge, that by some inveterate perversity nothing must be something. Even Parmenides, however stoutly affirming as the only "truth" that "being alone is, and non-being is not," confessed to an "opinion," held with all the conviction of empirical life, that there was a *being* of not-being, which yet should be carefully ignored.

(Even Shakespeare furthered the jest, in "King Lear." The king had retorted on some extravagance of his "fool," that it was "nothing"; and could Nuncle make no use of nothing? This was a pity, since the king had so much of it: all his rents footed up to just that amount; whereat the loyal Kent remarked, "This is not altogether fool, my lord.")

"Nothing" proves a very available stuff; it is at least half of the stock of metaphysics. In science too, it has indispensable uses. A couple of gallons of nothing, for instance, are indispensable in the experiment proving that *in vacuo* the guinea and the feather fall synchronously, and that a wheel will revolve therein for an unaccountable time. It would be necessary, too, in the proof that the resisting and negative air is the positive sustenance and fulcrum of a bird's flight through it, and that in fact a bird could not fly in a vacuum at all. This obvious inference is very consolatory in any conjecture as to the forces requisite to the motion of the celestial orbs; for if a planet's atmosphere is wholly its own, that envelope should not retard its motion in clear space; and as our moon has no atmosphere at all, one whiff from a goose feather should suffice to revolve it till time shall be no more.

Even thus we may gossip at the verge of the insidious maelstrom that has engulfed all the philosophic sails that have defied its vortex. The fault was not in their stars but in themselves that they went down as underlings. The rash assertion of Hegel in the beginning of his logic, that being and not-being are *the same,* should have been of itself a signal of logical distress. The same? Certainly, weighed as abstractions, mere topics of thought, they are as such the same. Even contradictions are facts, for discussion, or dialectic. Reality, negation, nonsense, the unutterable, the unthinkable, are alike real topics for metaphysical talk; but they have no basis or foothold in the dependable world; they are verbal concepts which have no perceptual corroboration — adjectives flying regardless of appropriate nouns. The moment that being and not-being are required to serve as qualifications of any objective reality, their difference is evident and fatal. All the value in the world, and all distinction of values, are in being, while all non-being is alike and worthless. When it is said that non-being has being, or that nothings are somethings, what are the empirical percepts that should staminate this fluorescent nonentity? They have no concrete life or force. No Kantian can affirm non-being.

Experience and history, reflection upon sleep and death, the admonition that there is no knowledge nor device in the grave whither thou goest, have indeed impressed upon us the sad truth that there is and was for us a condition of not-being; but these empirical considerations have no bearing on the similarity of being and not-being save as logical abstractions regardless of their concrete filling or special content. In saying that being and not-being are the same, Hegel could not mean that life and death are the same; his logical interest lay in the fact that it requires force to destroy as well as to create and that, therefore, in the self-relation of the ego as subject-object, the objective or *quasi* passive side implicates an equal subjective initiative. But the goal of his logic was development of the Absolute Spirit as the essential activity and process of self-relation.

Stoutly ignoring the unknown root of all sense and human understanding, Hegel fell back upon the purely logical and dialectic Inevitable of Heracleitus, and as a merely formal and speculative proposition the Inevitable is sure and simple enough, if we allow the single presumption that opposition is the basis of distinction — or, as Heracleitus phrased it, that "strife is the father of all things." If being is such and conceivable, not as an independent entity, but only as the opposite of not-being, they cannot be separated; either assures the presence of the other, and so the inevitable existence of both. Total non-being is impossible in or for thought.

The being of a hole is as real as that of a plug; as a mere topic of thought the one is quite as conversable as the other. But such conversation is mere diversion. If we were comparing reality and unreality, the one, *as a topic*, would be as real as the other; but that kind of reality is mere supposition, a play of fancy, the stuff that dreams are made on, a saying that the hole is essential in the doughnut.

Negation is mighty only by reason of its positive given force. In a world of purely logical forms and schemes this were the acme of triumphant thinking. But when the plain man asks after its results, he is put off with the glory of the action; the strength displayed in destruction is the same as that proper for creation. But if negation is positive in its results, wherein does it oppose assertion? and by what means shall we get any denial or any destructive result? Our only inference is that assertion and negation are alike merely verbally constructive, and that real destruction is logically impossible; the void remains.

Contemplating the field of psychological experience, Heracleitus seems to have been the first to signalize the fact that one is made by limiting, and that everything gets special existence not only by contrast, but by opposition and strife with its environment, which serves as background and frame, and gives it distinction, relief and individuality. In the consciousness of lights and shadows, and of pains and pleasures; in the contemplation of the ups and downs of fortune; in the estimation of size and value, and the appreciation of the present as in memory of the past, everywhere he found the One getting its distinction, emphasis and *éclat* through a compensation of the Other. This is the most striking and poetical lesson of experience, and it oriented his metaphysical speculation to the merely relative truth that being depends upon not-being.

We may say here, somewhat gratuitously perhaps, that this was rather a poetical than a philosophical observation on the part of Heracleitus. Had he enforced and brought home his principle — that "strife is the father of things," or, that opposition is the basis of distinction — he would have had to found reason upon unreason, as equally authoritative, and conclusion would have become impossible.

It is our instant necessity here to see that however contrast and compensation enter into and emphasize distinction, they do not infer nor require the opposition which has been utilized to construe the inevitable by making the mere contrast of being and not-being the productive ground of true being, on the theory that negation is positive in its result. This result, properly considered, is merely logical, formal and schematic. Let non-being, in its transcendent thought-world, be ever so much a reality and a proper topic for contemplation — whereof we may consistently discuss the existence, or the possibility, as well as we may the prevalence of the content of being — yet we instantly perceive that being proper embraces and identifies the whole real world, and that not-being is only a mental supposition of death, which, realized, would vacate the field of thought. It lives only as a hypothetic mental relation or supposition. The fact appears that mere opposition will not assure being, and that there may be difference and distinction without antagonism, peacefully side by side, however contrast may emphasize it: *this because contrast may come as well from new excess in nature as from the negation and non-being of the passing or the past.*

Granting that a relative non-being is necessary to logical or conceptual being, and that conceptual difference is necessary to logical and truthful identity; granted that dark lines and shadows are necessary and relevant to the "high lights" of the picture; granted that it were practically the same disaster, whether all the light or all the darkness went away; you are yet nowhere near the affirmation that darkness is necessary to light, or that non-being is the ground of being, or that opposition rather than friendly difference is necessary to subjective distinction. Nature solves this problem by her purely gratuitous and miraculous excess and bounty, putting all assertion into being, and outfacing all pretense of positive negation with her everlasting Yea. "God is light," said the ancient, "and in Him is no darkness at all." Yet "one star differs from another star in glory"; there is no cosmic shame; there is no cosmic evil; but there are degrees of light which afford æsthetic shadows of their own order and genius. The all-bounteous Good of Nature ruffles with compensating waves the deep that knows no change, and lends variety and beauty to the spiritual world as fortune favors one with ten talents, and another with five, and another with only one. And if he who has none at all shall renounce a losing game and

THE NEGATIVE 165

destroy himself, who knows what compensation may attend his faith in another world than this.

We may illustrate the utter relativity, or the purely mental hypothecation of "the negative," by the revolution of a spoked wheel. Fancy such a wheel before us, on a track that leads to the right. We first lift the wheel from the track and revolve it around its own centre, its top rolling to the right while its bottom goes to the left. If now, while the wheel is still revolving, we set it down upon the track, the bottom will catch and hold to the track in a punctual and motionless contact; the centre will move to the right with the same speed with which the bottom was before moving toward the left, and the top will go to the right with twice the speed of the centre, while the leftward motion of the bottom is lost, being shifted to the centre: there is no longer any leftward motion of the wheel in the real world. But if now we go with the wheel — fix our identity and viewpint at the centre of the wheel, regardless of its environment, the leftward motion of the bottom is as rapid and real as it was before it caught the track — but this motion is only assumed as relative to an artificial and unreal viewpoint — there is no one living at the centre of the wheel, and there is no such backward or negating motion for any observer in the world of real experience.

We may readily convert this demonstration to the assumed "positive result" of the negative as a factor in the sustenance or production of being. Let it be granted that in a static and changeless world, where contrast or even opposition were necessary to distinction, non-being would be necessary to being.

But such a static world is a purely mental supposition; there is no such world in time's reality. On the contrary in the gratuitous becoming of the excess of Nature, being gets vital distinction in the on-coming future, and becomes itself the negative or background in a world new-born. Here is no Heracleitic strife or struggle for mere being — no grudging result of the mere activity of negation and opposition, but rather the bounty of a miraculous becoming, ever new, and ever more.

We remarked above that in saying that "being and not-being are the same" Hegel did not pretend that life and death are the same. But why not, if he meant anything that concerns humanity? As a literary fact the words *life* and *death* and *truth* have no patronage in transcendental philosophy; neither does any fact of experience have weight in formal logic — a kind of esoteric toy which, like a fragment of looking glass in the hands of a mischievous schoolboy, can be made to throw artificial reflections into startled eyes.

It is logically true that one is made by limiting — that its determination is negation — as well by exclusion as by inclusion; and it is ever true that in contemplation, as in a picture, light and being get emphasis and *éclat* from darkness and death. But this contemplation is but artistic conception. When the inexorable sure method demands the *percepts* of this fruitful negation — the basic experience that should staminate this fluorescent inanity — it finds that the real negative, as the smouldering compost from which the negative concept is exhaled, is the sad fate of humanity when the lights are out and the curtain is down, and the voice of the Preacher admonishes us that there is no wisdom nor device nor knowledge in the grave whither we go. Transcendental dialectic, positive negation, truth as contradiction and essential opposition and inconsequent process — all this is but a house of cards, the baseless fabric of a vision, an insubstantial pageant that will leave not a rack behind. No less, it is the best that philosophy has done, or promises to do.

We should gather from the citations foregoing that in self-relation and positive negation the German genius has exhausted the only sources or ground of cosmic explanation. If the Whole is to be in any way exploited it must be by either itself or nothing — a desperate alternative surely; yet we have seen however that "nothing can come from nothing," the negative may be at least logically fruitful, and "not altogether fool."

But the transcendental exfoliation exhausted all the fertility of its ground. Poor Psyche became so soiled and mussed-up by dialectic manipulation that her sacred character was compromised. If mere logical concepts could be posed as realities, mind-stuff was no better than matter-stuff, which was equally feasible and less disputable. Besides, Hegel had insisted upon exalting his Absolute to the very questionable eminence of Personality: "The highest, steepest thought is Personality." Such a claim was shadowed not only by all the atrocities of the old, but by the present controversy over the Christian divinity.

The Good has a promising name, but it is not adequate as a first principle. It is tainted with passion and personality; it is partial and hence unjust; its favor to the present depletes the justice due to the unborn. There is but so much for all, and what comparative has a surplus to spare? Shall not justice suffice? The Good reeks with the old duplexity; justice alone is passionless and integral and safe: for what hinders that the unbalanced Good should turn into evil at its personal whim? It does not appear that the Good had been deserved, and the flush on its countenance argues distemperature in the bosom of fate.

Surely we must welcome the Good; the downpour of gratuitous Nature dissolves the logical necessity which renders negation positive in its results; but for philosophy as explanation the gift of nature still taxes the wonder which the charm of dialectic had for its moment meretriciously disenchanted. The secret remains intact. The Good is not the best.

In any event, personality is the last philosophical canon of divinity. "Ever not quite" is a motto particularly significant here. The groundlings of skepticism will degrade its most spiritual conceptions with visceral necessities which impeach the sincerity of unqualified devotion. There is a flaw in its supremacy, a fig-leaf on the statue. Not even hatred and bigotry shall be genuine while they spare a loincloth to the uplifted Christ.

We cannot wonder that a surfeit of personal idealism put forth a score of post-Kantian philosophemes in the direction of materialism, all in favor of a depersonalized intelligence which dispensed with God while utilizing at will His attributes. Schopenhauer charged in from the field of pantheism with

THE NEGATIVE

a blind and striving will, still abetted by an imminent clairvoyancy — most happily characterized by our Professor Howison as "a kind of Blind Tom." Hartmann followed with the Unconscious — a merely titular pose of the subconscious, as somewhat that can see without eyes, and speak without articulation — the voice of the heart, as of Jacobi, and the "something higher than science" which Schelling (with many others) said he surely knew. Then came Duhring with the Actual, freshly qualifying the "thing in itself" (which Kant had left as merely problematical), as the real thing that by a vacation of solipsism, and a restoration of practical sanity, would restore reality to the common sense which idealism had abused. And then came Lange (contemporary in time, and consecutive only in the process of mental evolution), overweaning the rallying cry of "back to Kant" with an impeachment of that Master himself. For Kant had rushed where Aristotle could tread only tentatively, and had rather conceitedly assumed to name all of the "categories" (the innate faculties or laws of thought) in accordance with some determinate principle. Lange, breaking down Kant's perfunctory bars to scientific progress, insisted that the a priori as well as the merely sensuous was divinely "given," and that the laws of the mind, even as the laws of matter, shall be codified by *induction* — so clearing the path for that trend toward materialism, or toward that mitigation of its esoteric crudity, which has encumbered the post-Kantian régime.

And Lange forthright staunched his criticism of the "Critique of Pure Reason" by the instance of *motion* as one of the "forms" of sense, equally with space and time, and possibly the key to various paradoxes, which it factually is.

I shall introduce in the next chapter a neglected handmaid of Truth, a sort of metaphysical Cinderella, under the title of Ancillary Evidence, hoping thereby to lend something of dignity to that catchword, "ever not quite," which Professor James adopted as Pluralism's heraldic device. Her credentials shall be at once signal and authentic. There are in philosophy many loose ends of the inevitable duplexity, many theoretical oppositions whose poles do not quite meet; *there is a penumbra that defeats every claim to explicit definition and contact.* For example, in the saying (as old as Heracleitus) "being and not being are the same," there is this discrepancy at least that they cannot be *quite* the same, so long as the means are different or supposing that they are the same, the same is not quite *the same*, for, logically, the same is another that is like — there needs two for a sameness, as well as an identity for a difference. So nothing is not quite that; if it were, one could not be a thinking being and make it topical.

But this ancillary penumbra has more serious importance in the larger fields of philosophy, where ultimate distinction wavers and confuses definition. The static and dynamic viewpoints cannot be held utterly asunder; they are both feasible, but if they did not somehow compromise their opposition thought and life would be impossible. Contradiction cannot utterly contradict, nor can being exclusive be. Kant said well that all entities have community, and that all value and quantity have intensive degree, which scales somewhere between entity and zero, but by the ancillary shading which our title adumbrates; there is no *modus vivendi* without it. The present tense, where we must live, is but a hole in the ground, if you withdraw the ancillary presence of the past and the future; yet the metalogical life, our Cinderella of all work, as a sprite rising from Truth's bottomless well, clings stoutly to the skirts of the vanishing past, while trembling on the verge of the precipitous future.

CHAPTER VII

ANCILLARY UNITY AND THE PRESENT TENSE

IT is written that there can be no science of the fleeting. If this is truth it should seem that for us, children of the fleeting time, there can be no science at all — a contingency which the experts have done little to assure. Kant at least, with his two inseparable stems of an unknown root, shall remain hopeless of any punctual unity of cognition in the present or in any other tense.

We have criticised Kant for inadvertence — as in his call for gravitation to "hold the universe together," and his description of space as "an infinite quantity," and his notion of reality "fading to zero by degrees"; but we have not heretofore charged him with self-contradiction. Yet it must now appear that his most recondite studies had neither united nor unravelled those intricacies of the present tense which ever recall that well of Democritus, between whose implacable walls Truth escapes in an infinite divisibility. Neither do we find the embarrassment much abated by the discontent of Messieurs Bergson, James and others with a merely conceptual division between the future and the past — they demanding a perceptual and empirical reality in the

ANCILLARY UNITY, PRESENT TENSE

present, which the past has lost and the future has not yet attained.

As for Kant, we may readily indicate the diversity of his viewpoints. In his "Transcendental Analytic" (M. Muller, tr., p. 150) he says: "In mere succession existence always comes and goes (?) and never assumes the slightest *quantity*."

Yet on page 169 this is explicitly reversed: "Between two moments there is always a certain time, and between two *states* in these two moments there is always a difference which must have a certain quantity. . . . Every transition from one state into another takes place in a certain time between two moments — a state between two states."

This naïve reverie merely shares the popular confusion, and lacks any principle of definition. Rather, in fact, he disclaims any defining principle, saying: "All laws of nature, without distinction, are subject to higher principles of the understanding, which they apply to particular cases of experience. . . . Experience furnishes each case to which a rule applies."

This is the essence of pragmatism: that experience furnishes the "rule" of reason. What works explains.

There is this to be said for Bergson, James, and their followers, that if there is any radical difference between life and death, or between being and not-being, or in fact between this varied and wonderful universe or multiverse and nothing at all (if this may have any meaning), there should be a radical difference between the present tense and either the future or the past. We can hardly outflank the postulate that only what it is real; yet neither can we conceive how a nature that is only as and while becoming can fully have become and wholly be. Yet if we know at all we know that we are. Life is real, it is earnest, it is punitive. A rap on one's head gives a conviction of reality that no idea can come forth from it and refute. However naïvely or unphilosophically, we do habitually assume a certain breadth and fullness of duration in the moment. Its apprehension is expansive. Our ancillary Cinderella clings to and drags back the skirts of the reluctant past with one hand, and with the other reaches forth to anticipate the future. And just here is the crux of philosophy: while the fact is real enough, what have we to *say* about it — is it a concept or a percept, or both, or neither, for explanation or truth?

Clearly perceiving that a merely conceptual or ideal *division between* the past and the future does not do justice to the vital and in one sense exclusively present, James proposed (to spite the "intellectualists," possibly) that reality must come in definite empirical "pulses," "drops," "beads." (M. Bergson say "explosions.") I quote James's posthumous "Problems of Philosophy," page 155:

"Either your experience is of *no* content, *no* change, or it is of a perceptible *amount* of change. Your acquaintance with reality grows literally by beads or drops of perception."

Had any one else made this assertion in the presence of my dear friend, the proponent would have been immediately advised of its crudity and onesidedness, as merely "one way of putting it."

Of course there is a certain warrant for this suggestion of beads and drops and pulses, in the nature of sensation, as involving the alternation of attention and rest. Sensation comes in change; there is no call of attention to *the same*. And the grades of difference, in the time during which an attention is held, determine the length of various functions and features — such as words and phrases, sermons and plays, visits, vacations, et cetera. There are many ancillary averages of stress and strain in the business world.

The earth itself has its tidal pulsations and climatic compensations; everywhere there is trend and check. The wound-up world delivers its resilience to the swing of some inexorable pendulum, else the too-eager bud would explode into its flower; the incontinent potential would rush into the arms of the actual, and "the secret too long pent" would dissolve in we know not what of fiasco and calamity.

But the philosopher's trouble begins with the attempt at explicit definition, in the shading of these beads and pulses into one another in a continual process. The fault appears in conceptually punctualizing the attack of thought upon experience, in a centre-to-centre directness which excludes all collateral and ancillary supplement or adumbration. There is a penumbra which defeats the exactitude of every assumed connection. There is no explicit categorical punctuality in either our physical or our mental vision. The pupil of the eye — and of "the mind's eye" as well — is large; it covers more than we look at. However we focus our attention, there is a field of vision in which any intrusion is apprehended.

It is but a whim, saying that while we may *see* one object we must *count* three. I can see three by the same intuition in which a proofreader detects an error in a word, by the shape of it. This is not as saying I can see seven. While my capacity is open, the entrance is limited; like Mercutio's wound, it is not as wide as a church door, but it will do. It is large enough to *see motion*, as several places in one time, Zeno to the contrary notwithstanding.

What have been characterized separately as understanding and sense are so pragmatically interpervasive that they are only hypercritically distinguishable. The large pupil of the mind's eye vacates conceptual contradictions by factual experience.

The empiricists have sought to staunch their specialty by citing the stoppages in the production of the connected sections of a cinematographic film. The theory claimed as exemplified in the manufacture of the films is that between the sections, photographed one after another, there is a distinct pause for each picture, determined by and known from the construction of the photographing apparatus — following the ingenious and interesting conceit that the light requires time in which to act upon the collodion. This dead stop in the current time appeals to the empiricists as the bead, or drop, or pulse of the present tense, disrupted, however briefly, from the current time.

But this is a very negligent hypothesis. Either of these beads, as a perceptible bulk, is capable of an infinite division, in search of its ideal centre, which alone could be the "true" present. And practically speaking, the machine can make the beads thick or thin, according to its rapidity in taking the pictures.

Moreover the notion of this dead stop may be rather clever than accurate. Possibly the light might act upon the collodion while passing, as well as when standing still. A stick swished through water does not need a stoppage in order to get wet.

But the chief interest of the cinema machine is not in its presumptive demonstration of a stoppage of motion to realize the present tense, but rather in its proof of the possibility of motion, which Zeno and his followers denied — claming that motion in the present instant would require that a perceptual object should have at least two places in one and the same time, which they regarded as an impossibility.

Speaking of Lange and his "History of Materialism," I remarked upon his calling Kant to account for omitting motion from his list of categories, or native forms of mentation. Kant himself in a single instance classed motion as of that character. It would be a borrowing of trouble, discussing here whether or not motion is within the grasp of "quantity, quality, modality and relation"; the possibility of motion will be determined by consideration of time, space and vision as punctual unities — which they are not.

Observe first, in the case of a "motion picture" — say of the uplifting of an arm — that the real motion of the film and the picture-motion on the screen, although synchronous are not coincident; the arm may move three feet in the picture while moving three inches in the film; and this discrepancy may be exaggerated by moving the screen. The fact to be noticed here is that the motion on the screen is not of the *identity* of the sections of the film, but of their *difference*, which is mental; the motion consists in the unity of several sensuous places in one mental time.

When you whirl a curlicue with a burning torch, and make a fiery ring, *the ring is motion;* it is the infinite present places of the torch in one instant of mental vision, or time. Your vision is not of the torch, which shows no form, but of the manyness of its own present tenses and places in a one time for you.

It may be helpful to recall here our observations on the subject of size, as to an eye supposed as large as the earth; that the 1,000 miles per hour of the earth's peripheral motion would be withdrawn into the potentiality of the eye — the Many of individual experience into the creative One, which is Creator not by effort or intention, but by essential and eternal reason. So in the motion-picture, where the movement of the arm is (not quite wholly) the difference of the sections of the film, the apparent sweep of the arm is graduated by the distance from the camera to the screen. The motion is relative, and real only in experience as seen from the dynamic viewpoint.

Some of these paradoxes of philosophy, and even of religion, are wholly gratuitous. Let Achilles himself propose the paradox, that he cannot overtake the tortoise, and we see at once that to be a philosopher he has to be a knave; the mathematical require-

ANCILLARY UNITY, PRESENT TENSE 179

ment of the feat is wholly impertinent to its empirical accomplishment.

The theoretical puzzle of Achilles is that in the punctual unity of each repeated effort he must achieve the distance between himself and the reptile at the outset — during which accomplishment the latter will of course have advanced *somewhat:* and this recurring somewhat, however short its space, renews the whole problem — for Achilles' next effort is assumed to be spent in the covering of *that* space, while the tortoise gains a new one, offering the same difficulty in the mathematical impossibility of exhausting a whole by taking away successive fractions of it, since the remainder will ever be a whole. The absurdity of the story appears in the assumption that the athlete is intellectually hobbled, in his repeated efforts, punctually one by one, so that he may not continue to do his best as in the first endeavor, but must waste a whole unit on the little space which his rival has added to the course; and it is this restraint, which in practice he would never dream of (and which might be in another country), that encumbers an empirical proposition with a conceptual impossibility, uncalled for and impertinent.

The paradox is equally trival when viewed mathematically. If Achilles must win in mathematical rather than in athletic form, he should have a "show" by the rules of the game. Given the premise that he has the superior speed, we demand the *percentage* of his superiority. If his excellence is 25 per cent., then in four units of any conceivable effort he will reach the tortoise, and win the race.

We may well doubt that Professor Zeno displayed

these paradoxes on his centre-table for the delectation of his philosophical friends. But I have a mounted owl, from whose beak hangs a card bearing this question:

Was ist nicht?

No one of my visitors has answered it.

We cannot dismiss and dispose of motion as manyness of places — any better than we can shade entity to zero by degrees. There is a word or a thought missing here that shall grasp a vital unity in continuity and process and vanishing intensity as a whole, a category, a unique and ultimate given mental fact. What boots a mere manyness without a limiting discretion telling how many? We are out for blood, for the life of reality in one entity. If motion's manyness has forty thousand places the category's great revenge has stomach for them all. Time warms us of a *continuity without discretion* — the matter of experience which conception violates by cutting it into formal pieces with which to effect a more punctual contact with the mind. Again we say the pupil of the mind's eye is large. The most punctual centre is adumbrated with ancillary circles through which our closest inspection dives into the well of Democritus — the infinite divisibility between matter and form.

The thinker may readily juggle the consistency of motion and time, saying that each is a process, and they may advance coincidently, side by side. Unfortunately for this arrangement, time has but one uniform speed, while motion in any one time may have various degrees of speed, and thus break the identity of that friendly adjustment.

If motion consists of manyness of places, a whole of motion demands a multiplicity and an extension in the imputed unity of time and attention. I see no hope for this in realization, as a science of the fleeting, except by an ancillary enlargement and a capability of the grasp of manyness in the nominal unity and identity of the spiritual one — a categorical faculty or thought-form for process, continuity, activity, motion, or in a word, time.

But all this is matter for philosophy, which the Mystic does not presume to explain.

CHAPTER VIII

JESUS AND FREE WILL

LET us hope that we have learned somewhat, even if no more than negatively, from the route that we have gone over. We should have learned that intelligence, as we realize it, is a gift from some "alien energy," and that it fails of any originating principle of becoming, or any necessity of being. Neither position nor negation is fertile; something cannot impregnate itself, nor know itself, nor move itself, nor assume any other self-relation; and as for negation or nothingness being actively or processively positive in its results; and as for being, as statically taken, being inevitable because logically posited in the necessity of contrast or opposition — we have seen that the miracle of gratuitous nature furnishes sufficing contrast by its ever-new position in the everlasting yea, and leaves the dead negative, with a mourning wisp of memory to be sure, to bury its dead.

But our most reverent humility and self-denial have still to consist with a sense of our real originality and unavoidable responsibility, which keeps our philosophy at war with religion and policy. There is no *philosophical* objection to "free will." There are unquestionable powers or principles, whether rational or blind, and their only philosophical de-

JESUS AND FREE WILL

termination halts between monism and pluralism. The miracle of originality is not at all degraded by its *quasi* appearance in human consciousness, nor is the wonder or the problem of it alleviated by its exaltation to a divine supremacy; on the contrary, such an exaltation disrupts it from psychological fact, only to embarrass its hypothesis with the objections to which we have found the sacred claims of monism to be not quite impeccable.

Time may prove that we have been far and away too "fresh" in our naïve admiration and wonder at autocratic prestige and impossible unity and supremacy, where there is really but a uniform democracy, an everywhere, uncentered, and no better than every here. If we should have the good fortune to touch bottom in the Mystery, and the sacred should become secular, it would be but a nine days' wonder; we may well doubt that it would greatly affect our religion or our politics, or our worldly ambitions. The obscure and sedentary nature of philosophy is not due to any settled conviction of its hopelessness, at least not so much as to indifference to its problems, whose solution promises no material advantage — nothing that would make a brave man happier, or a coward braver, or a sensualist more spiritual. On the contrary there are high considerations under which it seems better that the Secret should still be kept. The inevitable stales, while Doubt and Hope are sisters. Not for aught that philosophy might promise could Tithonus have been reconciled to an immortality which he could not escape.

We shall find that the problem of moral responsibility, as divided between human and divine authority, was promptly solved by the Master in pragmatical terms. When decision was required of him, as to submission whether to Cæsar or to God, he referred instantly to the emblem of the power prevailing in the immediate field of observation: "Render unto Cæsar of the things which are Cæsar's, and unto God of the things which are God's."

Of all the world's religious teachers, Jesus was the most explicit and persistent in the denial of man's originality, and especially of his self-relation. He spoke for the race when he said, "Of myself I can do nothing." And however he dwelt upon "work" to be done, its performance or its neglect was theologically construed as rather an evidence of divine guidance than as a ground for either reward or punishment by the omnipotent Ruler.

Despite all the talk of free will and personal responsibility, modern culture, especially since Gall and Spurzheim, frankly and even kindly condones the wide difference in human organization and temperament. Certain virtues, each to a certain degree, the customs and needs of society and the dictates of common sense will still insist upon; but "for the most part" a man is now held as little responsible for his courage or his constancy as he is for his mental endowment. Those tough old Romans did in law hold the witness of an action as participant in its results; and in our own courts, not infrequently in cases of assault, a spectator has been adjudged as *particeps criminis;* the officer is entitled to call upon any bystander for assistance; but in case of default on the part of a weak or timid man the jury is wisely permitted to consider and determine the personal equation: they are assumed to know how it is themselves.

For the philosopher, God is a logical point or postulate, a concerted position, intended to locate or focalize his main problem. For him all questions of responsibility and personality fuse into the logical possibilities of such an assumed position. To popular thought, which at first steadies its vision upon some fancied fetich of a halo and bust, He is mainly defined by negations: He must *be,* but of course, upon reflection, He cannot be *this,* and He cannot be *that* — until finally He cannot be anything; but in any case He must be "infinite" — a portentous adjective, which literally dissipates all conception, eviscerates all content, and means nothing. No man hath seen Him at any time; thou canst not find out Him to perfection; nor *is* He to any save as the Logos shall reveal Him.

Said Fichte: "I will not attempt that which the imperfection of my finite nature forestalls, and which would be useless to me; *how* Thou art, I may not know. Thou knowest and willest and workest, omnipresent to finite reason; but as I now and always must conceive of being, *Thou art not.*"

It is not strange that this bold expression cost him his professorial chair.

Freedom, attributed as a quality or property of anything, should infer the thing's exemption from any influence or bearing or determination from either its environment or its content. Any *creature* must, as such, have a natural content, and if active it will be a secondary cause; but so far as it is cause at all it has a given quality, and exemption from this quality would imply the nullification of its being. The hypothesis of anything being free of or undetermined in its own content, or as an actor independent of its creator, or as responsible to its creator in the very instance of its creation as an activity, should require at least a very difficult defense.

The popular notion of "free will" is that one is responsibly free when he can "do as he has a mind to." The State is not immediately (however ultimately) considering his originality, in declaring his responsibility to its own policy; in a round-about way it does wisely assume the mental cultivation of the citizen; but the immediate congenital quality of the creature, from the viewpoint of its puted Creator, can hardly involve responsibility.

The psychology of this predicament has been rather vaguely exploited. Doubtless there was always recognized (or at least since our "civilization") something determined in the natural make-up of the individual man. Socrates, for example, argued earnestly that virtue cannot be taught. But it was mainly subsequent to the observations of Gall and Spurzheim that physiological structure, either brute or human, was held to determine, in all but very exceptional cases, the mental and moral qualities of the individual. Ethical and religious objections have of course been raised against the theory, and Emerson even resented it, but intelligent people generally now admit its main contentions so far, that the frontal brain is efficient intellectually, the top and back brain morally, and the side brain more or less æsthetically. This is so taught in the common schools.

JESUS AND FREE WILL

Various mechanical bearings and compensations seem to rationalize the consciousness and disposition as naturally resulting from peculiarities of physical organization. In Scripture, the creature thinks "as he is," and as if necessarily so. The long fibre of the hound must render him sensitive, apprehensive and timid, while the compact bull-dog, with his teeth in advance of his nose, threatening execution before judgment, is sudden and quick in quarrel.

Such considerations should repress the flippancy of this "having a mind to." Mind is not so cheap a commodity; and the will is not quite amenable to one's ideals. No doubt, one could have the courage of Ney or Decatur if he had a mind to, in the right sense; or he might go up as climbs the steeple-jack, and standing on the cross, wave his cap to the thrilled and apprehensive crowd below; but the average man in the same position would feel his hair turning gray at the roots; his heart would fail him, and inconsequent and dangerous fancies might come to him.

The very place puts toys of desperation,
Without more motive, into every brain
That looks so many fathoms to the sea
And hears it roar.

Even our common honesty is amenable to the clearness of our natural memory and perceptions. Plato suggested the difference of the rogue and the honest man as largely mathematical.

The freedom of will and consciousness requires a delicate appreciation when it involves relations of the divine and the human, and especially, for us here, as implicating the doctrines of Jesus concerning it, for these afford little of favorable countenance to the current notions of free will, especially as affecting human responsibility and retribution. He was the first to so emphasize the divine guidance and government as to invest it in the business and bosom of humanity as a working thought of daily life, for its own sake and hereafter.

There seems to have been but little really scientific reflection upon the intimate relation of our puted originality to the Power that is our ultimate reference, or upon the infrequency of our consideration of it, although for the greater part of the time we are involuntarily using it, and are inspired and guided by it. From the causative viewpoint one hardly need pay any attention to himself, whether thinking or acting. One should be curious, even if not astonished, that, while he is giving attention to the fact, he draws his every breath voluntarily, yet his breathing goes on quite as regularly "of itself"; and also the fact that his thoughts and words come from sources of which he knows nothing, and whose current he can only with special effort control, and whose persistence he would often repress. Give the clever thinker a patent for a device that would *stop* one's thinking, he need never again work for wages.

Experts have differed almost diametrically upon the wonderful duplexity of what we call personality, especially as involving divine and human nature. To the egoist, personality is original: "the highest, steepest thought," said Hegel. Emerson would look no higher than the canon of Kant — the cultured consciousness — and to this our personality is a

JESUS AND FREE WILL 189

wavering and inconstant attachment, never quite identical with our more essential being. Indeed he would regard "genius" as subservience of the former to the latter, as " the virtue of a pipe is to be hollow and smooth." "We aspire and look up," said he, "and put ourselves in an attitude of attention, but from some alien energy the visions come." Even so held St. Augustine, Goethe, and many others. The thoughtful man, even with no regard to the consolation of Jesus, must find in this reflection the most intimate solace for his follies and his sins. It is his best and least costly reverence, the belief that he is the instrument of a higher power.

The adjustment of the citizen's inspired action to the requirements of national and social government was a problem which more than transiently concerned Jesus. He recognized a discrepancy in civil duties being excused by loyalty to divine commands. Though it needs be, in the divine scheme, that offences come, the state criminal shall suffer punishment — shall render unto Cæsar the tribute due to his function and vocation.

The Pharisees demanded of Him a reconciliation of his gospel of mercy with the punishment exacted by the Mosaic law. The case must bear citation:

"Jesus went unto the Mount of Olives. And early in the morning he came again into the temple, and all the people came unto him, and he sat down and taught them.

"And the scribes and pharisees brought unto him a woman taken in adultery; and when they set her in the midst they say unto him, 'Master, this woman was taken in adultery, in the very act. Now Moses in the law commanded us that such should be stoned; but what sayest thou?'

"This they said tempting him, that they might have, to accuse him. But Jesus stooped down, and with his finger wrote in the dust. So when they continued asking him he lifted up himself and said unto them, 'He that is without sin among you, let him first cast a stone at her.' And again he stooped down and wrote in the dust.

"And they who heard it, being convicted in their own conscience, went out one by one, beginning at the eldest, even unto the last; and Jesus was left alone, with the woman standing in the midst.

"When Jesus had lifted up himself, and saw none but the woman, he said unto her, 'Woman, where are those thine accusers? hath no man condemned thee?'

"She said, 'No man, lord.'

"And Jesus said unto her, 'Neither do I condemn thee. Go, and sin no more.'"

(How far this seems from the "jealous God, visiting the iniquities of the fathers upon their children even unto the third and fourth generation!")

It is theoretically impossible to pervert this episode to an exceptional case. The sin charged, the overt commission, the concurrent testimony, the unquestioned law and the prevalent custom, all confirm it as a recognition of the divine viewpoint, as to the responsibility of the creature to the Creator whose work shall be manifest in him. The pertinence and motive of the legend can obtain only in the divine purpose of the gospel to relieve the human conscience of any responsibility to the inspiring Power whose behest it powerlessly fulfills. There can be no vicarious or compensatory forgiveness of moral dereliction; the secondary orginality which burdens the human conscience must be relieved, not by any sacrificial readjustment, but by a wiping out of the record in the act of the divine Disposer as taking the burden and its responsibility upon himself, and setting the "sinner" free. [See Eucken to this same effect.]

Our discussion should have thrown some light upon the recalcitrance of Jesus against Jewish law in this instance. Our theologians, in their "plan of salvation," seem to still regard him as a sacrifice for the remission of our sins, not considering that only a truth can relieve the spirit. The central truth of the gospel of Jesus is that of himself the creature can do nothing; that God is rather a father than a governor, but more than either he is for his own purpose the inner and inspiring life and light, without which not even a sparrow falls to the ground.

However the creature may seem to himself original and responsible, the true light shows his power to be but secondary from the divine viewpoint, and the remission of his sins is possible only in the truth that the Divine assumes responsibility for them. Let one know that the follies he has committed are circumstantial, and not congenital in his proper stuff— that his shame and remorse are not ultimately attributable to him, but rather to the divine purpose, his conscience may drop the ball and chain; for the truth and the light will have set him free.

That Jesus conceived of himself as historically and generically singular in the fact of this annunciation, its previous repression may well have persuaded him.

The personal psychology of the Master is as obscure as was his social environment. The Grecian culture of 400 years before must still have glimmered through the régime of the Cæsars. Pontius Pilate was obviously a philosophical scholar. His chance question, partly to the crude Judean agitators, "What is truth?" is, barring the proem to the gospel according to St. John, the most important metaphysical expression in the New Testament; and the announcement of Jesus, "I *am* the truth," is the only plausible retort to that unanswerable question — since really truth is impossible. As to what Jesus knew of the world's inconsequent philosophy, no exacting occasion appears to have shown. His responses were ever timely and pragmatical, as fitted to his audience. A discussion with Pilate would have been in bad form. A logomachist or a professional sophist might well have regarded this as an eminently fortunate opportunity; but a fine genius, possibly entranced by an auto-suggestion of uniquity, could but stand for and live the only feasible answer to the Roman's fling.

Our more immediate interest in Jesus lies in the metaphysical weight of his emphasis upon what we regard as the philosophical fact, that personality can bear but a part of the burden of explanation. That the surd should be *absolute* is an extravagant conjecture. Idealism will have at least this admission, that the Mystery, even as ultimate, must be *known* to be such: there shall be knowledge or nothing. The problem was still for him, as it must be for all thought, that however humbly he denied himself, however utterly he submerged his originality in him in whom we live and move and have our being — a relation transcendently more intimate than that of father and son, or of principal and agent, or of ruler and subject — he had yet to construe, in his homiletic, a duplexity in his ostensible unity with the Father. The dialectic controversy which the succeeding ages have realized was imminent and unavoidable. But we should observe, as of the utmost philosophical importance, that in his treatment of this occult relation he credited to humanity no more of "free agency" than a personal individuality as such must socially infer. The Cæsar is enthroned in the material world; and life, with all the antagonism and self-seeking by which vitality accrues, is for divine purposes divided among the many; but the private aspiration of the individual, and his prayer to the paternal Power which shall exploit these individual antagonisms, recognizes as little as possible of the separateness between the secular magistrate and the subject of his official jurisdiction. The Lord's Prayer at once pleads and deprecates the fact that it is addressed to the very source of its own inspiration — to that which both prompts and enables the petitioner "to will and to do." It voices the helpless anxiety of a supplicant to the Power which alone can furnish the disposition which it demands, yet to which it acknowledges indisputable responsibility. Our interest in the complication is not so much in the sinner's psychological illusion of freedom as it is in the philosophical testimony against his original competence.

Matthew vi, 9: "Your Father knoweth what

things ye have need of before ye ask him. After this manner therefore pray ye:

"Our Father, who art in heaven, Hallowed be thy name. Thy kingdom come. Thy will be done in earth as it is in heaven. Give us this day our daily bread. And forgive our debts, as we forgive our debtors. And lead us not into temptation, but deliver us from evil. For thine is the kingdom, and the power, and the glory, for ever. Amen."

There can be no consistent interpretation of these sentences other than that all power and disposition are of God. How utterly impertinent were the adjuration, "Lead us not into temptation," in any other understanding than that all guidance and inspiration are of God! — Yet we have it from St. James: "Let no many say, when he is tempted, 'I am tempted of God'; for God is not tempted of any, neither tempteth he any man." This protest, however, came from the vulgar consciousness, "under the law," and lacked the refinement and second-sight of Jesus and St. John. The New Testament will go for nothing if such contradictions shall be allowed to outface its esoteric spirit.

This doctrine of St. James was the voice of that "categorical imperative" for which Kant, in the interest of Prussian orthodoxy, imperiled his philosophical reputation, refusing to consider that all exaltation of the power of the creature implies an equal derogation from that of the Creator — a dividing of the house against itself.

The title of Jesus, whether as the Son of Man or the Son of God, was questioned as exhaustively during his lifetime as it has been since. He read from

JESUS AND FREE WILL

"the law" an ascription of godship that left it quite other than unique; "to some gave he power to become sons of God"; and our advanced criticism has been quick to quote the precedent, and has so plausibly barricaded the human position, made it so dangerous, æsthetically, to attack it, that its discussion is socially regarded as bad form; we hear, occasionally, that "religion out of church is sacrilege." In fact the policy of the Church has always deprecated even the possession of the Scriptures in unclerical hands.

Protestant faith, for all its monism, is embarrassed by a too dull appreciation of the unique element in nature. There needs no more than common sense to admit that no one miracle should be more astounding than another, nor than the whole. A man rising from the grave, having a body already, is not half the miracle of a bird perfecting in an egg, with only an impersonal heat to promote its development. That a man was born of a virgin is as nothing to the fact that one was ever born at all. This wonder, like every other accomplishment of nature, is but a question of historical evidence, in which every incident, microscopically criticised, is in some particular unique. The miracle of a local fact fades in its cosmic background. One may readily class himself as a cad and a menial by truculently presuming upon Nature as intending consistency and law. The cataclysms of history, the wandering aerolites which have struck us, the frustrations of promise and the impossibility of final purpose, all give warning that our lesson is not of law, but rather of exceptionality and unreason. On the other hand, the wildest abnormity may recur in its cycle, and prove no miracle as such.

There appears a confusion in ecclesiastic affairs, obviously owing to neglect of the duplex vocation of Jesus as he apprehended and explicitly declared it. While he, as a Jew, loyally accepted the Messianic succession, and announced that jot nor tittle of the law should fail until all should be fulfilled — that is to say that he by vicarious sacrifice should still satisfy the law of retribution as it was written of old— he categorically proclaimed a *new dispensation*, of love rather than of vengeance, wherein, by the divine resumption of all efficiency, and the renunciation of all originality on the part of the creature, the conviction of sin should be alleviated, and its burden of responsibility borne by the Creator. Our only philosophical interest in the topic is, that Jesus, for himself and for all men, *renounced originality and free will*, in favor of divine omnipotence.

That Jesus was no philosopher — meaning that his insight was never blurred by dialectic problems — is of course, from our viewpoint, decisively in his favor; but that he was the world's most profound psychologist, as having the clearest intuition of the demands of honor and conscience, shall unquestionably appear. For who that has felt the horror of remorse for cruelty to another could assuage the pangs of conscience with the thought that another, more generous than himself, was suffering a penalty that was justly his own desert? "Whip me, ye devils!" cried the despairing Moor, as he gazed upon the evidence of his vengeance and superior strength. Could any vicarious suffering have relieved him, who truly "was great of heart"? Not thus is the forgiveness of sin. But if one could have assured him that he had been possessed, that he had been demented and overborne, "ensnared soul and body" — that truly of himself he could have done nothing — he might at length have been free, in the liberty of the Gospel. Not by expense of the blood of bulls and goats is salvation, nor mainly by his own blood itself — "my *word* shall make you free." The sin is no longer "imputed" to the creature.

It is not to be denied, however — and herein is one secret of the popular success of Christianity — that the satisfaction of the "law," the assurance that "Christ has died for you," that his blood cleanseth from all iniquity, is a postulate more appealing to the average sinner than is the metaphysical assurance of an illusive sense of responsibility. Pragmatic salvation is promoted by vicarious substitution, and is not over-critical as to method, so long as it gets results. The advice is not infrequent among men of approved sagacity and established credit: "Why trouble yourself over these insoluble however important problems? Better keep with the procession, join in the ordinances, take the safe side, and countenance respectability. The yoke is easy, and the burden is light." It is a natural consequence of this pragmatic objectivity that a thousand worshipers shall kneel to Jesus as the Son of God, where one may bow to the sublime wisdom and goodness of the Son of Man; but an appeal to the Court of Common Pleas would show that one judicious critic should outweigh a whole theatre of others, and that, freed from superstition and professional exploitation, Christianity is the religion of the scholar and the gentleman — neither more nor less for the twentieth century.

Accustomed as we have become to the Immanuel idea — the concept of "God with us," as meaning the homogeneity of intelligence — we can but faintly realize the weight of its obsession upon the consciousness which first discovered, or at least the personality that first rationally entertained it. Alone among men whose civic necessities emphasized their responsibility to an objective environment, and who had no notion of an inner and subjective connection with the divine intelligence or power, he could hardly avoid the conviction of singularity in his nature and his mission. More portentously, if not even more formidably, his distinction involved the Highest; and we get the hint that his brooding upon it grew into a temptation to thaumaturgically test its significance: Could he convert stones into bread? Could he cast himself from a precipice in safety? Could he go forth into the world and achieve wealth and political power? Whatever confidence the experiment did inspire was held in check by his recognition of an ancient Scripture: "Thou shalt not tempt the Lord, thy God." This quotation obviously was not wholly a retort upon the devil, but also a reminder to himself.

The astute critic will date from this temptation and its lesson, whatever that lesson may have been, the seemingly uncalled for and otherwise unaccountable persistence of Jesus in designating himself as the Son of Man, and in even homiletically defending that title as in itself a sufficient renouncement of that other title, the "Son of God," whose virtual synonymity he could not trust his enemies to understand.[1] Had he deigned to renounce his own singulartiy and join the rabble as one wholly of their caste, he might possibly have escaped as effectually as did his disciples, of whom not one appeared at his trial. Evidently he had no faith in the ability of his adherents to treat the topic of divine Sonship; and on several occasions he admonished them to "tell no man this thing."

There appears in the record a *special anxiety* of Jesus to forestall any accusation of his presumption to the Highest, however difficult his doctrine might render a due discrimination between the titles of Son of Man and Son of God. Obviously in the mind of Jesus there was for him no difference between them, whether or not all men, at their best, might be equally entitled; but the extraordinary significance then first apparent in his claim was a constant embarrassment to his discourse, seeming to demand of him a habitual classification of himself with his fellow-men. I count in the New Testament seventy-two instances of his adoption of the designedly apologetic or deprecative title of the Son of Man, while in but two instances, and these of very questionable literary probability, is he quoted as identifying himself generically and exceptionally with God. On the other hand, he reproached his disciples continually, in that only a lack of faith deferred their accomplishment from equality with his own.

[1] This consideration is strongly urged in "Christ's Secret Doctrine," an essay by H. S. Mories, published by James McKelvie and Sons, Ltd., Greenock, Scotland.

It was the profundity of his doctrine, not the overpresumption of his individual supremacy, that cost him his life.

This shall give no offense, our saying that Jesus was not a philosopher. His sense of explanation had attained only to God. The humblest Galilean had as much theology as had he, and could not have learned from him that he had traced the logical mystery to any higher source than the child finds in the father by a faith which forestalls all speculation — the same faith which Fichte came to substitute for impossible knowledge.

And who but he has left in the human record any food for the imagination that could picture the divine man? Who but he, in all history, has divinely posed, or said unto his fellow-man, face to face, Look into my eyes and see all of God that shall be seen at any time?

"Philip saith unto him, Lord, show us the Father, and it sufficeth us. Jesus saith unto him, Have I been so long with you, and yet hast thou not known me, Philip? He that hath seen me hath seen the Father; and how sayest thou then, Show us the Father? Believest thou not that I am in the Father, and the Father in me? The words that I speak unto thee I speak not of myself; but the Father that inhereth in me, he doeth the works. Believe me, that I am in the Father, and the Father in me; or else believe me for the very works' sake. Verily, verily I say unto you, He that believeth in me, the works that I do shall he do also; and greater works than these shall he do, because I go unto my Father."

Surely here spoke the Son of Man, with no un-

JESUS AND FREE WILL

due pretension above his fellow-man, if so be the latter would rise to a right faith in their common nature.

Obviously there should be a reopening of this cause — the charge of blasphemy as against Jesus, accused of posing as "the Son of God" — and a modern reporter should be assigned upon the case. It is true that the testimony was technically inconsistent, but an unbiased judge should perceive in the discrepancy of the evidence a warrant against any collusion or conspiracy of the witnesses, and find rather an assurance of occurrence so extraordinary as to provoke different intepretations, as well as to impart even discordant impressions. Not in all history have complications so intricate, involving property interests so extensive, come to rest in mere possession upon such unsettled premises, and under such conflicting titles. These material properties and perquisites are likely to hold the churches asunder long after the average culture shall have accepted Jesus under his own oft-reiterated title of the Son of Man — par excellence.

It seems long until the race can adjust the personal equation, rather by lifting up its own dignity than by dragging Jesus down.

Finally — and frankly and modernly — we have no immediate vocation to either account for or conciliate the popular prestige of Christianity. For people of mature convictions certain of its manifest discrepancies are swiftly righting of themselves, in ways which a boastful approval would only check and embarrass. It may be safely granted to "modernity" that the personality of Jesus is liable to exaggeration through the mist of distance and the crudity of his record, and that, born into our science and culture, his life and doctrine would have been differently interpreted — and it was false interpretation that destroyed him. But as against all skepticism of the unique in history, and in scientific and secular assurance of the faith in him that is so largely and devoutly cherished, we must hold it as not a syllable too much to say — and we challenge philosophical contention of the saying — that there is no other name given under heaven among men, as of one through whose truth the race can either forgive or be forgiven for its sins, than the name of Jesus of Nazareth.

Said Goethe: "Life, no less than scientific investigation, is confined within impassable barriers. All man's activity rests upon a given natural order; his work can only succeed when it strikes out in the direction prescribed by nature; it becomes empty and artificial if it tries to sever its connections or to act in opposition to nature. 'Let man turn whither he will, undertake no matter what; he will ever come back again to that path which nature has mapped out for him.'"

Said Emerson: "The ardors of piety agree at last with the coldest skepticism, that nothing is of us or our works — that all is of God. Nature will not spare us the smallest leaf of laurel. All writing comes by the grace of God, and all doing and having. I would gladly be moral, and keep due metes and bounds, which I dearly love, and allow the most to the will of man; but I have set my heart on honesty in this chapter, and I can see nothing at last, in success or failure, than more or less of vital force supplied by the Eternal."

Said Spinoza: "There is no bad, to God . . . to him there is no 'free will.'"

Said St. Augustine: "What is done by thee is done by God working in thee." . . . "Whatever he does or leaves undone, man can alter nothing; his rôle in life is minutely prescribed for him."

Said Eucken: "He who will not begin with wonder and admiration will never find entrance to the Holy of Holies. For his discoveries, his syntheses, his happy inspirations, the artist has to thank not his own reflections but a Supreme Power."

Said Eckhart: "All error and depravity come from God's creatures presuming to be or do something on their own account."

If we aspired to an apothegm, it would be that freedom, originality, and reason as in equation with the Mystery, shall be the last hopes of mortal explanation.

CHAPTER IX

THE ANÆSTHETIC REVELATION

I HAVE made the preceding digest of current philosophy in the hope of familiarizing its mental spectres, and of authenticating if not justifying the halting discomfiture of even the most cultured patients of the anæsthetic revelation. If I have rightly indicated the obstacles and pitfalls which disrupt the course of satisfactory explanation, and have sufficiently emphasized the confessed failures of philosophical endeavor, the reader should foresee that the seemingly promising rubric, "Anæsthetic Revelation," may forecast rather unutterable Mystery than satisfaction, although our better insight of the dialectic shifts, and the more familiar use of the logical conventions, may clear, to some extent, the mental area in which the Mystery is encountered.

Our hope is not so much to philosophize the Mystery as it is to signalize in it an unequivocal *impasse* whose obstruction can be neither obviated nor defined — if the confusion of philosophy may attest the fact.

The illumination, or the obsession, which has prompted this treatise, will have rarely arrested the attention of the boor or the bigot; but for the worldwise it will determine as his ultimate and only possible insight of the genius of being and the secret of

THE ANÆSTHETIC REVELATION 205

the world. Any essay upon the anæsthetic (or presumptively any other) revelation, as proposing a detail of what it is or is like, is immediately baffled by the consideration that its topic is and must be unique. It has no class, no relation to any comparable fact or theory whatsoever. Its best remembered impression is the sense of *initiation*, as into the immemorial, the inevitable, the time-out-of-mind, the something of fate or destiny which, in even justice, at least for once every sane consciousness should realize.

All analogies anticipate the concession that the unique cannot be articulate. Nor does the revelation require for its reception, however it may for its entertainment, the thoughts of language, wherein man excels the beasts of the field. One may be advised of a handicap which the lack of conventional language imposes upon a dumb intelligence, potentially as apprehensive, possibly, as his own.

An English dictionary, with its 2,000 pages, carries some 350,000 different words, of whose meanings the average citizen may know one tenth. Our Indians, of the time of Columbus, may have had 200 words, among which were a few adjectives, but no sign of an abstraction. Conceive then the utter latency — saying nothing of the potentiality — in the Indian mind, of such meanings as memory, objectivity, veracity, heredity, and ten thousand of the like, which were wholly beyond his faculty of expression, or even of focalization in his attention. Under strong emotion he could merely contort his habitually immobile visage, or gesticulate in rude imitation, while his heart might be voluble of an inarticulate and helpless meaning. He could not know, he could not connectedly think, he could not be said to *feel* the meanings which only culture could educate up to sane and conventional expression, even to himself. Yet the basis for all this exploitation was within him, his birthright as a monad and a soul; he was not a stock or a stone, but counted as one in the spirit world, where even the beast is open to some revelation which in the instant shall carry, however cryptically, the hint of initiation — the hint that Now You Know.

I have wondered at psychology and "natural history," that they have nowhere noticed or identified what has been long known to me as *the voice of the blood*. They should have heeded the injunction, to "search the Scriptures." For centuries ago, when there were cattle upon a thousand hills, and the patriarchs dwelt in tents, and had no abattoirs for slaughtering purposes, they bled the stalled ox and the fatted calf in the open field, and the blood sank directly into the grassy ground, where it must have frequently occasioned the metaphysical phenomenon which I have mentioned as the voice of the blood, so impressively quoted in Genesis, in these words:

"And the Lord said unto Cain, Where is Abel, thy brother? And he said, I know not. Am I my brother's keeper? — And he said, What hast thou done? the voice of thy brother's blood crieth unto me from the ground."

The dwellers in cities may live and die with no pathetic suggestion from this incident, they regarding its language as merely poetic and symbolical; but it undoubtedly grew out of a peculiarity well known to every plainsman, and which shall have been observed, however carelessly, by many a farmer's boy — a peculiarity of the following character: Where the blood of an animal has been freshly shed upon the ground — particularly, in my own experience, the blood of an ox, or of a cow or a calf — any other member of the herd passing over the fatal spot will be arrested and entranced, seemingly by some exhalation from the vital fluid. The animal stares, with a rapt and distracted expression, moaning and pawing the ground, as if in fierce remonstrance, though apparently "more in sorrow than in anger." This abstraction may last for several seconds; but any noise or intrusion which would ordinarily call attention will break the spell, which, as in the case of "bearing pain," seems to be instantly gone and forgotten. Having had largely to do with flocks and herds I have witnessed this wonder many times; but after all our Psychical Research I have never seen it in secular print.

I cannot make less of this phenomenon than a revelation, addressed to some atavism of the bovine race, wherein it is as susceptible of the genius of being as man himself has proved it. Of what cataclysm in the history of the creature's species may not this trance afford a reminiscence. The animal has no formal or consecutive thought, probably, but neither, so far as I have gathered, has the anæsthetic patient, save as an informal memory that baffles recollection.

One may ponder long the manifest elements of animal mentality, as transcending the passive receptivity of native instinct — considering not only how much the dumb creatures may be taught, but how many æsthetic traits they show, in the vanity of play and imitation and rivalry, and how deep and lasting their affections are — before he will attain any clear conception of the metaphysical possibilities of this animal trance, or reverie, or illumination, or whatever it may be called — learn, for instance, if it has any imagination, any hint of palingenesis, or metempsychosis, or any scintil of a past, or of being itself, or fate. Very probably it is the creature's supreme moment, his nearest relation to what we think of as spiritual life. And it is so pronounced, so wholly unique in scientific metaphysics, that I have come to regard it as the monad's most palpable connection with an unseen world.

There are various other instinctual obsessions or possessions which lend a superstitious atmosphere to animal life. A cow, when she leaves her calf resting while she roams in pursuit of her own forage, seems to have left a spell upon it that holds it motionless against her return. It will not leave the spot save for some extraordinary and threatening intrusion; but if really driven by some compelling apprehension to escape, it will run as for its life, and recall the mother with frantic and pitiful appeals.

So a brooding hen, however timid has been her previous habits, is so inspired by a courage and loyalty to her eggs — which must not be allowed to cool — that she will not budge for man or beast. We may easily generalize these instances as provisions of nature, and so forth, but they have a mystical appeal.

There is another supreme instant, often noticed

of the dying patient — a stare of seeming recognition, as of some wonderful import, just before but distinctly not inclusive with the "setting" of the eyes. We should consent that the meanest creature ever favored with this miracle of consciousness, this flower of all evolution, may well be given, at least for once, a glimpse of history, or some abnormal reality.

And here, again, the most astute and critical may need warning, against any skeptical and peremptory demand upon the mystic, as to *what* he knows or sees. This what gives the skeptic away, in his naïve presumption that the world-mystery can be of a *class*, and so comparable and definable. But the basis of all metaphysical insight is the primary fact that *being is unique*. Until one can identify this logical necessity he is not of the illuminati, although he may be wearing the broadest horns of the herd. He should see that this import cannot be writ on any scroll; he must have the background of its meaning in himself — if indeed he ever may, after our hopeless account, or discount of self-relation. Nevertheless, although we may not profane the one mystery as a topic among others, it seems possible that we should rise to it at our best, and learn that it is a mystery only because we are living on a plane below our best, while its higher sanity is still within the homogeneity of an intelligence which transcends the portals of formal enunciation.

It were manifestly absurd, claiming a "revelation" not amenable to intelligence; but if we may understand Socrates' proof that Meno's slave had latent geometry in his mind, or believe that a proud and sulky Indian may be chafing under the pressure of abstractions so easily connoted by us, the reader may at least "believe in" a revelation unique and manageable, and withheld from popular appreciation not only, but instantly unthinkable by the most profound of mental experts. The latter will claim, under his modern lights (which reveal below the "threshold") that he may *live* the secret although he has not yet language in which to formulate it, and so hold the world to the rule of reason, pound for pound. But it is peculiarly this flippant and chipper rationality and "matter of course" that the revelation embarrasses and disconcerts. Here is no static accountable equation, but rather a constant excess, and a going on simply *because* it is going on, in which the natural endeavor to account for itself proves to be of a piece with and continuing the same stuff that it is meant to account for. Strong in the revelation is this sense of an inevitable going on "because of" the curious interest in the fact that it is going on, helplessly and fatedly going on, with a sense of immemorial initiation into the truth that this is the inevitable and eternal world-condition, and however piquant or unique, as what inevitably and of course must be, and ever must have been. There never was a time that did not recognize the presumption of time and the push of its own necessity, and also that any question of its motive was itself a sufficient reason at once for its continuance and for its precedence, but with no relation to a beginning. This is what stultifies the argument for cause: that there is no possibility of a beginning, and therefore no place in which to locate a cause. Above all, it is a *revelation* of the one truth that

THE ANÆSTHETIC REVELATION 211

is supremely "worth while," but baffled of content by the too-evident fatuity of turning upon itself to achieve a self-relation — a real self-consciousness, in which concept and percept should unite in a whole cognition.

It is fairly presumptive that thought, newly wrought to its highest tension, should revert with curious interest to its remembered experience (or its self) and be baffled in its attempts at instant self-relation, while realizing at the same time that the effort of understanding is itself continuing (and in a certain sense accounting for) the very activity which arrests its attention — affording a presumption from the past as enforcing time's continuance.

With this sense of an effort of the soul to turn upon itself for an escaping and unachievable self-knowledge, the anæsthetic insight attests the only presumable or possible first principle of thought and being, namely, fact, philosophy, explanation, "cause" — all this curiosity and discontent, is to *get before the fact*, to surround and comprehend the fact of consciousness; and it discovers at last that, in a process of factual thought beginning is impossible, and hence fact is a foregone conclusion, or necessary presumption; and since here is everywhere, comprehension is inconceivable save as in this vain and continuous obsession of self-relation, which keeps the Hound of Heaven on his own trail.

"The wonderful thing is *fact*," said Carlyle. The gritty Scot was very near to the mystic sanity. And all through German philosophy crops out this desperate and illogical finality of fact, in such sayings as "it is because it is" — using the given fact of knowledge (or of process) as the "cause" of it, and as objectively before it — whereas (as I have laboriously sought to show) the cause is subjectively and miraculously *given* as the first of facts, and fact (not cause) is the prime reality of being as experience — the given percept which must ground all conception.

Now if this necessary analysis were all — this secular Kantian thought, which thousands of introspective people have revolved as the puzzle and crux of philosophy — our "revelation" would be none such! But the immemorial atavism, the sense of initiation, the voice of the blood, the unique assurance that it **is** a revelation of the historical and inevitable and the time out of mind — all this admonishes the philosophical parasite that he is not here as a cosmopolitan critic of worlds, with a vocation to put this being in its class, but rather that there is but this; and that, for his once and all, he knows reality. It was a strong saying of William James: "He that hath ears to hear, let him hear: for me the living sense of reality comes only in the artificial-mystic state of mind."

It should be obvious that a generalization of such an experience — involving as it must all the ancillary shadings of the present tense — would have to be told in tentative and provisional and poetical rather than factual terms. Continuous but reverting, sure and yet questioning, at once real, reminiscent and expectant, the genius of it might well regard sardonically any attempt at its factual expression.

We are not to infer that the status of the world

THE ANÆSTHETIC REVELATION 213

is necessarily weakened or undermined by this interpretation of it as a mystery to us and our philosophy. The spirit still transcends. There is no finite consciousness or conviction that should forestall the cosmic afterthought of our parasital and secondary nature, or authoritatively declare the surd ultimate in itself. We might say that for one as great as the world the world could be reasonable; but if we have any faith in our own judgment there is no such one, nor any such world. The cosmos itself is no unit, but rather an egotistic fetich, which the multiverse shall dissipate and overwhelm.

A proof that the revelation is homogeneous with intelligence at its best tension is, that it rarely follows recovery from the major operations which have required prolonged anæsthesia, and which have doubtless benumbed the reflective faculties of the patient. It attends rather the "coming to" from a trance of but a few moments' duration, when presumably the mental faculties are still fresh, although under abnormal exhilaration. It is of common knowledge that we think faster and more comprehensively at some times than we do or can at others.

That eminent psychologist, William James, was specially insistent — particularly in view of the notorious trances of Lord Tennyson — that *any* revelation, however occult, must still be *sane*, and that there can be no other than the homogeneous intelligence. While he was apt enough to agree that knowledge is unaccountable and insoluble, he could not consent that a really *false knowledge* might be imposed upon intelligence as such; he "felt" that hypothesis to be contradictory, however deeply the "unknown root" might be buried.

Of course, feeling can be no arbiter of contradiction; and "the prime fact of knowledge," as Prof. Ladd calls it, cannot be proved or authenticated; we cannot double-think, as Fichte assumed to do, in his doctrine of consciousness as transcending mere sense by a "knowing that you know." Kant firmly settled the ultimate authority as to knowledge — the canon and last word of human reason and certainty — in the plain "I think" — of course, of the cultivated man. For there is a plenty of error and illusion, which he would not consent to call *false* thinking, but rather would stoutly hold to be not thinking at all — he having himself determined the only sure method of thought.

Emerson, on the other hand, would seem to have favored the more intuitive confidence of Prof. James. He said: "We know truth when we see it, as we know, when we are awake, that we are awake." But this is rather high morality than astute metaphysics. ("Truth" is explicitly the condemnation of knowledge; it is a quality of resemblance, not of identity, which last is the only reality of possession. Knowledge cannot realize the life of that which it in fact is not. Truth is a false pretence of the representation of an originality which does not appear in its portrait. In other words, the truth of a mere — *i. e.* pretended — re-presentation would disqualify the original, as being no more essential than is a copy.)

However, the same self-reliance appears in the consciousness of Tennyson, as shown in an anecdote

THE ANÆSTHETIC REVELATION 215

which has been extensively published, as related by John Tyndall:

Tennyson and Tyndall had been in consultation with "Master" Jowett, of Balliol College, and Tyndall relates that after the Master had retired the poet resumed the previous discussion, which had involved his peculiar trances, and had provoked certain rather cavalier suggestions by the eminent translator of Plato as to their possible illusion. According to Tyndall's account, Tennyson immediately retorted upon the animadversions of his late guest with the utmost seriousness and (for him at least) extraordinary heat. He said: "By God Almighty, there is no illusion in the matter! It is no nebulous ecstasy, no confused state, but a condition of transcendent wonder associated with absolute clearness of mind."

This striking expression — the very ideal of what one must think the announcement of a "mystery" should be — comports perfectly with the definition which the poet vouchsafed to me in 1874, and which, with his implied permission, was widely published at that time. I quote partially this letter:

"*Faringford, Freshwater, Isle of Wight,*
May 7, 1874.

"Sir: — I have to thank you for your essay. . . .

"It is a very notable sketch of metaphysic, ending yet once more, apparently, in the strange history of human thought, with the placid Buddha, as verified by nineteenth century anæsthetics.

"Although I have a gleam of Kant, I have never turned a page of Hegel — all that I know of him having come to me *obiter*, and obscurely through the talk of others; nor have I ever rigorously delivered myself to dialectics.

"I have never had any revelations through anæsthetics, but a kind of waking trance — this for lack of a better word — I have frequently had, quite up from boyhood, when I have been all alone. This has come upon me through repeating my own name to myself silently, till all at once, as it were out of the intensity of the consciousness of individuality, individuality itself seemed to dissolve and fade away into boundless being, and this not a confused state but the clearest, the surest of the surest, utterly beyond words — where death was an almost laughable impossibility — the loss of personality (if so it were) seeming no extinction, but the only true life.

"I am ashamed of my feeble description. Have I not said the state is utterly beyond words? But in a moment when I come back to my normal condition of 'sanity' I am ready to fight for *'meine liebes ich,'* and to hold that it will last for æons of æons."

On page 158 of Vol. 2, of the "Tennyson Memoirs," is given a previous draft of this letter, found among the laureate's papers. The first paragraph is nearly identical with the first of this; but the latter part runs to an account of Tennyson's only occasion of being subjected to anæsthetic treatment and this for a surgical operation. He wrote: "The friend who held my hand and supplied the handkerchief, told me that first of all" (after he came to) "I blurted out a long metaphysical term which he could not re-word for me."

THE ANÆSTHETIC REVELATION 217

Had Tennyson repeated the experience he would have recalled this expression.

In 1880, Sir William, then Professor, Ramsay, conducted certain experiments upon himself, with anæsthetic agents, chiefly ether, the results of which experience, and others of later date, appeared in the *Journal of the Society for Psychical Research*, of 1893-4.

In opening the topic Prof. Ramsay says (in view of the fact that the various anæsthetics afford various kinds of mental effect upon different persons): "On me all anæsthetics produce the same mental state . . . they all produce the same curious delusion." He had a kind of culture in his process, which in the early stages was oriented by natural preconceptions and habits of thought; but these, ever recurring at first, came gradually to be suppressed and ignored, as he settled into one clear and permanent insight, until at last he ceased to observe them. Of this permanent insight he says: "An overwhelming impression forced itself upon me that the state in which I then was, was *reality;* that now I had reached the true solution of the secret of the universe, in understanding the secret of my own mind; that all outside objects were merely passing reflections on the eternal mirror of my mind — something quite trivial and transitory. The main and impressive fact *for me* was that *I* was self-existent, and that time and space were illusions. This was the real ego, on whose surface ripples of incident arose, to fade and vanish like the waves on a pond. . . . Any remark (of others) wearied me because I had heard it so often before; I conceived a low opinion of the being who could pass his life in saying such a trivial and unimportant thing, and I disdained to answer. . . . I not merely knew that it had happened before, but that I could have predicted that it would happen at that particular moment."

He speaks: "Absurdly self-conscious all through — every little event so signal and important as eternally the item for this particular instant. I swallow — *important* . . . this is a stage in the cycle of the universe (all events led up to *this*). . . . Each time I am under the influence of an anæsthetic I am able to penetrate a little further into the unfathomable mystery. The recognition of past stages does much to render the path familiar." (All this is soliliquy, recorded by his secretary.)

"I do not think that I am a follower of Bishop Berkeley in my ordinary everyday existence; my tendency of mind is by training and by the nature of my daily avocations, to suspend judgment — a condition of scientific skepticism. But under the influence of an anæsthetic all doubts vanish; I *know* the truth of Berkeley's theory of existence — that all fellow creatures are products of my consciousness, and that although they may be real to themselves, and have each a world of his own, to me they are only parts of my thoughts, and moreover not very important elements in the chain of my life.

"But the feelings evoked are *disappointing*. It is not satisfying to realize that the goal of the universe is of this nature. The circumstances are so trivial as to make it painful to believe that *this* is

THE ANÆSTHETIC REVELATION

the scheme of nature; that 'that far off divine event to which the whole creation moves' should have in its progress no higher deeds, and for its outcome no nobler aim than I am then conscious of."

(Observe here how this scientist has then forgotten, in the primordial secret as it is for all, the world of later man's achievements — the wonders of astronomy and politics and religion and art.)

"My feelings are sometimes those of despair at finding the secret of existence so little worthy of regard. It is as if the veil that hides whence we come, what we are, and what will become of us, were suddenly rent, and as if a glimpse of the Absolute burst upon us. The conviction of its truth is overwhelming, but it is painful in the extreme. I have exclaimed — 'Good heavens! is this all?' Such impressions, exceedingly difficult to express in words, pass off gradually. After five minutes they begin to fade in intensity; the conviction of their absolute truth is less deep-seated; that there exists an ordinary workaday world, in which I and innumerable others play our parts, is again realized, and in ten minutes or a quarter of an hour the state of mind is again perfectly normal. There is no after impression, and my nerves are as steady as usual."

(It is to be remembered that these impressions are not *crescent* in anæsthesia as such, but occur as the effect is passing off. In his experiments Prof. Ramsay kept renewing the dose at intervals of from one or two up to fifteen minutes and then reporting.)

Prof. Ramsay furnished in his account certain notes taken by his secretary, giving some of his exclamations at different stages of his anæsthesia, of which I copy a few. Observe that "the universe" is his constant burthen:

"Everything has recurred before — sense of having been here before . . . the table, mantel, etc., having been *always* there. . . . This one little piece of enormous coherence of universe — utterly ridiculous in its smallness. . . . Every bit of these events *recurred;* cycle of events recurring bothers me greatly, because I expect each stage to go further — that is, stage in evolution of the universe. *This* is the scheme of the universe and my being here, but I never before reached the point of having taken ether before. I will stop short and explain (here he was nearly in his normal state of mind): In the ordinary workaday world this is an untenable theory — I mean the sense of 'myself alone' — of what affects me — there is a sense of precisely similar events. I believe, as far as I can comprehend, that this is the universe. Here I have recognized the ultimate scheme (genius?) of the universe as far as I am concerned up to a certain stage. It will probably be worked out when I die. Yet that is not the end — I shall go on after that, but to what?" (Resumes the ether.) "Oh, by Jove! Yes, I know: After all it comes to this: It is one or the other theory of the universe, and mine must be the most probable — mine or somebody else's. Well, I may be the central person in the universe — I don't mind — I can't help it. . . . Have I been unconscious for a considerable time? By Jove! if one only knew the whole thing. This may be the truth; it is my own view, and *deserves* to be known. . . . People choose to imagine that there are

THE ANÆSTHETIC REVELATION 221

worlds — that is to say, build mental cosmogonies. Of course it is an open question, whether other people have existence as well as one's self. By some chance I am picked out for the central purpose of the universe. In this state of mind quarrels and reconciliations, woes and fears, are no longer the chief things of the universe, but one asks, where does it come from? what is it all for — which is the normal, which is the abnormal state of affairs? When I come back to my sane consciousness I hold the ether state to be abnormal, and *vice versa*. Of course this is utterly absurd in ordinary life. Now I am sane again — but under ether there is only me."

Sir William then recalls a work by Sir H. Davy on nitrous oxide, published in 1800, at the end of which is an account of a symposium of twenty-nine persons who took the gas with varying effects, of which he (Sir William) recognized chiefly those upon Sir Humphrey himself. He quotes Davy as follows: "As I recovered my former state of mind I felt an inclination to communicate the discoveries I had made during the experiment. I endeavored to recall the ideas; they were feeble and indistinct. One collection of terms, however, presented itself, and *with the most intense belief and prophetic manner* I exclaimed to Dr. Kinglake, 'Nothing exists but thoughts! The universe (sic) is composed of impressions, ideas, pleasures and pains.'" Sir William adds: "It is curious that this, with Davy, was an isolated occurrence — with me it was a permanent impression." It should be remembered, in this regard, that Sir Humphrey was probably the first to discover this effect of modern anæsthetics.

At the conclusion of his paper Sir William offers the following reflections:

"It is somewhat startling to be confronted with an unexpected condition of one's own mind. The saying '*in vino veritas*' is, I suppose, intended to imply that an intoxicated person will blurt out the truth; but the intoxication of anæsthetics forces me, while in that condition, to believe that what I think is true. The theory attributed to Bishop Berkeley is a perfectly consistent one, and can be disputed only on grounds of what we call 'common sense.' I do not, in my ordinary state of mind, attribute any importance to this theory, beyond regarding it as a somewhat improbable, but incontrovertible speculation; but I confess that, since my experience with anæsthetics, I am disposed to regard it as worthy of a little more consideration than it usually receives. The difficulty in accepting it is our practically absolute certainty of the existence of our fellow creatures; and the deduction that if A and B receive the same impression at the same time, that impression must be caused by some *thing*, external to both. But in my anæsthetic state this objection presents no difficulty to me; I conceive each ego (monad?) to have its orbit, and to stand absolutely alone, conscious of but uninterfered with by the other egos."

(Observe that this is his inference, and not his insight — which was of himself as the only centre.)

"To choose a crude illustration: two mirrors reflect, but do not influence each other in any mechanical or material sense. The recollection, which remains after return to the ordinary state of mind, of *having had* such Berkeleyan views, is, perhaps naturally, not without some influence on the normal mind, and, as I have said, it appears to me not wholly absurd to reconsider the usual postulates of 'common sense.' In short, I am confronted under ether, with what I may term 'recurrent events.' It is necessary to form some theory which will reconcile myself with this new environment; and the idea that the universe centres itself in one appears to me, while in the anæsthetized state, to be a satisfactory one. The fact remains that, while anæsthetized, my belief in that theory of existence which we may call for short the Berkeleyan hypothesis, is *immeasurably more firm and decided* than, in my normal state, is my belief in the ordinarily accepted views of matter and motion which regulate the lives of most human beings."

He finally declares that in giving this account he has been careful to exclude any intimations which might otherwise have lingered in his mind as to experiences of which he had heard or read of others under anæsthetic conditions.

We may remark that Ramsay's disappointment or disillusion is in the fact that the revelation makes so intensely secular, inevitable and homely what he had before regarded as necessarily sacred and imposing and foreign.

The adumbration of Sir William Ramsay on the seeming inconsequence of the anæsthetic revelation — such as his protest, "Is this all?" etc. — recurs emphatically in the following letter addressed to me in May, 1911, from No. 19 Chester Terrace, Regents Park, N. W. London:

"*Dear Sir:* — It is interesting to find that your experiences under anæsthetics have been similar to mine. I fancy that a good many people are thus affected. I have been at least fifty times. But I don't think there is anything 'behind.' Anyhow, I don't intend to study it further, for one gets no further by repetition, and I am sure it is bad for the nerves. "Yours faithfully,

"W. RAMSAY."

This phrase, "anything behind" — doubtless meant to repress any metaphysical expectations from the experience — has for the philosopher a practical significance. There is nothing imminent in it for one whose outlook is expectant of a royal and monistic explanation. If any really great intellectual achievement is to be recorded, I fancy it rather in the Egyptian style, in which England said to Pharaoh, "I will make a man of you":

It was not a duke or earl, nor yet a viscount,
  'Twas not a big brass general who came,
But a man in khaki kit, who could handle men a bit,
  And his baggage labeled, Sergeant What's His Name.

Sir William's depression under the commonplace and secular tone of the world-mystery accords very well with our democratic multiverse, which dispenses with the brazen general Absolute, and the tape-tied Infinite, whose *quasi* prestige is that it is unlimited; but just therefore it has no definition, and consequently it has no practical use. Perhaps our heavenly expectations have been too prodigious to

THE ANÆSTHETIC REVELATION 225

prove either possible or just. Strictly, we have no right to an opinion *about* anything. The moment that anything is *classed*, as "this," or "the," it is emasculated of the subjective element, and for idealism cannot be real.

About ten years after the publication of these experiences of Sir William Ramsay there was held a symposium of persons who had been led by his example to test the anæsthetic vision for themselves, at No. 20 Hanover Square, London, June 24, 1904. The gathering comprised representatives of quite distinguished literary and social eminence, and the current discussion of the topic had the advantage of not only frank and ingenuous expression but of scientific and historical criticism. A considerable number of the associates related their individual experiences, which, however various in seemingly temperamental details, fell generally under the summing-up of Mr. Ernest Dunbar, the lecturer of the evening:

"After the first effects of ether have passed off, there comes a time of profound intellectual stimulation, during which the mind reasons with astonishing rapidity, choosing, in some individuals, transcendental lines, appearing to solve, *once and for all*, the mystery of the universe."

The hundreds of letters that came to me after the distribution of my pamphlet in 1874 gave a feeling or sentiment indited by Emerson, as if "all the books in the world were written by one man." An expert knows the hand. Why do we call a certain class of unsophisticated persons "naturals"? The charge carries nothing against them, either moral or intellectual, often quite the contrary, yet they are — simple. (We need not to dwell upon their psychology.) So when we look at a good portrait, we know there was an original behind it, although we may have never seen the party who sat for it: such an artist could not be so depraved as to have misrepresented his subject. Even so with these letters: they all struggle with an ineluctable purport that shames the best definition. I select one that is rather more "literary" than the average:

"I haven't got what you would call an intellectual memory. Things come to me in flashes out of experience, and pull me up short, and I say to myself, 'Yes, that's it — *that's* it, I understand; I see why it is so, and what it means, and how far it extends. *It is five thousand years old.* Adam thought it after Cain killed Abel — or Abel thought it, just before he died — or Eve learned it from Lilith — or it struck Abraham when he went to sacrifice Isaac. Sometimes things like that hit me deep, here in the desert. I can see just over on the horizon the tents of Moab in the wilderness. I feel that yesterday and to-day are the same; that I have crossed the prairies of the everlasting years, and played with Ishmael in the wild hills, and fought with Ahab; and I feel that time and the world are small affairs. You see how it is: I never was trained to think, and I get stunned by thoughts that strike me as from right out of the centre. Sometimes I'd like to write them down, but I can't write — in fact I can't think. You'll know how it is."

Is not this fine, however tantalized by "*cacœthes*

scribendi"? Here was your poet of the light that fails, of the matter that cannot rise to form. Given the something born but never made — the something that touched Isaiah's hallowed lips with fire — this fellow might have voiced the intelligible forms of ancient poets and the fair humanities of old religion; he too, like the lost Keats, might have stood with Ruth amid the alien corn, or with stout Cortez and his men, silent upon a peak of Darien. He too — why not? might have sniffed the Paestan gardens, where the air is sweet with violets running wild through broken friezes and fallen capitals:

Sweet as when Tully, writing down his thoughts
(Turning to thee, divine Philosophy),
Sailed slowly by, two thousand years ago,
For Athens, when a ship, if northeast winds
Blew from the Paestan Gardens, slacked her course.

The reader shall need to consent to this being of genius, however at last we fail of the genius of being. We have read, of those explorers for the Pole, that he who once enters the Arctic dream can never recur, with his former interest, to the temperate vocations of his race; for evermore the loadstone draws him, and evermore his fancy kindles the opaline splendors of the eternal ice. And it is even so with those who have discarded the sensuous limitation of reality, and realized that a comprehension is unthinkable; there is a *wanderlust* of the monad that is ever tangent from the fabulous One. There is a larger sanity and a surer fixity for the far stars whose orbits know no centre of pluriversal space.

To these experimenters, whose besetting and baffling thought is ever of the "universe," and again the universe, we may say, You are sane, although, so far as explanation is concerned you are using the wrong words. For holding the revelation strictly to the homogeneity of intelligence, and as due to pure thought at its highest tension, the solipsism that puzzled Ramsay and Tennyson and Davy and so many others is scientific sanity at its best. Until one has realized that his present thought is the ultimate triumph of nature — that all history has led up to this — that all the efficiencies of the universe have resulted in this, and pre-eminently in the criticism of this, as the iris reflected from the highest bubble on the last wave of time, he has not been wholly and truly sane.

Your solid Englishman or German appeals to the great world, and deems the Frenchman extravagant when he calls the universe to witness his exploit; but the French spirit is of the three the most highly generalized; its enthusiasm shows no distraction, however averse to the company of less volatile dispositions. It will rather stay at home than emigrate; your Frenchman belongs in France. He has the deepest sense of national solidarity and fatality, inspiring a financial faith beyond that of other nations. His national debt, which no one cares to have paid — and why should it be, if rightly incurred? was, at the beginning of the world war some five hundred million francs more than the debts of England, Germany and the United States combined.

It shall not be surprising, then, if the high tension

THE ANÆSTHETIC REVELATION 229

of the Gallic spirit appreciates certain æsthetic values, among which a blunder might be worse than a crime, and the angels of high heaven, who weep at man's fantastic tricks, should be less grieved at the exceeding sinfulness of sin than they are discomfited by the utter fatuity of foolishness and fudge.

(An American, however, can hardly accept any foreigner as the highest æsthetic result. Our mongrel breed has absorbed and submerged all racial peculiarities. An American actor will imitate the speech of any alien people, but on no foreign stage can be heard any attempt to mimic plain United States. This is what Walt called "the tasteless water of souls.")

The following letter, characteristic of a large class, was sent to me through the kindness of Prof. Hodgson (45 Conduit St. Regent Street, London, January 18, 1883), he having furnished the writer (Edmund Gurney, 26 Montpelier Square, London, S. W.,) a copy of my essay:

"I had this extraordinary experience myself last year, under nitrous oxide, harmonizing with your description; but the result was almost ludicrously disappointing. For half a minute or more after I had 'come to,' I was quite sure that the problem was solved and that when I got my breath I could tell the dentist about it, and that it had something to do with time. When I got my breath I found that I could not get it out, then and there; but walking home I meditated an article about it in a philosophical journal. Somehow this conception dwindled in the course of the evening, and my plan reduced itself to a letter to William James, which, however, would (I felt sure) teem with interest; but when, after a few days, I sat about the writing of the letter, there was no more to tell than I have told you."

Many patients who have recovered from near drowning have reported wonderful reminiscences of their past lives. Probably the pressure of an unusual volume of blood distends the wrinkled and faded palimpsests of the brain, and freshens the field of memory under anxious introspection. And doubtless the exhilaration, of which anæsthesia seems to be or to follow an excess, is still vivifying the mentation of the patient while he is "coming to." Nor is it surprising that one under high stimulation should be lured to the more poetical regions of his own culture, which for us are apt to be in the historical and sacred past, and to savor of the problems of philosophy.

Dr. Holmes, "The Autocrat of the Breakfast Table," etc., although sharing that contempt for human nature and its manifestations which characterises the medical profession — whose patrons are mostly lying on their backs — was yet thoroughly loyal to the ether revelation as a unique concernment with the universe as the Mystery and the Whole, or as he oftenest said, with Being. I quote a reminiscence of his conversation with Moncure D. Conway, a literary cosmopolite:

"He told me that when ether was discovered he had such reverence for it that he thought it might possess some spiritual virtue, and resolved to experiment on himself to find if it had any psychological

THE ANÆSTHETIC REVELATION

effect. He prepared the ether, and having placed beside his bed a small table, with pencil and paper to record his impressions on awakening, he lay down and applied the drug. Sure enough, he presently found himself just sufficiently conscious to seize the pencil, and with a sentiment of vast thought wrote something down. It proved to be these words: 'A strong scent of turpentine pervades the WHOLE.'

"But he was not satisfied with that, and made another effort. 'This time,' he said, 'I felt as I wrote that I really had seen the secret of the universe. The *words* proved to be, 'Put Jesus Christ into a Brahma press and that's what you will get.'"

I need hardly remind the serious reader that there was a humorous quirk in the fibre of Dr. Holmes, that was sometimes prejudicial to his really fine genius. As more to our purpose, and in justice to him, I will recall in poor prose a poem of his, entitled "The Parson's Mare":

"She was a shambling nag, of unknown antecedents, that had come to the old clergyman in the way of a 'donation,' and at the county fair the neighboring boys, for a lark, had brought her, hitched to the parson's dilapidated sulky, as an entry on the race track, a burlesque to the more pretentious contestants. The managers humorously gave her a place and a start with the rest. . . . But suddenly there was a surprise; the nondescript was forging to the front, and actually setting the pace. The experts were dumbfounded at her. What, in the name of all professionalism, possessed her? Could they but have looked within, and caught her inspiration, the atavism of a long-forgotten record was relighting the vestiges of a great career; it was a palingenesis out of the past. Sometime, somewhere — maybe when the Assyrian came down like a wolf on the fold — maybe when the warhorse laughed at the shaking of the spear — maybe while the dames of Rome their gilded hair waved to the wind — she had romped the stadium through victorious cheers! — She left them all behind. The confusion was such that her time was not taken (a shrewd omission on the part of the story teller), and having exhaled her inspiration she was led halting back to her stall."

There is an unpublished supplement to the story, in which it appears that the ill-requited pastor had an authentic record of his shabby assistant, that he had trailed her marauders, and had observed the denouement through a crack in the fence.

Had my issue, in 1874, of "The Anæsthetic Revelation and the Gist of Philosophy" brought no other responses than such as I have quoted here, I should have despaired of the audience on which the fate of the present essay may depend. There are plenty of people who have learned the impossibility of the old-fashioned "truth" — the false pretense of a genuine re-presentation of fact — and have characterized this as "a queer world" — which helps its psychology about as much as does the reminiscence of one who has overeaten of mince pie for supper, and had "a glimpse of his grandmother." But there are well-practiced experts in the mechanism of thought who have clearly realized in this experience the impasse which halts the logical conception of self-knowledge.

Among the cleverest of these I recall Xenas Clark,

THE ANÆSTHETIC REVELATION 233

a young philosopher of Amherst, who died in the '80's, much regretted. In connection with the anæsthetic revelation he is quoted by James, in "The Varieties of Religious Experience," as follows:

"It is the one sole and sufficient insight why (or not why, but how) the present is pushed on by the past, and sucked forward by the vacuity of the future. Its inevitableness defeats all attempts at stopping or accounting for it. It is all precedence and presupposition, and questioning is in regard to it forever too late. It is an *initiation of the past*. The real secret would be the formula by which the 'now' keeps exfoliating out of itself, yet never escapes. What is it, indeed, that keeps existence exfoliating? The formal being of anything, the logical definition of it, is static. For mere logic every question contains its own answer — we simply fill the hole with the dirt we dug out. Why are twice two four? Because, in fact, four is twice two. Thus logic finds in life no propulsion, only a momentum. It goes because it is a-going. But the revelation adds: it goes because it is and *was* a-going. You walk, as it were, round yourself in the revelation. Ordinary philosophy is like a hound hunting his own trail. The more he hunts the farther he has to go, and his nose never catches up with his heels, because it is forever ahead of them. So the present is already a foregone conclusion, and I am ever too late to understand it. But at the moment of recovery from anæsthesis, just then, *before starting on life*, I catch, so to speak, a glimpse of my heels, a glimpse of the eternal process just in the act of starting. The truth is that we travel on a journey that was accomplished before we set out; and the real end of philosophy is accomplished, not when we arrive at, but when we remain in, our destination (being already there) — which may occur vicariously in this life when we cease our intellectual questioning. That is why there is a smile upon the face of the revelation, as we view it. It tells us that we are forever half a second too late — that's all. 'You could kiss your own lips, and have all the fun to yourself,' it says, 'if you only knew the trick. It would be perfectly easy if they would just stay there till you got round to them.'

"The Anæsthetic Revelation is the Initiation of Man into the Immemorial Mystery of the Open Secret of Being, revealed as the Inevitable Vortex of Continuity. Inevitable is the word. Its motive is inherent — it is what has to be. It is not for any love or hate, nor for joy nor sorrow, nor good nor ill. End, beginning, or purpose, it knows not of.

"It affords no particular of the multiplicity and variety of things; but it fills appreciation of the historical and the sacred with a secular and intimately personal illumination of the nature and motive of existence, which then seems reminiscent — as if it should have appeared, or shall yet appear, to every participant thereof.

"Although it is at first startling in its solemnity, it becomes directly such a matter of course — so old-fashioned, and so akin to proverbs, that it inspires exultation rather than fear, and a sense of safety, as identified with the aborginal and the universal. But no words may express the imposing certainty of the patient that he is realizing the primordial, Adamic surprise of Life.

"Repetition of the experience finds it ever the same, and as if it could not possibly be otherwise. The subject resumes his normal consciousness only to partially and fitfully remember its occurrence, and to try to formulate its baffling import, with only this consolatory afterthought: that he has known the oldest truth, and that he has done with human theories as to the origin, meaning, or destiny of the race. He is beyond instruction in 'spiritual things.'"

If one had casually asked in an esoteric circle (possibly antedating the incident), "What is the anæsthetic revelation?" this rather ambitious version of Clark would "stand him off," at least for the moment, as the right psychology of the experience, with little or no claim to any philosophy of it. As for that, so much depends upon one's viewpoint. I have just now brushed a wandering gnat from my manuscript, smearing the paper, and summarily effacing an ephemeral existence. This little citizen was one of us; yet the Congress will proceed with its enactments; the world war will not be ostensibly affected by its fate. And in a certain large sense it is not "considering too curiously" (as Horatio protested) to adjust our own parasitic humility by the gnat's unimportance — providing that we do not erase its cosmic significance. For although we and our monuments and our memory are doomed to thus sink out of the sensuous reality of the everywhere-as-here (at which event no autocratic One shall make light of our poor individuality), the fact may remain that *all* centres are identical (though not coincident) in this illumination, having each a significant importance and a dignity that gets no shadow from the fabulous and impossible Whole: nay, rather takes on a dynamic originality (if such may be) wherein the monad may strike heroically about him, for good or ill, assuming fearlessly that "the throne and equipage of God's almightiness" have no deeper nor other realization than his own — that the pluriverse is of many, and that he is at least one, and as good an authority as are innumerable ones.

It was as aiming to reach this position that I arraigned the inconsequence of philosophy, having long observed its failure of any ultimate generalization or comprehension. And although neither have I achieved in thought any masterful conception of the dream which we inhabit, I feel that by eliminating the needless task of impossible comprehension and beginning, and more determinately orienting inward the path of explanation, I have brought to bear upon this anæsthetic expression a criticism of philosophy as the soul's endeavor to envisage itself, and to adjust itself to an environment which, however to be admonished of a due humility, this insight cannot forego.

Not that I am expecting from this orientation of thought more determinately inward — as in fact it is modernly disposed — any clearer solution of the classic problems of philosophy. The microscope and the telescope alike fail of finality or ultimate limitation; the Midst is everywhere. Although the Many evaporate and disenchant the mystical One, as an outwardly objective expectation, still the infinitesimal route is as well bottomless as "the infinite" is indefinite. These are all scientific facts; and it were an idle and impudent esoteric pretension that the anæsthetic insight affords a clearance of them. If it were a revelation in that sense the reader might fairly demand what it is, while the proponent is merely trying to indicate where it is to be encountered. There is no pretense in our treatise of philosophising either this or anything else.

That there might have been a world of dead fact is a supposition comparatively easy to us; but when we add to the fact a knowledge of it, and are driven by idealism and solipsis to assume that the knowledge, so far as we are concerned, determines the nature of the fact, there results a convolution and confusion which a modest citizen may confess himself to not quite understand. But that these conditions culminate abnormally in the anæsthetic experience (still possibly as mere sanity at its best) only a negligible bigotry should hereafter deny.

It was said of old, "the fear of the Lord is the beginning of wisdom." I shall not further arraign the translations of the Vulgate; suffice it that in the most critical usage the word "fear," above, means a reverent cognition, which can only by implication carry a punitive inference. But surely, however the heart of the monad may be coincident with the only possible centre, and send its pulses through the pose of Ajax (who in our day would need only a rubber suit for his defiance of the lightning), we must perceive that as a transient visitor his rôle is one of humility, as in so large a sense ancillary and dependent. He has ample ground for reverence; and though he may conclude that no personal one is comprehensively all-important or controlling in the multiverse — and that all notions of beginning and cause are but shadows cast by the rims of his finite binoculars — it is a transcendent necessity of spirit to declare and wonder at THIS, and to regard it as so far One, and a wonder or miracle into which his entrance is attended by a sense of initiation as strong and definite as if some "all obliterated tongue" had warned him, in the voice of a common fate, Now You Know!

Doubtless there is a Mystery, but it must not stigmatize reality; the mystery is on our side of the fact. Despite Schwegler's "certain existent unreason," it were the height of presumption on our part to proclaim the ultimate surd. The factual world needs no such accounting for, *in itself*, as we need for it. We are late, we are ephemeral, and mainly inconsequent; yet the fact that the mystery is in our own incompetence only lends dignity and charm to its revelation, and to our initiation into a prestige supremely worth while. Even though by great progress we should come to a stage where this insight would be normal — and why not, since even now, if we cared, we could wire the round earth, and whisper into our own ears? — yet let it become commonplace, scientific, secular where now it is comparatively sacred, still in the culture of the newcomer it must ever be what Clark characterized as "an initiation of the past."

The revelation, for us, is of sanity at its utmost tension and interest, realizing at once the effort and the fatuous incongruity and impossibility of self-vision, and having a clear and unquestionable consciousness that this condition and this effort realize the genius of being, and effect the process of time; but above all is a sense of admonition — perhaps an after-glow from our religious associations — that this is the secret of the world, inevitably such; no other account of it can be mentionable in the same connection.

I have to reiterate that this clear vision has nothing to do with philosophy. It stands alone, "like Adam's recollection of his fall." What we intend by "the genius of being" has no relation to the empirical facts of the world, nor to any purpose or process of "life." The problems of metaphysics — the reconciliation of the static and dynamic viewpoints, the question as between a sufficient and managing intelligence and a fated collocation of monads and atoms, or as between a comprehended one or whole and an unlimited diversity of ones which carry the prime secret each at its own centre — all this is as nothing in the transcendent solipsis where the Monad is the only One. The rest are the things which are Cæsar's.

We have now to gather up the dangling threads of our story, and knot them for a religion and a life; — hoping that the fasces may have a consistency and strength which may not have been apprehensible in the individual shafts; and that the fond monism that we have dialectically disparaged may be at least transcendentally and mystically rehabilitated. Our essay would be wholly impertinent (as possibly it is in any event) if it did not so far countenance the professorial obsession as to regard the world as *this*, and this *one*, at least as a topic for discourse — such discourse, maybe, as Emerson satirised as "puss and her tail."

The pretensions of professional philosophy have been heartlessly disingenuous. Even with Fichte, they were oriented less toward a livable faith than to a triumphant demonstration of the ignorance in which faith habitually reposes. Your even Christian does but dream of the contradictions involved in what he calls "the truth."

Firstly then, our philosophical curiosity arises as to the world's beginning and its making; for we ourselves begin, and we do some making, and we naturally assume that the world at large should have such an accounting for — all the time forgetting that any objective thing accounting for it would have the same mystery as involves the thing itself, and serve to merely postpone or push back its "reason" — which must be in us if anywhere, and not otherwise required; *i. e.*, the secret of a creation can be realized only in our own actually creating; to see the fact as being done were not to detect the motive force employed. Wherefore the saying, "the reason of things is reason."

Here the vulgar psychology comes in, and claims the whole secret of so simple an effect as the reason of reason, in the self-relation of consciousness — the "prime fact" that such is knowledge that it knows itself, and is its own ground and reason — showing the basic principle of all explanation and all being. But we have sufficiently shown that self-relation as a theory is not a philosophy or a logical account of our inspired thought and will.

Nevertheless all our advices from the anæsthetic field — and especially such as that of Xenas Clark — show that sanity at its highest tension (and interest) not only inheres in but evolves by a curiosity and effort for self-knowledge, never dreaming that it is but an orifice of the supernal deep — a mouthpiece or mask, to be sure, but the supernal has no other voice; the monad is your only one; for no man hath seen God at any time, save as the Son hath personated him.

(We should connote here the solipsism of Ramsay and Tennyson; for the world is full of worlds, as many as there are organisms; and to whom a thing appears, that thing is.)

But now, for a life, we turn back from philosophy, as from the green-eyed jealousy which makes the meat that it feeds upon, to the psychology of Jesus. Dropping all theological controversy as such, and listening only to the voice of experience and common sense, is it not pragmatically true that every creature is secondary and inspired, regardless of his instant conceit of originality — and yet more profoundly regardless of the mystery that in that conceit may lurk the only hope of ultimate and divine explanation?

Said Hegel: "It is truer to say not that we think, but that thinking goes on with us."

Every breath that we voluntarily draw is, in the cosmic sense, an irrelevant interference with divine providence. We have no need to *do* it; with or without our volition it will be done; and the determination *not* to do it — which would be in the least violent method of suicide — is one that nature most essentially abhors. We have no account of any man succeeding in such an attempt, although many have thus experimented.

Have we not here, in this insistence of nature, the occult basis of that admonition of the Master, to take no thought for the morrow, nor for what we shall eat or drink, nor for wherewithal we shall be clothed? How shall a man's sins of the past be remitted in the divine assumption of their responsibility; unless it shall be equally true of the present that our heart-strings are in divine hands, and that our native impulses are entitled to the second-thought of God with us?

But this taking no thought for the morrow, and the rendering unto Cæsar of the things which are Cæsar's, require transcendental interpretation. Of course one shall take thought, lest he starve, or walk into the fire. These things will be according to intention, and faith without works is dead; but to intend them in the expectation of impunity were to "tempt the Lord, thy God." But there should be obvious here the possibility of a serene composure, as of a double nature, at once active and passive, that should advance with a lofty courage, subject only to the categorical imperative of its better self, as interpreting all the divinity that concerns it.

What is hardest to express, or to believe that one has expressed, in this connection, is the unique fact which I have again and again reiterated, that it is a *revelation* — *the* revelation of the genius of being. When this in its turn is made a topic for criticism and gossip, and the assured and busied commonsense retorts that one knows as much as

THE ANÆSTHETIC REVELATION

another about that; or when the metaphysical expert recalls the dialectic difficulties of knowledge trying to know itself, or of a becoming that continues with only becoming for its result, or of a *quasi*-reality between a future and a past — then the inveterate skeptic must have his fling: These puzzles, which philosophy has mumbled over for thousands of years, are in your tenser ideation only more emphatically intricated — *i. e.* you are more aghast at the Mystery which still baffles definition — else why not define it? There needs no ghost come from the grave to proclaim the Mystery; any pretense of a revelation should rationalize and resolve it. In brief, wherein are you didactically the wiser for it, as an instant generalization of the classic problems of philosophy?

Now, humbly begging pardon, philosophy has had heretofore no such generalization as is here so superiorly announced. I would respectfully recall the animadversion of William James, that there is no complete generalization, whether in theory or in fact, *for us;* I have but added my own conclusion that there can be none such for any one. (The notion of a finite God, if not utterly preposterous, is incongruous at its best.)

As Dr. Johnson remarked to the aspiring youth who sought his advice as to the best dictionary, "either of them is good enough for you," so this treatise, which, eliminating monism, comprehension and self-relation, should clear the haze of what has been called philosophy, may well prove, if not a revelation, at least a clarification to the average student, especially if his culture has utilized the regretful sentence of Herr Eucken that philosophy as a pursuit has failed.

But all this pseudo disparagement or deprecation and *quasi*-explanation of the classic Mystery drifts idly over the weird and solemn consciousness — "clearest of the clearest, surest of the surest, weirdest of the weirdest" — of an intimate and personal relation to the Inevitable, whose continuance is in and through its wondrous appreciation of its own precedence and consequent necessity.

I have tried often, but cannot come nearer to the Anæsthetic Revelation. But what then? It is no fad or bantling of mine. On the contrary, as Sir William Ramsay noticed, many people have encountered it, and like Edmund Gurney have passed it as unthinkable in set terms — without which we can neither know nor remember. But the boasted progress of the race will be shamelessly inadequate if we have come to a time when the historical secret which philosophy has coveted is empirically accessible, only to be inconsequently neglected.

After this, our best (however unsatisfactory) pronouncement, the persistent reiteration, "What is your revelation?" or, "What is it about?" is in bad form — a kind of counting of the spoons. Knowing is the soul's all, whether in her birth, her bridal, her business or her vacation. Man fell for knowledge. Knowing is the excellence and the ecstasy of being; *it is everything, to be* — a constant gratulation over what is not, or is potentially or conjecturally. It is investiture in the purple, in the divine right, and it is sufficient in itself.

And now inexorable Time admonishes me to have

done with this world. I am thankful at having seen the show; and although, after eighty-five years, the stars are flickering slightly, and the winds are something worn, I am still clear and confident in that religion of courage and content which cherishes neither regrets nor anticipations.

Yet one little dream I would have come true: Somewhere, anywhere, though hopefully at some not-unfrequented garden-side, my dust, with its "all-obliterated tongue," should seem to inspire the legend — low by the veiling grass, but cut deep into enduring stone:

GREETING — IF THOU HAST KNOWN!

SUPPLEMENTARY ESSAY,

THE POETICAL ALPHABET

A JURY of common-sense men might well be excused for a verdict, over their book oaths, that there is no important sense in what follows here; but the same jury, asked if they had ever heard
> *The horns of elfland faintly blowing,*

would probably make some haste in the protestation that they never had. Common-sense men as such are not philosophers, and they are not concerned with the fact that logical truth is held to the arbitrament of language, the production and determination of which are therefore of prime importance in philosophical explanation.

It was on a June morning in 1854 that I entered the publishing house of James Munroe and Company of Boston (and Cambridge) with a manuscript which soon evoked a discussion as to why the word *icicle* was not a fit name for a tub. That it is not was promptly agreed, but its unfitness grew into so many varieties of discrepancy which no single principle would account for that the seeming levity of the question sank under considerations of philogical interest and importance.

THE POETICAL ALPHABET

Something in the natural sound of the spoken words was the first relevant suggestion; when you set down a tub it responds to that name. The shapes of the two things are also responsive: the tub is short and stubby, while the icicle is spindling and slim.

These points were very well taken — *i. e.*, the differences of sound and form; but numberless other characteristics appeared. The icicle is delicate, it is clear, brilliant, fragile, with at least a suspicion of moisture, while the tub is merely fibrous and dry. All this goes without saying, in a certain æsthetic appreciation, which does not yet generalize the genius which vulgarizes the tub. To illustrate this, consider the use of the words *entrails, reins, bowels* — all good in scientific and social discourse, but for some unmentionable reason classic culture draws the line at *guts!*

"Well, what is the trouble with guts?"

I expounded here that they were vulgarized by the absurd genius of u flat. And did a letter have a genius? and would I refer to my manuscript and oblige with the genius of *u* flat? I responded as follows, to wit:

"*U*, guttural, or flat, is a humorous savage, best described in his own words: a huge, lubberly, blundering dunderhead, a blubbering numskull and a dunce, ugly, sullen, dull, clumsy, rugged, gullible, glum, dumpish, lugubrious — a stumbler, mumbler, bungler, grumbler, jumbler — a grunter, thumper, tumbler, stunner — a drudge, a trudge; he lugs, tugs, sucks, juggles, and is up to all manner of bulls — a musty, fussy, crusty, disgusting brute, whose head is his mug, his nose is a snub, or a pug, his ears are lugs, his breasts dugs, his bowels guts, his victuals grub, his garments duds, his hat a plug, his child a cub, his dearest diminutive is chub or bub or runt; at his best he is bluff, gruff, blunt; 'his doublet is of sturdy buff and though not sword, is 'cudgel proof'; budge he will not, but will drub you with a club, or a slug, nub, stub, butt, or rub you with mud — for he is ever in a muss or a fuss — and should you call him a grudging curmudgeon he gulps up "ugh, fudge, stuff, rubbish, humbug" in high dudgeon; he is a rough, a blood-tub, a bummer, and a "tough cuss" all around; he has some humor, more crudity, but no delicacy; of all nationalities you would take him for a Dutchman."

It is rather remarkable, in so far as the muscular effort of utterance might be relevant, that the continuous or long *u* serves for the very opposite effect, as we see it in the *true*, the *pure*, the *sure*, the *beautiful*, the *gude*. "True blue" is a proverb of the highest worth.

As for the Dutchman above, it may be recalled that formerly we had a religious association called the Dutch Reformed Church. For a long and struggling time its sturdy independence clung stoutly to the name Dutch, but with assured prosperity came a more amenable style, and the Dutch prefix was omitted from what is now called the Reformed Church.

Yet it was not wholly the *u* flat in Dutch that disqualified it for devotional suggestion, but the *tch* was exceptionable: *itch, bitch, pitch,* all defile; but when the bard of natural history congratulates himself that

THE POETICAL ALPHABET

The gray bitch holds to the death,

we realize a manly poetry which the tea-table would resent.

All the reading of my serious years has been attended by this side consideration: that each of the sounds represented by the several letters of the alphabet is specially effective in conveying a certain significance; and wherever language is popular and happy it is so in accordance with these early intuitions. That I was not singular in this sensitiveness I was assured by hints dropped by Swedenborg and the poet Burns; but I had not as yet chanced upon the "Kratylus" of Plato when I anonymously issued a characterization of the meanings of all the alphabetic sounds. The subject of that essay came up to me again, some years afterward, on the occasion of Mr. Stephen Pearl Andrews's issuing his theory in the *Continental Magazine*. Seeing his article therein, I sent him my essay, and received in return his cordial astonishment at the fact that I, an unread tyro, had come by nature or instinct upon mainly the same results which he claimed to have deduced as scientific necessities. He said his next article in the *Continental* should include the gist of my essay; but, sadly enough, the magazine had come to its final end. In 1868 I made some extracts from my essay for *Putnam's Magazine*, and that periodical also soon after went under in the current of literature. In all this time I knew nothing of the "Kratylus," and I do not know even now whether Mr. Andrews was better informed than myself. These statements are to be considered — and, fortunately, it is the custom of gentlemen to believe one another — otherwise what follows might seem at best only a lesson improved; but when it truly appears that as a youth of inconsiderable reading I in English unknowingly concurred with Plato in Greek, in the interpretation of the sounds of a half dozen of the letters, the fact has philological value as an unprejudiced approval of Plato's observation. For my own part I can cheerfully forego the originality for the comfort of the coincidence. There is good assurance that Plato did not borrow from my list, in the fact that in any case he left several of the more significant letters behind him; and even those meanings which he did express seem to have only a brawny immediacy which would be useless in the far and fine suggestions of modern poetical art.

The use of words of mere onomatopy — buzz, hiss, wheeze, sneeze, splash, slush, hum, roar, jingle — requires little or no skill; but the meagre and savage art which produced these imitations was precursory and prophetic of a later and more delicate and more complex suggestiveness, reaching beyond mere sounds to the faintest modes and qualities of fibre, surface, lustre, distance, motion, humor, solemnity, contempt — characters won out of all the phenomena of life, and answering to the fullest knowledge, or intuition, or inspiration, of all the mental phenomena of the world at the moment of its use — to the true estimate of the comparative age and æsthetic value of thought and things — in brief, to the universality of experience. The essence we would precipitate rises as an aroma out of the process of the growth and

THE POETICAL ALPHABET 251

decay of all things, and it is effected by considerations the faintest and most remote, in the attenuations of which a great poet may transcend the apprehension of his less devoted readers.

I give here my alphabet as at first printed, with a few merely abstract sketches taken from my quite elaborate essay — little known and long forgotten. The reader shall judge whether or not it deserved its fate.

MAN'S NATURAL ALPHABET

ā: vastness, space, plane.
ă: flatness.
b: brawn, bulk, initial force.
c: soft, as s; hard, as k.
ch, tch: a disgusting consistency.
d: (initial) determination, violence.
d: (final) solidity, end.
e: convergence, intensity, concentration.
h:
t: } ethereality, fineness of fibre.

g: (hard) hardness.
gl: hardness and polish.
gr: hardness and roughness, grit, grain.
ī: thinness, slimness, fineness.
ĭ: inclining directions.
k: fineness of light and sound.
l: polish, chill, liquidity.
m: monotony.
n: negation, contempt.
o: volume, solemnity, nobility.
p: volume without fibre, pulp.
q: queer, questionable.
r: roughness, vibration.
s: moisture.
sh: wet confusion.
u: crudity, absurdity.
v, w, y: vehemence, general emphasis.
z: haze, dry confusion.

Diphthongs:

au: vaulting, curving upward.
ou: roundness, downward.
oi: coil — external
ei: coil — internal.
ia: downward and away — flourish.

As the compositor locates his types before him in his case for his own convenience rather than as following the conventional order of the alphabet, so we must treat firstly the five vowels, on which all the other letters expend their force.

ā. — "Far, far away, over the calm and mantling wave" — so begins the boy's first romance — the poetry of the ocean, of vastness, space, plane. The word *ocean,* is used only for rolling and dashing effects; the *wave, the main, vast waters, watery waste, or plain,* are the poetical synonyms of ocean. *Lake, vale, straight, chase, race, trail, trace, away,* give distance and plane. Near at hand, long *a* gives effect to *slate, scale, flake, plate, cake,* etc. *Waver, shake, quake,* show horizontal vibration.

ă. — The flat *a* shows its effect in *mat, pack, strap, slap, platter, flap, pat, flat, clap,* etc.; *dash, splash, thrash,* give flat and lowdown effects. A stone much broken, yet retaining its bulk, is said to be *crushed,* but if its form is borne down it is *mashed, smashed,* etc. Burns, in his poem, "The Vowels," calls *a* "a grave, broad, solemn wight"; this character belongs to *a* only as in *ah,* or *o* flat.

e. — Swedenborg said that the angels who love most use much the sound of *o,* while the more intellectual and penetrating use more the sound of *e.* Burns's notion of *e* was that of intense grief, as in

THE POETICAL ALPHABET 253

"*greeting*" (that is, in Scotch, weeping). The general use of *e* is for concentration and convergence, or intensity, the bringing of thought to a focus. All the pet names and endearing diminutives end in *e* — the *wee* things — the *lee-tle*, *tee-ny* things. The child dwells on the *e* in *pe'-ep*, or *pe'-ek*, and in *me'-an*, *ke'-an*, *sne'-aking*, etc. Not so the baby when he gives you his rattle-box; he opens his mouth and his heart with the instinct of the dative case, and says "tah!" — outward and away. So when he gets the wrong thing in his mouth his mother cries "*Ka!* spit it out"; whence possibly, the Greek *kakos* — bad, as applied to things. The introspective Hamlet says, "making night hideous and *we* fools of nature," instead of *us*, the objective case. *Zeal, squeal, screech* — to *be*, to *see*, to *feel*, are strong by the use of *e*.

ĭ — I, short, as in *pin*, has a *stiff, prim, thin, slim, spindling effect*, as of the "bristling pines"; or when "Swift Camilla" "skims along the main." It has a thinning, perpendicularly attenuating effect. A "light skiff" is well mentioned; and a "thin whiff."

O hark, O hear, how thin and clear!

Short *i* has a very lightening effect in sounds: as in *tinkle, clink, link* — thin metallic sounds of a perpendicular vibration. But flat, or horizontal vibration uses ă, as in *clank* — as of a sheet of zinc slapping the floor; how different from the *clang* of a bar of steel! *Tin* is a good word for that metal in the thin shape most commonly known; but in the native bulk and volume we call it *block*.

ī — Long *i* gives inclination. "The clouds *consign* their treasures to the field." "In winter when the dismal rain comes down in slanting *lines.*" *l* long and *a* give a poetical curve, downward and away:

"Once in the flight of ages past."
"Many an hour I've whiled away."
"Swilled by the wild and wasteful ocean."
"Some happier island in the watery waste."
"O when shall it dawn on the night of the grave?"
*"Athens, and Tyre, and Balbec, and the waste
  Where stood Jerusalem."*
"O, wild enchanting horn."

o. — Plato seems to have done miserable injustice in characterizing for simple roundness the vowel *o* — the noblest Roman, or Greek either, of them all. Roundness is well enough — although roundness proper is represented by *ou* diphthong — but roundness is merely the key to *volume, solemnity, nobility,* and *wonder.* Read this most solemn sentence in all literature, and see at once the more serious meaning of *o:*

*For man goeth to his long home, and the mourners
  go about the streets.*

Not all the trappings and the suits of woe can so pall the sunlight in the homes of men as does the fit reading of this sombre verse. Burns's idea of *o* was expressed in "the wailing minstrel of despairing woe." Swedenborg's insight was rather one of adoration or devotion. But these comparatively incidental expressions give way before the philological art of more modern writers. All things *noble, holy, adorable,* or *sombre, slow, sober, dolorous,*

THE POETICAL ALPHABET 255

mournful, devotional, or *old, lone, sole, glorious,* or even *bold, portly, pompous,* find their best expression in the *o* sound. *Jehovah, Jove, Lord God,* exalt the soul. *O, ho, lo,* are exclamations which nations use with little variance.

> "*O Rome, my country, city of the soul,*
> *The orphans of the heart must turn to thee.*"
> "*O sad Nomore, O sweet Nomore.*"
> "*Roll on, thou deep and dark-blue ocean, roll.*"
> "*Their shots along the deep slowly boom.*"
> "*The lowing herds wind slowly o'er the lea,*
> *The plowman homeward plods his weary way.*"

Most people think of a *boulder* as a big, bulky stone; the dictionaries use the word for a *class* of stones of which one need not be greater than a pea. The *o* gives the volume, and the initial *b* gives the bulk and brawn — which make a favorite dictionary so popular as the "*unaBridged.*" Yet in *pebble,* which is one third made up of *b,* we get no bulk at all, owing to *e* and *p.*

u. — Burns had some notion of the effect of *u*; he speaks of it as "grim, deformed, with horrors entering"; but obviously this was only a careless glance of that great genius, who probably had never thought of the character before, and who possibly never thought of it again. But we have had enough of *u.*

Of the diphthongs, *au* seems to me effective in *vault* (to leap or swing), *flaunt, toss* (taus), *saunter, jaunt, haughty, walk, halting,* and the like. *Ou* is the curve of *roundness,* as in *bough, bow down, crown, around, mound, bound* (tied around).

"Down the shouldering billows borne." *Oi* strikes me forcibly in *coil*. *Iou* is a favorite curve with the poets.

> *"And false the light on glory's plume."*
> *"The wide old wood resounded to her song."*
> *"Of love's, and night's, and ocean's solitude."*

But the vowels are weak and delicate when compared with the consonants, which give to language its fibre and its nerve.

b. — As a special intensity, *b* represents the disposition to swell out the cheeks and utter an exaggerating and sometimes contemptuous explosion, such as *boo! bah! bosh! bully! bravo!* etc. *B* gives volume in a crude and semi-humorous mode. Thus *brawny, brusque, blunt, burly, bulky, big, bully, brazen,* besides carrying a certain direct and proper meaning, reject all refinement in favor of a humorous *brag, burlesque,* and exaggeration of the *Brobdignagian,* "unabridged" order. It is especially strong in connection with *u* short — a regular *"buster,"* a *"big bug,"* bugbear, Bluebeard, and bugaboo — a bombastic, brazen buck and blower.

c. — This letter is only *s* and *k* as convertible, and has little individuality; that little is a kind of slipperiness; *ch* and *tch* are used for absurdity as bordering on disgust. This in *itch, bitch, botch, kutch, scotch* (to haggle or wound), *smutch, smirch, screech,* etc., a class of words avoided by refined society, because their humor is offensive.

d. — Plato used *d* and *t* alike for determination or binding at an end. We see the effect of *d* immediately in *wad, sod, clod, load, rugged, leaden, dead.*

THE POETICAL ALPHABET 257

The short report of a heavily loaded pistol is well caught in the word *explode.*

> "*Earth's cities had no sound nor tread,
> And ships were drifting with the dead
> To shores where all was dumb.*"

As initial, or beginning a word, *d* shows a resolved or violent disposition, as if the teeth were set: thus in *damn, dare, do, dig, drive, dogged,* etc. The metal *lead* is well named; so are iron, tin, and silver. What little effect *t* has, as apart from *h*, is certainly similar to that of *d*, as Plato averred.

f, h, t, and *th.* — These are the ethereal, softening letters, whose fibre is the most fine and attenuated, as of breath without resonance. Thus in *smooth, soothe, breathe, feathery, Lethean, muffled, smothered, far, faint, forgetful, Sabbath, suffocate, froth, stuff, muff, whiff,* etc.

> "*The effusive South*
> Warms *the wide air, and o'er the vault of heaven*
> Breathes *the big clouds, with vernal showers distent.*
> At first a dusky *wreath they seem to rise,*
> Scarce staining *ether.*"

> "*Lethe, the river of oblivion, rolls
> Her watery labyrinth.*"

g, l, and *r.* — These are the giant consonants, expressive of unquestionable and unequivocal power. There is no humor, chaff, or nonsense about them, and "baby talk" excludes them. Each has a distinct force, which yet is most effective in union with one of the others. *G* is the hard letter, *r* is the rough and vibratory letter, and *l* is the chilling and polishing letter. Thus *gr* gives the hard roughness to *grit, grate, grind, grained, gravel, grim, grudge, growl, groan, grunt,* etc., while *gl* is effective in *glass, glary, glide,* etc. *R* by itself is strong in *bur, mar, blur, scar, rude, roar, rush, writhe, scour, crisp, fry, fritter, fragment, broken, gnarled, burly, torrent,* etc., etc.

"*The hoarse, rough verse should like the torrent roar.*"
"*The wrinkled sea beneath him crawls.*"

"The crisped brooks," says Milton, and a hundred poets after him.

Though the ocean's inmost heart be pure,
Yet the salt fringe that daily licks the shore
Is gross *with sand.*

Foreknowing that *s* is the wet or moist letter, note how the brackish wash, the grit of the sand in the brine, is rendered in the word *gross* above. Tennyson, also, has a quick expression of this briny wash, where the sail-boat is said to "cut the shrill salt," etc. But how dry and deep-carved is the figure following, of a sleeping poet:

Dropt in my path like a great cup of gold,
All rich and rough with stories of the gods.

L, by itself, makes all *clear, lucid, placid, liquid;* it is the polish of *glow, gleam, glide, glassy, glance, glitter,* etc. The *l* lends the cold, metallic quality to the solidity of *lead;* it gives lustre and ring to silver, as the *r* roughens and darkens *iron.* "Hear the sledges with their bells." For the little bells we have "the tintinnabulation that so musically swells."

k. — *K* must be taken into all account of fine sounds and lights, usually with *i* and *a;* thus in *twinkle, tinkle, flicker, sparkle, crackle, link, chink, trickle;* so in fibrous attenuations: *nick, splick* (the quarryman's name for a chip of stone), *skin, skiff, skip, skim, skive, sketch.*

> "How they tinkle, tinkle, tinkle,
>   In the icy air of night,
>   While the stars that over-sprinkle
>   All the heavens seem to twinkle
>   With a krystalline delight."

This of Poe is comparatively cheap work, but the reader must detect in it the same instinct by which the far-seeing Tennyson makes the steeds in "Tithonus"

———— shake the darkness from their loosened manes,
And beat the twilight into flakes of fire.
  "———— *e'er my steps*
Forgot the barefoot feel of the clay world."
"*Like scaled oarage of a keen, thin fish.*"

  "———— *whose diapason whirls*
The clanging constellations round the pole."

I cannot, of course, be sure that the general reader is with me at the insight of these fine distinctions, and I beg him to consider that I might well exchange my confidence in his mutual appreciation for a vindictive and scientific criticism, which should prove my positions out of the preferences (some might call them thieveries) of the poets themselves. Take these letters, *k* and *l*. Burns sang:

> "*Peggy, dear, the evening's clear,
>   Swift flies the skimming swallow.*"

Both Tennyson and Alexander Smith appropriate the *skimming swallow*. Or take the word *clanging*, quoted above. It first appears in the "Odyssey," applied to *geese*. Mr. Alexander Smith (who gave promise of poetry) grasped the situation as his own. He sings:

*Unto whose fens on midnights blue and cold
Long strings of geese come clanging from the stars.*

Shelley, in "The Revolt of Islam," is so beset by this notion of clanging that he uses it twice:

*With clang of wings and scream the eagle passed.
With clang of wings and scream the eagle flew.*

In spite of this repetition the Laureate *clangs* three times more: in "Locksley Hall" he "leads the clanging rookery home"; in "The Princess," "The leader wild swan in among the stars would clang it"; and again, in the same, "But I, an eagle, clang an eagle to the sphere." There may seem little apposition of *clanging* and mere flesh and feathers, according to the genius of the letters as herein assumed; but if one will consider *eagle* a hard word, for a hard, metallic bird, fit to fight a golden-scaled serpent in the air, then the clanging may come in with high poetical advantage. So midnights "blue and cold," with a glitter of crystal stars, and the yelling, and jangling, and mingling of geese, may find voice in *clanging*.

m. — This is the letter of dreamy murmur and monotony; *hum, rumble, moan* are onomatopoetic. *Memory* is the poet's dearest word.

n. — All nations agree in saying *no*. There is hardly a language in the world in which *n* is not the chief element of negation. Plato makes *n* the sign of *inwardness* (as translated); intensity of withdrawal were better. It is a nasal sound, which is intensified by drawing up the muscles of contempt at the sides of the nose — as when we dwell upon *mean, sneaking, n-asty*.

p. — This letter shows the character I have given it in such words as *plump, lump, pulp, voluptuous, sleep, dump, ripe, lip, purple*.

q. — *Queer, questionable, quaint, quizzical, quip, quirk, quiddity, quillet, squeak, squeal, squint, squeamish, squelch, qualm, quit, quash*, etc. show *q* as the organ of the whimsical and *outré* — the very opposite of *o*.

s. — *Moist, misty, nasty, sticky, steam, slop, slip, slush, dash, swash, drizzle*, all suggest water in its different stages; even *ice* is kept wet by the *c*. *Luscious, delicious, nutri(c)ious*, suggest juicy substances.

sh, either initial or final, suggests moist confusion; thus, initially we have *shiver, shatter, shake, shrivel, shrink, shred;* finally, we have *dash, clash, lash*, *thrash, swash, smash, trash, rush, gush, mush, slush,* etc.

——" *the sun new risen*
Looks through the horizontal misty air
Shorn of his beams."
"*The stars obtuse emit a shivered ray.*"

v. — Perhaps one tenth of the words which begin with *v* have an element of vehemence: *vim, violence, victory, vanquish, velocity, vigor, vice, vengeance, villainy.*

W and *y* also have general emphasis.

z. — This is a dreamy letter, of *hazy, mazy,* dry confusion; a *lazy, drowsy, dozing, furzy, dizzy, vi(z)ionary* atmosphere attends it, in which the genius of Thomson delighted.

A pleasing land of drowzyhead it waz.

There was a question as to a certain Turk: Did he wear the fez?

O. Henry answered: "No, he was clean shaved."

The most indulgent reader will almost necessarily suspect that as a youth with these prepossessions I occasionally dropped into poetry on my own account; and for purely psychological purposes — where any literary pretension would hardly obtain — I quote frankly a specimen of what then seemed to me poetry of the best:

THE PIRATE

On a haggard rock in the Middle Sea
Where grizzly waves lash dismally
And sullen horror reigns,

There the wind went by with a crazy moan,
And the gibbet creaked with an iron groan
 Where the Pirate hung in chains.

And beneath, far down, the sea birds gray
Winged slow and cold through briny spray
 With lonely, yelping strains,
And the phantom ship with its twilight sail
Leaned far away, on a hopeless trail
 From the Pirate, hung in chains.

Lo, the lightning struck in the iron-work
When thunder storms rushed grim and dark
 O'er ocean's nighted plains,
But the morning came with a ghastly smile,
And blue with fire, on the rocky isle,
 The Pirate hung in chains.

BIBLIOLIFE

Old Books Deserve a New Life
www.bibliolife.com

Did you know that you can get most of our titles in our trademark **EasyScript**™ print format? **EasyScript**™ provides readers with a larger than average typeface, for a reading experience that's easier on the eyes.

Did you know that we have an ever-growing collection of books in many languages?

Order online:
www.bibliolife.com/store

Or to exclusively browse our **EasyScript**™ collection:
www.bibliogrande.com

At BiblioLife, we aim to make knowledge more accessible by making thousands of titles available to you – quickly and affordably.

Contact us:
BiblioLife
PO Box 21206
Charleston, SC 29413

Printed in Great Britain
by Amazon